AROUSING
THE GODDESS

AROUSING
THE
GODDESS

~

Sex and Love in the Buddhist Ruins of India

Tim Ward

MONKFISH BOOK PUBLISHING COMPANY
RHINEBECK, NEW YORK

Canadian Cataloguing in Publication Data

Ward, Tim, 1958–
    Arousing the goddess

    ISBN 0-9726357-3-4

1. Ward, Tim, 1958–   – Journeys – India.
2. India – Description and travel.   3. Buddhas.
4. Buddhism.   5. Tantrism.   I. Title.

DS414.2.W37 1996   915.404'52   C96-930119-7

Design: Gordon Robertson
Cover photograph: John Bigelow Taylor
Author photograph: Wendy Ward

Printed in Canada
Arousing the Goddess cover art, Copyright ©1990 by John Bigelow Taylor
Collection: Robert Ellsworth

Monkfish Book Publishing Company
27 Lamoree Road,
Rhinebeck, New York 12572
www.monkfishpublishing.com

Distributed to the trade by Consortium Book Sales and Distribution

Bulk purchase discounts, for educational or promotional purposes, are available. Contact the publisher for more information.

Grateful acknowledgement is made to the following for permission to reprint material used herein. Every reasonable effort has been made to ensure that the correct permission to reprint was obtained. Should there be any errors in copyright information, please inform the publisher, and a correction will be mady in any subsequent editions.

K. Dowman, from *Masters of Mahamudra*. Albany, New York: State University of New York Press, 1985.

Swami Saradananda, from *Shri Ramakrisha, the Great Master*. Mylapore, Madras, Sri Ramakrisha Math, 1952.

The Gospel of Sri Ramakrisha, tr. Swami Nikhilananda. New York: Ramakrishna-Vivekananda Center, 1969.

Omar Garrison, from *Tantra: The Yoga of Sex*. New York: Harmony Books, 1964, 1983.

Excerpts from *Living with Kundalini* by Gopi Krishna; © 1995. Reprinted by arrangement with Shambhala Publications, Inc., 300 Massachusetts Avenue, Boston, MA. 02115.

For Wendy

About the Cover:

The Supreme Bliss Wheel of Integration Tantra

The male-female couple on the cover of *Arousing the Goddess* is taken from a 15th century Tibetan Buddhist icon. It symbolizes the ecstatic union of wisdom (the female figure) and compassion (the male figure). According to Tibetan Buddhist/Tantric tradition, the Buddha adopted this split archetype deity form in order to teach this highest tantric yoga to Shiva and his consort Parvati (Kali) as a means of controlling their destructive energies.

Images so holy and so powerful were never displayed in public in Tibet, but would have been revealed only to advanced meditators with the appropriate instructions. The fiery, ecstatic union is not at all physically sexual in meaning. Rather, Tibetans consider the *Supreme Bliss Wheel of Integration Tantra* the most sophisticated technology for contemplating the union of wisdom and compassion, and cultivating the clear light of freedom.

Acknowledgments

A dedicated group of friends weathered the course of this book with me, reading various drafts, correcting my imaginative spellings, and asking thoughtful questions about abstruse or sentimental passages. First among them is Jim Flint, my buddy from Buddhist boot camp. Jim kept me topped up with decaf latte and durian while I finished my rough draft in his Seattle apartment. His rapier-like editorial skills skewered my every cliché and his prodding made me more honest about the details than I would have been on my own (and he disclaims any connection with the last half of chapter 14). Teresa Erickson and Melanie Choukas-Bradley also read multiple drafts. Their comments and queries gave me feminine perspectives on the book which proved invaluable—for example, the universal meaning of a white bikini. Conversations about Tantra and the Goddess with Deepti Gupta helped me better understand Indian mythology, and engendered much inspiration. Thanks too to Paul Cohen and Georgia Dent of Monkfish Book Publishing Company for their enthusiasm and creative energy. It's a joy to know my book has found a good home on Monkfish's list. I'm also grateful to Georgia for the cover design, and for actually listening to and incorporating an author's input. My deepest appreciation to my agent, Ashala Gabriel, for hooking me up with Monkfish in the first place. Thanks for your faith.

Thanks to John Taylor, who released rights to the cover photograph of the original Tibetan artwork, and to Patrick

Crean who edited the original manuscript. Bernice Eisenstein took on the much appreciated job as copy editor. Jennifer Glossop worked as line editor, Shaun Oakey as proofreader, Cathy Daigle as inputter, and Maggie MacDonald coordinated all this detail work which turns a messy manuscript into crisp pages. My appreciation to them all for a great job.

Many others encouraged me along the way: my parents, Jane and Peter, my brother Mark, Wade Davis, Gail Percy, Jim Steen, Heather Mastel, Mary Pole, Jim Allen, Nick Harris, Tracey Stuart, and Jane Somerville.

Finally, I'd like to thank Wendy, my sister, to whom this book is dedicated, not only for her love and understanding, but for saving and typing all my letters from Asia. And my gratitude to Sabina, wherever she is: a remarkable woman who inspired a book.

Tim Ward

CONTENTS

AROUSING
THE GODDESS

CHAPTER ONE

FLYING HIGH IN THE AGE OF DESTRUCTION

Ladakh

S EX AND LOVE: these were not what I sought when I came to India. I wanted to sit at the feet of Buddhist lamas and Hindu yogis, learn esoteric meditation techniques, and then see for myself how the teachings could help me face India's maimed and poor without turning away. Instead, I fell in love, and the rest just happened. Ten years have passed, and I have written two books about my experiences with the monasteries and mysteries of Asia. Yet I know that loving Sabina, and entering into those strange, electrical states of sexual ecstasy with her, changed me more than anything I learned in a temple. Though it may seem strange, a fanatical Belgian Buddhist monk played a key role in this affair, and it is with meeting him that the story begins.

Lama Philippe lived in Gutsang Monastery, just a kilometre up the mountainside from me. He had a large, narrow nose, and pale blue eyes that burned with intensity. His ears stuck straight out from the sides of his shaven head, and he was so thin that his arms and legs looked like white sticks poking through the maroon bundle of his robes. He had come to Gutsang to complete an advanced meditation practice that involved chanting one million repetitions of a complex mantra. Each morning he scaled the barren red cliffs beside the hermitage and intoned his sacred syllables until dusk. Then he climbed down and ate his daily bowl of rice or barley paste. He explained to me that the intensive repetition of Tibetan mantras and other rituals is the "short path" to enlightenment and has its root in ancient spiritual practices called *Tantra*. If a student of the tantric path pursues it with diligence, he can gain enlightenment in as little as three years, forever freed from all suffering and delusion, or so Philippe said.

We had met in the daily line-up of visitors outside head lama Drukchen Rimpoche's receiving room in Hemis Monastery. Philippe had been forced to come down to Hemis to sort out a visa problem with Drukchen's secretary; I was in line to give a progress report to Drukchen on some problems I was having with my meditations. As the only two white guys living in this remote corner of the Himalayas, we talked. I told Philippe I was an independent student of Drukchen's. Although I was not a Buddhist, the head lama told me certain basic meditations a non-Buddhist could undertake without psychic danger. He agreed to take me in for the summer and approved the translated Tibetan meditation text I had brought with me from Canada as a workbook. Once settled in the monks' quarters in Hemis, I pored over my text for a few hours every morning, and then meditated four to six hours a day. I bused into Leh Town every other week to buy vegetables and chocolate bars. When I met Philippe, I realized what a Sunday school beginner I still was.

I told him I envied his intensity and that, although I'd been in Hemis almost three months, I felt my serious meditation had not yet begun.

"But of course," said the monk, "your *serious* meditation will start only as soon as you cease to be *serious* about it! Me, I can't really say I meditate. I don't levitate or see into the future. I just do what my guru tells me. If you want to develop meditative concentration, you can't do it by trying to meditate. Practise generosity, then meditative awareness will develop."

Attempting to be generous, I offered to bring him something from the marketplace on my next trip to town, suggesting fruit and vegetables. He said he didn't eat them on retreat, but I could bring Tibetan prayer flags, and we could plant them together on the mountain ridges.

On the day I arrived with the flags, Philippe said it was good *karma* I had come. He needed a break from his daily routine. He took me around to the back of the decrepit stone-and-wood chanting halls. From there we could see the mountain ridge that half-encircled Gutsang—itself more than four thousand metres above sea level. The sky was a cloudless, dazzling blue. The thin air sharpened the focus of every red crag, and harsh sunlight etched deep shadow lines around the fallen boulders and outcroppings of rock. Ladakh was an alpine desert. It seldom rained, and virtually nothing grew without human cultivation. Nicknamed "Moonland" for its lifeless, otherworldly terrain, Ladakh made a perfect landscape for disciples of the Buddha intent on contemplating emptiness.

"We can put the flags all across the ridge," said Philippe. "But those ones on top, the high winds have torn them to shreds. They really need to be replaced."

Squinting at where the mountains opened wide to the sky, I could just make out a toothpick of wood, high and far away, with something tattered clinging to it. Distance was difficult to judge. Lama Philippe explained that planting prayer flags produced excellent karma for all sentient beings. Each bright-coloured flag bore the wood-block print of numerous Tibetan prayers. Whenever the flags fluttered, the prayers flew across the sky, and all who could see them would receive a blessing. The higher the flag, the farther the blessings could fly. Thus the peaks were the best locations for planting.

We climbed next to each other to avoid the loose rocks that rolled and ricocheted downhill towards the rapidly shrinking monastery. Eventually we reached a stunted tree which had given up its struggle against desert and rock. We tied one blue and one red flag to the dead limbs, ripping the corners and then knotting the tattered strips around the wood to hold the flags in place. Philippe tore off a few

3

dry branches to use as poles farther up the lifeless slope. Then he chanted a prayer over each flag. He drew two tiny brass finger cymbals from his bag and pinged them together. A single clear note sang out. He twisted the cymbals back and forth, causing the sound to swell, diminish, and swell again as he brought the cymbals in and out of resonance. He seemed to relish the ritual, drawing it out for more than a minute until the note was completely washed away by the wind.

By mid-afternoon, the peak seemed as far away as it had in the morning, and the climb was becoming ever more vertical. We scrabbled over patches of loose shale, both of us sliding with little control. The leather straps on Philippe's sandals began to deteriorate. We stopped to catch our breath, clinging to an outcropping of rock. We sucked the cold thin air and shared a drink of water from my flask. While resting, and to delay more climbing, I told Philippe how my interest in Buddhism had started.

"Back in Canada, when I was eighteen, I became a Christian and was very evangelical for a few years. I tried to save drunks on skid row and that kind of thing. At university, even though I majored in secular philosophy, I was also active in a local Baptist church. My friends in the philosophy department thought religion was nuts, and my church friends got nervous when I said Christianity might just be one interpretation of a vast and mysterious world with many paths to God. I wanted to learn more about the other paths, so after graduation, I decided to explore the temples and shrines of India. I was pretty naive, but I really admired the cool, analytical approach of Buddhism. I liked the idea of looking the human condition in the face, not flinching from the worst of it, but meeting it with compassion. To save money I had to work as a waiter, a janitor, and even did a stint on an oil rig. Soon as I had enough cash, I bought a backpack and a one-way ticket to New Delhi. Ladakh was the first place I headed, and here I am."

Philippe seemed barely interested. His eyes studied the route to the ridge top. When I asked how he got started along the Buddhist path, he shrugged.

"I was a monk in my last several lives."

"I mean in this one."

"Oh. I was thirty-one years old, leader of my own atonic hypnotic jazz band. One night we had a gig at this hotel in northern Scotland. These guys with shaven heads and red robes were staying down the hall. They were Tibetan monks, checking out a site for a new monastery. The vibes were amazing. I knew nothing about Buddhism, but I knew this was for me. The morning after I met him, I told the lama my bags were packed, I was ready to go to India. Now, what did he want me to do? And so here I am."

He fell silent, his eyes still scanning the mountains.

"So do you think what we are doing—you far more than me—is going to make a difference? I mean, do you think Buddhism will catch on in the West?"

"Buddhism will soon be destroyed," he said calmly.

"What?" His answer, delivered in such an offhand manner, almost made me lose my grip. "Why?"

"This is *Kaliyuga*," he replied, "the Age of Kali, the Black Goddess. She wears a wreath of severed heads and dances on a corpse. In Kaliyuga, destruction reigns. My lama tells me that in two hundred years there will be no more Buddhist teachings left on earth. Sometimes I think, Why fight it? If this is the Age of Destruction, why not destroy?" He grinned. I saw that his teeth were long, his gums receded, perhaps the result of malnutrition. It made him look ghoulish when he smiled. "Sometimes I think I should take off my robes and become a rock star," he continued. "It's easy for me to transfix thousands on stage."

"But you don't."

"No. My teacher urges me to continue despite the obstacles. There is so little *dharma*, true Buddhist teaching, in the world, so much suffering. So for now, I persevere."

We mounted the top of a hump. Rubble and boulders covered the mid-ground ahead. Beyond, a cliff face rose to the ridge top.

"It's impossible to climb much higher," I said. "But see that thornbush over there, round to the right? There's a flat spot where we could both stand. We could tie on the last of our flags, then keep going to where the ridge drops lower, and maybe get a view over the other side before turning back."

"That's the grandmother route," he fixed me with his blue eyes. "The spirit of my guru tells me to go straight to the peak!" A skinny arm stuck out from his robes, pointing up at the pinnacle.

I balked, and we split the remaining flags between us, agreeing to meet farther along the ridge where it dropped. I watched as he disappeared over the boulders, sandals slipping, robes flapping in the wind. Fanatic, I thought grudgingly. My climb proved surprisingly easy. Within half an hour I was tying green, white and orange flags in place on the thornbush. When I looked back, Philippe had vanished somewhere in the cracked jumble of split-off cliffs and huge boulders. As my eyes wandered over the terrain, a little ledge wide enough for a mountain goat suddenly became visible. It climbed diagonally across the cliff face from near where I stood, leading in the direction of the pinnacle, and possibly running right to the top.

Unable to believe my luck, I decided to follow the ledge and beat Philippe to the peak. The drop fell over fifty metres to smashed boulders below, but the ribbon of rock looked deceptively secure. At first it was wide enough that I could walk cautiously along it. As the ledge began to narrow, my hands gripped the rough surface of the cliff. By not looking down I kept my growing fear at bay, alternately chanting Buddhist mantras and Christian prayers, staying focused on the task in order to prevent my mind from dwelling on my stupid lack of judgement. Soon only my toes gripped the ledge, while the rest of my feet hung out over the drop. Finally, about forty metres from the top of the ridge, the last inch of the ribbon dwindled out, leaving me clinging to the bare rock face. For a while I hung there, too scared to move, sweating in the cold. Up seemed easier than back, so I started climbing, grabbing fingerholds and kicking little footholds in the shale surface of the cliff with the tips of my sneakers. I kept thinking that my mother would disapprove of this most strongly.

My head poked over the ridge. A howling wind hit me in the face. The ridge was a knife edge, sloping down at about forty degrees on the other side. For a second I struggled against the force of the wind, pulling my arms over the top to keep me hanging safely. Then I looked up and saw the mountains of the Indus Valley spread out to the horizon, and to the east, the distant ranges of Western Tibet. My arms and legs shook. My lungs heaved. I felt delirious. On hands and knees I straddled the knife edge and crawled towards the tattered flagpole. The pinnacle was actually a huge oblong boulder perched on the ridge. I scrambled up to its wind-rounded peak, stripped off the shreds of old flags from the branch poles, and fastened one yellow and two bright red ones in their places.

I hollered Philippe's name as loud as I could over the side of the cliff. No reply. I got on my belly, crawled to the edge and looked down into space. I watched a brown-backed kite circle far below, searching for something to eat. My pleasure at beating the monk disappeared. Why wasn't he here? He was the one taking the short path to the top. How the hell was I going to climb down that cliff and search for him? A few more hours and we would be trapped by the dark. The winds would turn icy. And what would I do if he had fallen, but was still alive? Helicopter? I doubted there was one in all Ladakh. If there were, things moved so slowly in India that getting one out here would take a week. I had to stop thinking about this. I tried to meditate like a good Buddhist, but could not keep myself from inching over to the drop every few minutes and searching the rocks for a blotch of maroon.

A long time later a white hand reached up over the edge of the boulder. Philippe shook a little as he sat down beside me. He had run into dead ends, crawled through an eagle's nest, and more than once swung out across splits in the cliff face to grasp handholds on the other side.

"A few times there, I had to call to my guru," he said.

"I was led here by the spirits of several grandmothers," I told him. He gave a thin smile.

When he recovered, we tied his flags in place, and then consecrated them as they whipped straight in the high winds. Our task completed, we sat cross-legged and gazed at the distant snow peaks.

"So tell me about Kaliyuga," I said at last.

"To both Hindus and Buddhists, time is cyclical," Philippe began, almost yelling to be heard above the wind. "One cycle is divided into four ages, or *yugas*, much the same as those of the ancient Greeks: the Gold, Silver, Bronze and Iron Age. The last age the Indians named after Kali, the Black Goddess, devourer of time. She destroys the universe at the end of each cycle, which is where we are now. As the goddess is aroused, chaos breaks loose. The destructive aspect grows stronger. This happens inside each of us too, for we are mirrors of the cosmos. In Kaliyuga, destructive passions run wild, causing much pain and suffering. For this reason, it is also a great time for Buddhist practice: the door of liberation becomes most appealing. The dedicated practitioner can escape the endless cycle, if only he can keep his balance in the whirlwind."

"How?"

Philippe looked up, and I followed his eyes to the flags. "The same way as the prayer flag, tied to the branch, flies straight in the wind. The branch is the Buddha's teaching, and we are the flags. When the branch is firm, the stronger the wind blows, the straighter we fly, and the farther the blessing travels to all the lands below. With no teaching, the wind carries us swiftly to destruction."

"And with no wind, no blessing," I mused. "But what's the fate of the flags tied tightly to the branch? We just spent all day replacing shreds and tatters."

Philippe smiled and revealed his long teeth once more, but said nothing.

"Then why resist?" I asked. "Why not go with the wind and wait for the Golden Age to come round again?"

"Because for Buddhists reincarnation is a horror," he replied. "These days in the West, reincarnation is so *chic*. People think it is a wonderful thing to live many lives. Oh yes, and regress them all in therapy: 'I'm King Ferdinand of Spain! I'm Joan of Arc! I'm Leonardo da Vinci!' No, the world of the Buddha was one that understood reincarnation. Each karmic act is like a stone dropped in a pond, a ripple spread through your lifetimes that rebounds and interferes with other ripples until the water is turbulent and dark. That darkness pushes you around, first one way, then another. You are in chains to your past deeds, and their consequences bring you torment. As both human and animal, you have been butchered, choked, strangled, crushed, impaled, burned, flayed, dismembered, starved, drowned, hunted down by predators and your entrails gnawed out while you are still alive. Your children have murdered you, your spouses forsaken you, your parents raped you. Diseases have ravaged you and sucked out your life a million times over. All of this has happened, and all of it will happen to you again and again, life without end! This is the true meaning of reincarnation."

"I thought it was about spiritual evolution."

"No!" he said vehemently. "Nothing evolves, the wheel of karma just goes round and round, like a Ferris wheel. You may accumulate good deeds and work your way up from the hell realms to the kingdom of the gods over many lifetimes. But then your good karma is exhausted. The terror for celestial beings is that when they die, they know they are descending back to the torments of hell. In the human realm all that prevents us from going insane is the ignorance of our limited brains—the very ignorance that at death causes us to flee blindly into another womb, and keeps the karmic wheel going round. This is why the teaching of the Buddha is so important: so that we may feel the fire of our suffering, and take action to put it out!"

"But if I don't feel that suffering now, why should I believe that it exists, and I'm just ignorant of it? There's an old Western philosophical principle called Occam's razor: it says that the fewest possible assumptions are to be made in explaining a thing. In other words, don't believe in something if your experience can be adequately explained without it."

Philippe cracked a lopsided grin at me. "You're a tough one, Tim. I'm glad I'm not your lama."

It was twilight by the time we returned to Gutsang. Philippe invited me to his cold, stark cell for a bowl of rice. We were both exhausted, and his feet were caked with blood from sliding in his sandals down slopes of loose shale. He gave us each a spoonful of

Tibetan strengthening medicine. As we ate our rice, his left foot suddenly began to twitch.

"Ah, my early warning system," he grinned, pulling a bottle off the window ledge and popping a pill. "Not to worry. Before I started meditating, it was right out of control. Now the pill stops the seizures before they get going. Epilepsy"—he smiled at me—"my personal taste of Kaliyuga."

October 8, 1984, New Delhi
Dear Wendy,

My flight south from Ladakh landed in the Punjab, home of the Sikh religion. It was not a wise time to be there, Sis, because a few months ago the Indian army stormed the Sikhs' holiest shrine, the Golden Temple. Many Sikhs died inside. The army brought out lots of weapons and claimed the bodies were of separatist terrorists. Even moderate Sikhs thought it was a set-up, and the radicals declared they would seek revenge. I actually tried to see the temple while I was there, and made it to the city of Amritsar.

At the army checkpoint just outside the temple, a soldier told me I needed a pass. He directed me to ask a senior officer for one. The officer's eyes bugged wide when he saw me.

"Foreigners are forbidden to be in the Punjab!" he told me, more astonished than anything else.

"I suppose that means you're not going to grant me a pass to the Golden Temple?" I replied.

He said, stone-faced, that I was very lucky I hadn't been caught by the authorities, and offered me an army escort to the train station right away. I accepted.

After three months in the serenity of the mountains, it's jarring to return to a country in a state of crisis. One unfortunate side effect of the raid is that the government has changed the visa regulations for British Commonwealth citizens, who up until a few months ago could stay in India without a visa for forty-nine years. As of late June, six months is now the maximum. That means I've got less than three months left. There is so much to see, and I can't stand the thought of doing it like a superficial tourist. I'm hoping to wrangle an extension in Nepal, which fellow travellers have assured me should not be too hard.

In the meantime, I'm back in New Delhi after Buddhist boot camp in the Himalayas. I shed about fifteen pounds and have a hard flat ass from sitting cross-legged on rock for hours at a time. More than anything else, I think the mental training of the monastery has prepared me to travel through India intact. I can see two main advantages to the quasi-Buddhist viewpoint I've acquired.

First, handling human suffering. India is such an in-your-face kind of place. People everywhere. And when I say "in your face," I mean like lepers shoving their arm stumps at your nose until you give them something to make them go away. When I first arrived, there was one little boy with a crippled old man who had me trapped in a bus seat. I refused to give alms because it was plain the old man was just using the kid and it sickened me. The boy got down on his knees and reached out to touch my sandalled feet with his hands. They were clammy, like a cold tongue lapping at my toes. I felt revulsion like I have never experienced before. I keep wanting the rest of humanity to stand shoulder to bony shoulder with me, and it fills me with such horror when it bends to touch my feet. Buddhist detachment, I hope, can help me keep my inner balance in the face of misery that I can do nothing about.

Second, handling sex. You know, Wendy, it was so great having you just one grade behind me in high school so we could explain the mysteries of the opposite sex to each other, or at least share our mutual confusion. I felt so awkward in front of girls I was attracted to, so mumble-mouthed and ashamed of my hormones. I know I seemed really weird, after finally getting into a sexual relationship with my first girlfriend, coming back from a summer alone on the pipelines, barely eighteen, suddenly so radically Christian, and so determined to be celibate. I always felt you understood, even though Beth couldn't. At the time I thought the voice of God had said to me that premarital sex was selfish, bound to cause hurt, and so Saint Paul had forbidden it. I wrestled with that voice for four frustrated, sublimated years before arguing myself into the more moderate position that times have changed since Saint Paul, and if you really loved someone, well, you could get away with it. Of course, I moved in with Tina right after university, and we were both pretty miserable together until I left two years later on this trip to India.

Travelling has been so freeing. I spent three weeks with an Italian woman in Kashmir, living on a houseboat much of the time. She was headed to Ladakh to study Tibetan medicine, and I was off to a monastery, so we knew it wouldn't last. In the end, she got altitude sickness and had to leave the mountains. It was too bad, but I was kind of relieved, because it would have been most difficult to be satisfied with my cot in the monastery if I knew Anna had a bed in the town of Leh.

My three months in the temple, however, have given me a whole new insight into sex. The first section of my meditation text was an exercise in rooting out sexual desire. Now, don't get me wrong, I don't think I'm cut out for a life of celibacy. It's just been my experience that what complicates the joy of sex is the misery of attachment. That last part is strict Buddhist philosophy: not getting what we want is suffering, and losing what we've got that we want to keep is suffering too. What my new discipline has taught me, I hope, is to watch desire arise, note its presence without clinging to the sensation, without feeling driven to act on it, and then watch as it passes away.

When you solo travel, you naturally spend a lot of time lonely and horny. At least I do. If nothing else, the summer's meditation is going to help me resist the temptations of the flesh as firmly as the anti-fornication stance I once held, but without the guilt. So if I do yield, and I quite probably will at some point, I'll be able to do so without losing my inner balance. I hope.

I guess I am lonely now. Fortunately, I'll soon get a chance to see my teacher again. Remember I told you about Drukchen

Rimpoche, the head lama of Hemis Monastery? Well, the ritual mask dancers from his temple are going to perform here in New Delhi at an upcoming conference on Buddhism and Culture. Drukchen said if I was going to be in the area, I should attend. He said I could tell the organizers I was his student and there should be no trouble getting me registered. So I'll get to see him again, as well as getting to meet a lot of Buddhists. Several hundred monks, scholars and dignitaries will be coming from all across Asia and the rest of the world. The Indian government, which is sponsoring the conference, is promoting it as a great event in the history of Buddhism, the first international gathering of its kind. Prime Minister Indira Gandhi herself is going to give the opening address.

So for now I'm hanging out on the plains, waiting for the great event to begin.

With love, your brother,

Tim

P.S. Before I mail this, I have to add something interesting that happened today. I was wandering through Old Delhi, when an adolescent boy attached himself to me. He wanted to take me to his uncle, a Hindu astrologer and palm reader. He said the first five minutes would be free. For years I have scoffed at these things like a good evangelical, but the offer intrigued me, especially the freebie, so I went along. Uncle was a round man with a fringe of grey hair and thick glasses. His nephew went to fetch tea, and the two of us sat down on a flat bed. He picked up my hand, turned it over in two seconds, back to front, and released it.

"Interesting," he said. "You have a complicated hand. The square hand shape means you like to live a simple life, speak your mind honestly. But you have artistic-shaped fingers, and the inward curve of your index finger means you are philosophical by nature."

That was good enough for me. We settled on a price for the rest of the reading, and he continued: "You have a long thumb with an arch. This means you have deep feelings for the poor, and wish to help. Before you were twenty-four, you have done volunteer work. The wide spread between thumb and forefinger means you have many friends in your own country and abroad. Your middle finger shows that your philosophy gives you respect for all religions, but a close attachment to none." He asked my birth date, consulted his charts, and then added, "You have recently been drawn to Buddhism, find it very appealing, but you will not settle there. You are more concerned with the harmony of man than ideas about God. So you are like an observer on the shore of the sea, watching the tide ebb and flow. Your ring finger is straight, so you will be an administrator or director of some organization, probably a literary society, and you will be quite successful in such work. The little finger shows a love for truth and a need to speak it.

"But see the gap between your fingers? This and a small island in your economic line show you have little money, and that materially you do not possess much. Your heart line, though, is deep. When you love, you love with all. But if you hate a man, you can't stand the sight of him. Your mental line is long, and your brain will be active up until your death."

He also predicted I would marry a woman I did not currently know and have three kids. My brother would become rich, and my sister, who likes gardening and animals, would take care of my parents' property.

Well, from an initial good start, he went on to hit and miss. In terms of philosophy, I think I'm far more into mysticism than social justice, and a career as a literary society director seems like hell on earth. I love with all? That's never been my experience. The interest in Buddhism could reasonably be inferred from my close-cropped hair. Overall, though, I'm sure you'd agree it's a fairly accurate portrait. I especially liked the part about being an observer on the beach, watching the ebb and flow. That feels so true. Especially here in India, where if you're not attentive to the tide, it'll suck you under pretty quick.

CHAPTER TWO

THE EARTH-TOUCHING GESTURE

New Delhi

ACROSS A SEA of shaven skulls I glimpsed a wave of golden hair. It glittered, then vanished out of sight. I pressed my way through the different coloured robes on a sudden quest to find it, navigating my way around clusters of red-robed Tibetans, Theravadan monks from India, Thailand, Burma, Nepal and Sri Lanka in yellow, orange or dull ochre, Chinese and Koreans in sombre grey and blue, and Zen rishis swathed in black. There were hundreds of them, all sipping tea from china cups and munching English butter biscuits at the mid-morning reception the first day of the conference. The heads with hair were mostly grey: foreign and Indian scholars, artists, and a few younger students of Buddhism.

I found her standing between a tall European with a black goatee and a tiny Indian monk in tightly wrapped saffron. All three were speaking Hindi. The man with the goatee watched her face intently, while she focused on the little monk. The monk, in turn, kept his eyes to the floor, perhaps consciously averting his gaze, I suspected, because to think lustful thoughts is against a monk's vows, and to touch a woman, absolutely forbidden.

I was almost a month out of the monastery, and my Buddhist equilibrium had held, so far, back in the heat of the plains. The woman with the honey-blonde hair was a test: no doubt the most attractive woman I had seen in, well, at the moment it seemed like many years. Her skin was smooth, with a light tan along her neck and throat. Her jaw was a little large, her mouth wide, showing perfect teeth when she smiled. High cheekbones and something almost haughty in the way she held her head gave her a distinctly aristocratic air. She wore a black patterned silk pantsuit embroidered with gold thread that drew attention—drew *my* attention—to the perfect curves of her breasts and her bottom. I stood well back to watch her, and it caught me off guard when suddenly her eyes flashed straight to mine. The look shook me. Deep blue, the eyes held me for a fraction longer than what would seem normal, appraisingly, surprisingly welcoming. They communicated, it seemed, an invitation to stay and wait my turn. I felt awkward, self-conscious. I couldn't disappear back under the cover of the surrounding Buddhist robes, but it appeared suddenly so obvious that I was in line.

The diminutive monk raised his hands, palms pressed together prayer-like at his chest in the Indian gesture of greeting and parting which acknowledges god within the other person. She returned it gracefully, and he sped off into the crowd at a rather brisk pace. She put a hand on the coat sleeve of the European, whispered something to him. He nodded. He was much older than she, balding, chunky, perhaps in his mid-forties, while she looked under thirty. He forged his way through the crowd, following the monk. She smiled at me.

Without thinking, I pressed my palms together in the gesture of greeting. She laughed lightly.

"So you are Indian?" she said in a slight German accent.

"No, Canadian. Does that mean we should shake hands? I'm Tim." I didn't put out my hand, and neither did she.

"I'm Sabina, from Vienna."

"You come here often?" I winced inwardly at the stupidity of this. "I mean, to India."

"This is my fifth stay."

"So what brings you here?"

She gave a light shrug, as if to say it was a shame that the conversation was so banal. But her eyes stayed on me.

"I'm doing my doctorate in Buddhist art. My adviser is giving a lecture for the conference, and he wanted me to come so I can make contacts for my research. Afterwards, I go to Kashmir."

"Was that him you were talking with?"

"Who? Professor Strauss? Oh no, he's just here from Germany for the conference. What about you? Are you a student?"

"Well, no. I was. Sort of." Words sputtered out of my mouth of their own accord, out of my control. "I was studying at a Buddhist monastery in Ladakh, just working through a text on my own, and before I left—I'm just travelling through India—he, my teacher, invited me to attend here . . ."

Her eyes floated away from me as I spoke, searching the room, no doubt, for someone with the ability to speak even one language fluently.

"So," I rallied lamely, "are you making lots of contacts?"

She took a step towards me and lowered her voice, so that I naturally drew closer in response. "Actually, I think I have made a mistake today." She placed her slender fingers lightly on my arm, just for an instant, and smiled as if I was an insider to the joke: "I think I shouldn't have worn these clothes to the conference. It's not helping me with the monks."

I took a step back in mock seriousness, as if to examine her. Her touch felt too good. I was suddenly glad I was headed for Nepal in a few more weeks, back to the mountains. But as I moved away, someone else stepped forward.

"Hi there!" came a loud American voice right next to me. "I saw you in the opening session and thought you might like a copy of my book on Buddhism, *View from the Valley.* I'm Jerry."

A freckled hand stuck out towards her. Sabina clasped it, redirecting her eyes at the new face. Jerry wore a pin-striped blue sports coat with a blue-and-black shirt, white slacks and a string of big black prayer beads the size of gum balls around his neck. He was wiry, energetic, his carrot hair short and neat, as if ready for TV.

"I'm Sabina. Are you—"

"A Zen monk? Yep."

"But you're not wearing robes," she said, smiling at him, then glancing back to me.

"Oh, I don't go for that. Sure, when I meditate, I put on the robes. Daily life, I wear trousers. Trunks when I swim, ha."

"Hard as hell for most monks to make it across the pool."

"Huh?" Jerry's eyes stayed fixed on Sabina. He seemed perplexed by the sound of a third voice, as if he couldn't figure out where it came from.

"Their legs get all tangled in the robes," I explained. "It drags them under."

Jerry wrenched his eyes away from Sabina and for the first time looked at me.

"I'm Tim, from Canada."

"What do you do?"

"Fine thanks, and you?"

He looked me over top to bottom, eyebrows raised, head drawn back in mild disdain. Until that minute, I had not been self-conscious of my clothes. I was dressed in baggy, maroon Kashmiri-style pantaloons, and my best handwoven *kurta*—a long-sleeved cotton pullover. Under Jerry's gaze I felt more like an Old Delhi rickshaw driver than a conference participant.

"What's your book about?" Sabina cut the silence.

"Oh, it's like my other books, autobiographical fiction"—Jerry's gaze settled again upon her golden hair, occasionally wandering down her pantsuit—"like Henry Miller."

He stuck out the book in his hand, offering it, and followed through by stepping in towards her at just the right angle to block her from my sight and effectively sever me from the conversation.

I don't need this. I directed the thought to the back of Jerry's jacket. I spun around and stalked away. "It's not what I'm here for. I don't need it, I don't need it," I chanted as if it were a mantra. "Where are the biscuits?"

Next day, after conference proceedings were over, I was still chanting self-made mantras in the buffet line at the five-star Ashoka Hotel.

"I will not compete, I will not compete," I mumbled, plate in hand, eyes fixed on Sabina and Jerry sitting close together on the far side of the banquet hall at a small table, wrapped in conversation. She and I had spoken briefly a couple of times during the day, and joked about her clothes and our mutual preference for Indian dress. She had exchanged her silk pantsuit for a sky blue sari which, though more traditional, set off the deeper blue of her eyes and revealed the smooth tanned flesh of her midriff. Whenever she left me, I would, like a good novice Buddhist, observe desire arising. By simply feeling the sensation, rather than repressing it or acting on its urge, it had no power over me, gradually diminished, and passed away. But whenever I saw the two of them together, the feelings came in waves and would not subside. I chanted through clenched teeth.

"Hey, man, look at those Tibetans go for the chicken! I thought all Buddhist monks were vegetarian," said Manjoor, an Indian from South Africa I had met the previous day at the biscuit table.

Manjoor was studying medicine in Bombay, and had come to Delhi for the conference. He was angular, almost bony, never out of his blue jeans. His eyes were large and his mouth almost constantly moving. Over biscuits the first day he had persuaded me to move to his flophouse dormitory near Connaught Place, the cheapest uninfested deal in the city, he assured me. Had we been monks, our relative poverty might have passed as virtue. But as independent participants we ranked among the rabble of the conference. Adapting to our lowly status, we decided to make the best of it and skipped breakfast each morning in order to fill up at the free lunches and dinners.

"But who can blame the monks?" he continued. "The food's fantastic. Oh Christ, will I stuff my guts tonight!" Manjoor paused in his rapture to glance quizzically at me as I mumbled morosely to myself.

"Hey, Tim, what's the matter? Load up! Don't shrug like a monk at me. Who you trying to kid? I saw three bowls of ice cream go into your belly at lunch."

"So it's food. Don't worry, I'll eat my share."

"It's that chick, isn't it? I don't believe you, you lose your appetite over some woman! But hey, man, I can't blame you. God, she's gorgeous. You see those legs? Holy Krishna, I've never seen a white woman look so good in a sari. Like, you know she's wearing nothing underneath her clothes. If I didn't know how you feel about her, wham! I'd be in there in a flash. That rat-face American who hangs over her wouldn't stand a chance. Women like it, you know, men breaking teeth for them. I think you could take him."

"I'm not interested in taking anybody. Sure, I like her. She's beautiful. But she's going to Kashmir and I'm headed to Nepal. So what's the fight over?"

"Come on, you white lama, don't shit me. You tell me if you had one chance, now, tonight, just twenty minutes alone with her, you'd sit and meditate? No. You'd be in there like a cobra. She likes you. I can tell. God knows why. Why don't you rescue her from the American monk?"

"She doesn't need rescuing."

"Chicken, chicken, ah—at last we get to the chicken! Come on, grab a breast while you can. Next week it will be back to lentils and chapatti for both of us."

Passing the end of the food line, I led Manjoor to a table as far away as possible from where Jerry and Sabina were sitting. I set my plate down across from a lone maroon-robed monk who was holding a chicken leg in both hands and chewing vigorously. The elderly, purply-brown face bobbed in greeting as we sat down.

"Wow, you recognize this guy?" said Manjoor. "He gave a talk in my seminar today. He's the Great Protector of Mongolia."

"Pleased to meet you," I said with a small bow and the gesture of respect.

"No Englisi, no Englisi!" said the holy monk, grinning broadly through a mouthful of chicken, his face and bald scalp beaded with perspiration.

"Never refuse what's put in the begging bowl, right?" said Manjoor. "He's got a lesson for you about thankfulness, Tim. You know the story of the monk and the leper's finger? It got cut off accidentally, see, fell into the monk's alms bowl and—"

"Just eat, Manjoor."

"Ooh, are you touchy tonight! The Indian government spends all this money on us spiritual leaders and freeloaders—God, don't you waste any of it, think of all the starving children in England—and you're going to sulk. Bloody sacrilege! Tomorrow I'm bringing a bag for your dinner."

Manjoor watched critically as I mushed my saffron rice around on my plate without enthusiasm. The Great Protector of Mongolia excused himself for a second helping at the buffet.

"Christ, you're such an ascetic tonight. Who are you fooling? You could take her away from him in a minute."

"I'm not interested in taking anyone."

"Don't shit me"—a long brown finger pointed across the plates at me. "I know you, man. You're like a lion. Once you've made a kill, you fill your belly and then won't sniff at a young gazelle within paw swipe. Oh, you screw that Italian chick on your houseboat in Kashmir for a month, then go to a monastery in Ladakh, virtuous and calm. Four months? Now the lion's getting hungry again. Beginning to prowl. Aha! He spots his prey, the beautiful, blonde—"

"Sabina!" I blurted out, my voice squeaking up an octave. With my back to her, I had not seen her cross the dining area towards our table.

"Hi. Can I sit for a moment?"

She sat next to me, blue sari rustling. Blood started pounding in my ears.

"This is Manjoor," I said. "We're staying in the same hotel. He's from South Africa."

"Oh, I thought you were Indian."

"Parents, yes. But don't let the skin fool you. I've no Hindu inhibitions."

"Well, I just stopped to say hi. I've got to—"

"No, no, Tim said you would join us for coffee after dinner."

"Really? No, thanks but."

"Ah, we insist, right, Tim? God, he's been awfully quiet all evening. I don't know what's gotten into him. Tell me, Sabina, what do you make of him?"

She studied my face, held me in her eyes, a smile playing on her painted lips. I felt embarrassed at what she might see, almost ashamed, yet so glad for her gaze, for how she lingered with it.

"Innocent, I think," she said quietly, her face soft. I wanted to reach out and touch her cheek.

"What? Him?" said Manjoor.

"Something of a little child."

"Ho ha!"

"Yes, a bit. I see it. Now must go. Bye."

Manjoor shook his head after her. "You should take her, man. She's obviously insane for you."

But I no longer wished to argue. I wanted only to hang on to the gentleness of her gaze, the stillness I felt when, just for a moment, the lion lay down with the lamb.

That night Manjoor rambled on endlessly in the cot next to mine at the Royal Hotel flophouse. Occasionally he directed a comment at another South African Indian who stayed completely zipped up inside his sleeping bag like a giant brown larva in a puffy red cocoon. He said nothing, except when Manjoor punched him.

"Shit, you going to sleep all night, you lousy fucker?" Manjoor delivered a kick to one end of the cocoon. Head or foot, it was hard to tell.

A muffled "Piss off" came from the kicked end.

"Tim, as a budding doctor, this guy Marlow's a case."

"I've never seen him out of the bag."

"No kidding? He's gorgeous. Here—" Manjoor tugged at the zipper, grabbed two handfuls of curly black hair and wrenched a half-conscious face up out of the bag for me to see. "A beauty! Look at those eyes! You could fall in love with those eyes!"

"Piss off, piss off," the brown larva protested feebly with a bit of a laugh.

Manjoor dropped the head and stuffed it back in the bag. I laughed uncomfortably at his playful abuse. He looked at me sharply.

"Innocence, ha! You got her fooled all right. But let me give you some advice, my friend. Women don't want to be fucked by innocence. You got to let 'em know who's on top. Treat 'em rough, little child. They like it."

"Not my style. Besides, the conference ends tomorrow. Then we go to different lands."

"Go to Kashmir with her."

"I've been there. Besides, too many memories."

"The Italian chick again? Oh shit, are you for real? Beneath the pseudo-monk, a quivering Romantic!" He wagged a finger in my face. "I don't buy it."

"Anyway, it's too cold there this time of year."

"Cold? Jesus, it's your pecker that's cold. I should stuff you in the bag with Marlow."

I did my best, despite Manjoor, to focus all my attention on the conference proceedings, noting with interest that even among monks, conflicts flared up from time to time. The Theravadan Buddhists of south Asia scorned the northern Buddhist sects for turning the Buddha's original philosophy of renunciation into a religion of rituals and magic; the northern, or Mahayana, sects tended to look down on the old-school fundamentalists of the south, claiming that literal interpretations missed out on the cosmic truth of which the historical Buddha was merely one manifestation. Some members of the Tibetan delegation protested that the Indian government had left the Dalai Lama off the invitation list as a deliberate political snub to appease Beijing and keep China's occupation of Tibet off the agenda. Even Japanese Zen monks got into the fray. They complained their culture was being smeared by Sri Lankans (strict vegetarians) who criticized as un-Buddhist a 1,400-year-old Japanese dance number, "A Snake Eater Expresses His Joy upon Finding a

Snake," which was included in the evening performance schedule. I heard Indian Buddhist monks (for whom conversion to Buddhism was a way of breaking out of the rigid Hindu caste system) argue shrilly with a smug Brahmin pundit who maintained the Hindu view that Buddhism was merely a branch of the Vedic tradition, and the Buddha just another incarnation of the god Vishnu.

To mute such conflicts, the organizers revived an edict of the ancient Indian-Buddhist emperor Ashoka. They made it the virtual motto of the conference: "Anyone who tries to damage another sect merely brings harm upon his own."

In one seminar I did witness doctrinal differences being resolved with genuine Buddhist grace. During a Zen monk's lecture on Japanese haiku, a scholarly Tibetan monk objected to a quoted line of verse: "The Buddha-nature of the mountains and streams."

"Only sentient beings have the Buddha-nature," said the lama. "Where in the *sutras* is it written that mountains and streams possess it?"

Theravadan monks in the audience murmured assent. Japanese participants fought back in defence of *their* poem. Open conflict broke out, art versus scripture. Finally a Japanese-Canadian from Vancouver rose and humbly resolved the debate:

"I am a teacher of Buddhist history, and a Japanese by birth. So perhaps, standing in the middle as I do, I can offer my opinion. No, there is nothing in the sutras to back up this idea that the mountains and the streams contain the Buddha-nature. That point is clear. But if you could see the mountains and streams of Japan—they are so beautiful—you, too, would believe the Buddha-nature fills them."

Still, most of the lectures I attended seemed dry and academic, rather than a meeting of Buddhist hearts and minds. Other participants complained that there was no time in the schedule for inter-sect contemplation. So, on the last day of the conference, the organizers agreed to hold special demonstrations of various meditation techniques practised throughout the Buddhist world.

I slipped out early from a seminar on Buddhism and socio-economics to get a good seat in the demonstration room. Sabina turned the corner ahead of me. She was wearing a gold-embroidered maroon sari that swished with every step.

"Be calm, be calm, be calm!" I chanted ineffectively, walking swiftly to catch up with her.

"Oh hi, Sabina," I said casually, completely in charge of my words. "You going to the demonstrations?"

"Um, first I'm going to the toilet."

"I'll join you."

Her eyes flickered on me a moment, uncertain.

"Next door, I mean."

We walked together. I noted my pulse quickening.

"Tim, tell me, what do you think of this American monk? He's invited me to his villa in Bombay."

"Really? Oh."

"But what's your thought. Do you think he's real?"

"I don't know. I don't really know him. Not really."

"But why won't you say?"

I took a deep breath. "Because I do have a bad feeling about him. Could be intuition. Could be jealousy."

I banged through the swinging doors into the white tiled men's room, and stared at my face in the mirror.

"How old are you?" I asked my reflection.

"Twenty-six, and puberty has just hit," it said back, shaking its head.

I waited the appropriate length of time, then dived back out into the hallway right into the middle of a passing group of sari-clad women, all young and pretty conference aides. I felt I had stumbled into a living flower garden, surrounded like this, five of them suddenly chatting with me at once, well within paw swipe. Sabina swung out through the other door, gave me a little smile, then swished down the hallway out of sight.

A few minutes later I creaked open the door to the meditation demonstration room. A bearded lama with long black hair in a top-knot sat in the lotus position in the middle of the room on a table-top, chanting sacred syllables in a deep, resonating voice. I'd never seen long hair on a Tibetan monk before and thought perhaps he belonged to some obscure sect. About a hundred observers lined the walls with dozens more in student chair-desks surrounding centre stage. Sabina stood on the far side, next to Professor Strauss. Head bent, he was whispering in her ear.

I noticed my teacher from Ladakh, Drukchen Rimpoche, seated listlessly in a chair. I worked my way through to a vacant seat next to him. We had seen very little of each other throughout the conference. As a young but important lama, everyone wanted his time. The chanting monk abruptly stopped, stood and bobbed his topknot in all directions. The spectators clapped. Drukchen turned to me and smiled wanly. The conference had obviously been an ordeal for him. The lectures, debates, lavish banquets, artistic performances, they had nothing to do with the things he had told me he cared most about: the spiritual welfare of his monks, his efforts to spread the practice of compassion in the villages, and his longing for time for private meditation, which was so scarce amid his many public responsibilities, such as attending this conference.

The tabletop stage of the meditation room was next occupied by—Jerry. Fraud! Charlatan! I wanted to stand up and denounce him. With a toothy smile he folded his legs in kneeling position, hands resting in his lap. A Japanese chant boomed from his turtlenecked throat. His assistant, a burly, curly-haired man who resembled a bulldog, began taking flash photographs from every angle.

"Showing the monks how to meditate," I grumbled to myself. "Great cover for his next book."

My anger was abruptly dispersed by a gentle stroking on my arm.

It was Drukchen. The lama was playing with the fine brown hairs on my exposed forearm resting on the desk next to him. Throughout Ladakh, my body hair, a rarity among Tibetan peoples, had often fascinated them, especially young children. Occasionally they reached out to grab it. Drukchen, with the innocent absorption of a child, stroked me with his fingertips. I held still, as if a butterfly had landed on my arm. Drukchen lived so purely, I thought. He could reach out and touch and enjoy. My vain pretensions of conquering desire vanished under that soft stroking. I wanted to cry. Why could I not reach out and touch as the young lama did?

"It's sad, Tim, it breaks my heart. Last night of free food, and Vishnu help me, I've got the shits."

"Me too, Manjoor. Must have been the banquet last night. Bloody five-star hotels. I've lived for months on grimy restaurant slop and thrived on village water that should have killed me. A high-class buffet does me in instead."

"But I see you're still eating. Shit, a little Himalaya on your plate. Where did you find the vanilla ice cream?"

"Past the crowd of lamas round the back. Those young ones, last night for them before they go back to barley dough and butter tea. It won't be easy after five days at the trough of plenty."

Manjoor shot off through the crowd of red robes. Gentle fingers touched my arm.

"Tim, I'm going now. I wanted to say goodbye. I didn't see you all evening."

"Going, now? But it's only eight-fifteen!"

My heart jumped as if jolted. I tensed with panic, then felt a sudden flush of relief. She was going. I would never touch her, never see her again. Tonight I would be sad. Tomorrow I would be able to get back to the business of exploring India on my own, calm, balanced, a spiritual seeker once more. I was fortunate to be free of her. Yes. What was she saying?

"... and I'm not feeling well, so I go. It's been nice to know you."

"Enjoy Kashmir."

"Oh, didn't I tell you? Professor Strauss says there is nothing for my research in the museums up north. Besides, it's too cold alone up there, this time of year."

"So, what will you do?" My mouth went dry.

"Stay in Delhi a few more days, then go back to Varanasi. I still have some work to do here at the Archeological Records Library."

"Lunch?" I croaked, involuntarily.

"What?"

"Together. After the conference."

"Why, why not? Is Wednesday good? I'll give you my number. You'll call?"

I nodded.

"You're so quiet."

She wrote her number on a card, handed it to me, then put her fingers lightly on my arm again.

"Must go. Professor Strauss is waiting for me. Goodbye."

"Hey, man, give me a bandage," said Manjoor from his cot. "A cat bit me last night. My toe's bleeding."

"Cat? There's no cat in here."

"It's new. Jesus, you want me to bleed to death, get all infected and lose my foot?"

"Maybe it was a rat that bit you."

"A rat? Oh Christ! Rabies! Marlow, Marlow, you lazy bastard, maybe I got rabies!"

Manjoor stuck his head inside the red sleeping bag and began snarling and snapping over Marlow's hollers and curses. At length Manjoor pulled back, wiping spittle from his lips.

"Then you better give me some ointment or something too."

"Shall I wash the wound and suck it for you?"

"Ugh. What are you? Pervert? Vampire? Jesus, she really said she'd have lunch with you? I'll make sure the dorm is clear if you want to bring her back in the afternoon. Oh, spare me the noble brow. I know you wouldn't think of such things. Just a goddamn goodbye lunch. Sure."

"In fact," I said, voice calm and detached as I levelled my eyes on him, "I'm going to ask if she wants a research assistant."

For the first and only time, I saw Manjoor open his mouth, and not a word come out.

I found Sabina in a gloomy room of the Archeological Records Office lined with library shelves containing huge black books like leather tombstones. She sat at a dusty wooden table, surrounded by several stacks, head bent, turning pages. Her blonde hair was pulled back into a bun, and it looked far darker than it had at the conference. She wore a black T-shirt and a dark brown skirt.

"A little black smeared on the cheeks and you could be a jewel thief," I said.

Her eyes flashed up. "Isn't this place a mess? I have to go through all these books of photographs. Every picture. They are from museums all over India. Already this morning I've looked through these"—she put her hand on two of the stacks, each about half a metre tall. "You see, for my research I have to find every single statue in India of Buddha seated in the Earth-Touching Gesture."

"What's that?"

"I'll show you."

She pushed her book aside and climbed up on the table, pulling her legs up into cross-legged meditation posture, and touched the fingertips of her right hand to the table.

"This is what I look for. Underneath, there should be a small old man dressed like a general. That's Mara, god of delusion, *samsara,* or 'the world.' He's the Buddhist devil, if you like. He tried to prevent Buddha—this is before he became Buddha—from gaining enlightenment. According to the mythology, after several years of practising ascetic meditations, Buddha realized this would not lead him to enlightenment. He gave up this extreme path and took an offered drink of milk from a village woman. Once he had regained his strength, he took his seat under the Bodhi Tree, and vowed he would not move until he had comprehended the nature of suffering and how to be free of it. Mara realized this wisdom would threaten his kingdom, so he sent an army of demons to frighten Buddha and break his concentration. But Buddha saw that the demons were all chimeras, and could not harm him. Next, Mara sent his three beautiful daughters to seduce Buddha. But they could not break his concentration either. He saw that they too were illusions, and when he looked at them, they turned to withered hags.

"Mara grew very angry, but he was still a master of lies. He tried to trick Buddha into giving up his plans to spread his wisdom to others.

Appearing to Buddha himself, Mara congratulated him on his efforts of many past lifetimes which brought him to this crucial moment. Then he added that although Buddha was bound to gain enlightenment, his efforts would bear no fruit. There was no one to speak for him, no one to bear witness to what he had accomplished. Without a witness, who would be able to understand what the Buddha had done? No one. He would be alone with his enlightenment. So the wisest course would be for Buddha to leave Mara's realm and enter Nirvana at once, alone.

"But instead the Buddha touched the ground where he was sitting. He said, 'The earth will be my witness.' The Earth Goddess rose from the ground where he touched it and said, 'I will bear witness to your attainment.' Mara fled in defeat, and at that moment, Buddha was enlightened."

"Wow. What a great story to choose for your research."

"Oh, I didn't choose it. It was assigned to me by my faculty adviser back in Europe for my Ph.D. thesis."

"Still, it sounds like real detective work."

She shrugged. "Well, mostly it's just looking at pictures of statues and writing descriptions. Keeping track of everything is the hardest part."

We flipped through the photos together for an hour, then took a motor rickshaw to Connaught Place and Delhi's only pizza parlour for lunch. Sitting across from me in the greasy vinyl booth—the restaurant was disorientingly *faux* American—Sabina told me more about the next phase of her work, which involved searching the museums and ruins of India for Earth-Touching Gestures that were not in the catalogue. It was original research, and it had to be thorough. If she missed one statue that someone on her committee knew about, her thesis defence could be ruined. Though the task seemed daunting, she sounded confident about completing it. I munched the doughy, undercooked pizza, admiring her determination, yet struggling hard to keep my mind on her words and not on my impending proposition.

"Do you think you'll visit Sikkim?" I asked at last, hiding my hands under the table in case they started to shake.

"No," she said slowly. "It's not really part of my research area. Why?"

"Well, there must be a lot of Tibetan-Buddhist statues there, and, well, I want to go there sometime. Here, I brought you some pamphlets on the place."

"That's kind of you." She placed them on the table without looking at them, and kept her eyes on me, head tilted slightly to one side, seeming a bit puzzled.

I struggled to get my words in sequence. "You see, I told you I was going to Nepal. But I'm in no real rush. The mountains will be there a long time. And, well, Sikkim or anywhere"—I took a deep breath—"I'd like to be with you for a while. I like you a lot. Do you think you could you use a research assistant?"

Sabina's eyes dropped and traced the curves of our pizza crusts as if discerning a toss of the I Ching. "I . . . I'll have to think about it," she said.

She looked up suddenly, eyes piercing me just as she had done at the banquet.

"You have such clear eyes," she said.

"Your eyes—you have a way of holding me in them."

"You remind me of my dentist."

"What?"

"No, no, please understand. My dentist was a beautiful person. I was in love with him. I used to go for extra check-ups just so I could lie on his chair."

She sat silent, studying me with her eyes, her elbows on the table, chin resting on her folded hands. I felt helpless, as if I had fallen into a blue sea, floating, but unable to touch bottom.

She sat back. I held my breath. Slowly she smiled.

"Yes," she said at last, "I think you would make a very good research assistant. I accept."

October 16, 1984
Dear Wendy,

I met this Austrian woman at the conference who is doing her doctoral thesis on Buddhist art. For her work, she has to visit all the Buddhist ruins and museums in India, and she has agreed to take me on as an unofficial research assistant for a while. I can't think of a better way to penetrate Buddhist India. Sabina speaks good Hindi, and this is her fifth trip to the subcontinent. She seems to really know her way around. I know there's a lot I can learn from her.

Okay, who do I think I'm kidding? Certainly not you. Truth is, I fell for this woman hard from the first moment I saw her. At a Buddhist conference, of all places—about as likely as getting mugged at church. I guess I had my guard down with all those monks around. I tried to watch my desire rise and pass away, but it just kept rising. We met after the event was over. I told her I wanted to travel with her, and asked for the job. It was excruciating, being so open about my feelings. What happened to the Buddhist equilibrium I wrote about in my last letter? I don't know, but I'll bet I still need it. Although it was implicit in my offer, she hasn't exactly agreed to be my lover yet. In fact, I hardly know her. Tomorrow we leave New Delhi for Varanasi, where she's studying. We will travel together for about two weeks. Then she has to return to Delhi to meet a girlfriend coming from Austria. I'll go on to Nepal, and if things really work out, we could meet again at another Buddhist conference she has to attend in early December. It's an ideal set-up.

I haven't seen much of her, post-conference, except for one lunch and a folk festival we went to this evening. The last performance was a series of three martial arts dances performed by tribal warriors from the jungles near Burma. The first two acts were impressive displays of swordplay, but the finale began in a most bizarre way. Two warriors in loincloths came out on stage, one carrying a sword, the other a large cucumber. A man in pants and a shirt came out with them, holding a double handful of green powder, like chalk dust. The warrior with the sword knelt down and threw back his head. He closed his eyes and covered his mouth while the chalk dust was dumped over his eyes. Then a blindfold was tied over top of the dust, so there was no conceivable way he could see. The other warrior then walked to front and centre stage, lay down and placed the cucumber lengthwise on top of his naked belly. The man in the shirt grabbed the blindfolded warrior from behind, under the arms, picked him up and spun him around several times. He dropped him and walked off-stage as the drum began to beat.

The audience hushed as they realized what was about to happen. The blindfolded and dizzy warrior straightened as his feet hit the floorboards. He took four quick steps across the stage and brought his sword down hard, gouging the wood. He danced back and forth, slashing with every step, until he was right next to the supine warrior. The beat quickened, the sword flashed. The dancer straddled the other man's body, the blade flickering inches from his flesh. He moved in some dark, intuitive world in which he had perfect control. The drum accelerated, the warrior leapt high in the air, spun to land with his feet in front of the helpless man, and he plunged the sword down.

"Thut"—two split halves of the cucumber flew into the air. The warrior jumped up and spread his arms wide to show the audience that there was not a scratch on his belly. A bit less pressure and the cucumber would not have been cut through. A bit more, and blood would have flowed.

This is the first time I've seen anything tangibly paranormal in India. I've heard stories, yes, but actually watching a man see without using his eyes—it makes me realize afresh just why I'm here. I said this to Sabina, anticipating she might tell me some of the wonders she must have encountered in her many trips. She said such talk was foolishness. The warrior dancer just practised and learned his steps. Why did I have to make it all magic, she wanted to know? She sounded annoyed.

I told her I thought she was the one who spent all her time studying tales of the Indian gods and their magic.

"Study them, yes," she said, very prickly. "But I certainly don't believe any of it. Indology is a *science*, Tim. We observe, describe and interpret. We don't rub ash on our faces and walk on hot coals."

I was taken aback by this burst of academic rationalism, Wendy, and suddenly realized that what she apparently wants from India is much different from what I'm after. Not incompatible, certainly, just different. She's collecting data to fit another piece of India into a scientific system. I'm searching for the inexplicable, something to crack open my metaphysical prejudices. But her swift debunking strikes me as ironic, because the most paranormal part of my journey right now is that soon I will be travelling with this beautiful woman whom I know next to nothing about. To me the world seems full of mysteries, ready to be explored.

Love, your brother,

Tim

CHAPTER THREE

GREEN GRASS, MANY COBRA

Varanasi

O N THE OVERNIGHT train ride from New Delhi, an irritated conductor informed Sabina and me that we were on the wrong train to Varanasi. Our train was the 8:10; we had mistakenly boarded the 7:01, which had departed at 8:15, whereas the 8:10 had not yet arrived at the station. He said we would have to return to Delhi and exchange our tickets.

"I think we better get off," Sabina said.

"Whatever for?" I replied. "This train is going to Varanasi. We both have comfortable seats and sleeping berths, and nobody else has claimed them. It may be the wrong train for him, but it's right enough for me."

The conductor grabbed at Sabina's bag. I clutched the strap and glared at him.

"Why can't we just wait at this stop for our train?" she asked reproachfully.

"I'm sure we can," I grumbled, annoyed at her for breaking solidarity, "and if it stops at this station at all, and if it's only two hours late instead of twelve, our seats will likely have been resold and we'll be at the mercy of the next conductor anyway."

"All right, you go to non-reserved section," the conductor said. "Seats are reserved only until Bareilly, then you can come back here."

Sabina got up. I followed her, against my better judgement, to the nearest non-reserved car. We wedged our way inside. It was packed to the doors, the aisle jammed with dirty, sweating bodies and staring eyes.

"All he wanted was to get rid of us," I said, frustrated. "Let's go back."

She agreed. But the wily conductor, anticipating our return, stood blocking the entrance to his carriage and would not let us re-board. Sabina spotted a blue-uniformed official on the platform and pleaded our case. He seemed transfixed by her golden hair and beseeching smile, and said that although any Indian who made this mistake would certainly be sent back to Delhi, he would help us. He led the way to a special "women's carriage" at the rear of the train, where single women could travel unmolested. I wasn't too sure how this was going to help me, but when he ushered both of us on board, I saw half a dozen Indian men inside, trying to hide from the official under the saris of their wives. We squashed ourselves into the only vacant upper berth just as the train jerked forward.

At the next stop, soldiers boarded our car, rifles in hand, under orders to clear out the men, who cowered against their wives and refused to budge. Voices rose, then rifle butts. Strong hands grappled with skinny arms. The leader scanned the upper berths and spotted me. He pointed his weapon at my face, then jerked it towards the door. Sabina turned on her smile again, and broke into Hindi. I listened to the music of her speech, and watched, amazed, as after a minute the soldier began to grin, almost sheepishly. The train started to move once more. He signalled to the others. Dumbfounded, they released the male passengers they had collared and followed their commander off the car.

"You charmed him like a snake," I said, impressed.

"So often in India, hair this colour is a problem. You have no idea," she replied. "It's nice to make it work for you, once in a while. If I were alone, I wouldn't dare try."

"You'd get offers you didn't want?"

"Offers?" she laughed at my naiveté. "I'd get raped."

When the lights went out in the compartment, she shifted on the cramped berth to lie with her head in my lap. She reached up and stroked my hair. We touched arms, intertwined fingers, and whispered stories about our lives.

"I suppose a lot of men have asked you to marry them?" I asked.

"No. Only one. He was crazy jealous over me, and trouble. He had been in prison. He kept trying to control me, so I ended it. Most men just want me around for sex."

The matter-of-fact tone of this remark stunned me. Suddenly I resented these men from her past. They seemed so, so, numerous. Didn't they realize she was intelligent, talented, independent, skilled at negotiating her way through a difficult and even dangerous land? At the same time, the casual way in which she threw this out made me wonder, would it be enough, perhaps, if I just wanted her around for sex? I'd never do that, of course, I told myself. An image of Manjoor appeared in my mind, his brown finger wagging at me. I argued with the finger: Look, sure I want the sex, but I don't want the complications, the attachments, the guilt when it's time to go our separate ways. She's obviously adept at handling men, and to me that's most appealing. I won't have to worry about hurting her.

"They didn't appreciate you," I said.

"Oh, it's not as if I wanted them to marry me," she said lightly. "You know, so many men have given me keys to their Porsches. But there is a word in German for a man with a Porsche: *Porschole*. It rhymes with what it means in English."

When we arrived in Varanasi the next afternoon, tired and dirty, Sabina told me she knew a secret about the city: a genuine, germ-free modern swimming pool we could use. We took a three-wheeled cycle rickshaw from the train station to the posh Taj Hotel on the outskirts of town. There, the manager permitted foreign visitors to lunch and swim for thirty-three rupees—about three dollars. The pool was completely insulated from surrounding India by a high cement wall. I came out of the change room first, wearing my Adidas running shorts, and plunged into the blue water, marvelling at the strangely familiar taste of chlorine in my mouth. Since arriving in India, I had learned to treat water as something poisonous. Just the occasional unsterilized sip had made me wretchedly ill a few times. To splash about so freely without having to worry about contracting cholera or dysentery seemed an incredible luxury. Gliding along in a breaststroke, I watched the waiter bring out bottled beer and clubhouse sandwiches and set them on a poolside table. I hadn't seen such exotic delicacies in ages.

Sabina emerged from the change room wearing a white bikini. She lay down on one of the chaise longues and began covering her legs and shoulders with suntan oil, not speaking a word. For over four months I had not seen a woman wearing anything more revealing than a sari, and could hardly bear to look at her. I swam back and forth until I was nearly exhausted.

"Rub some on my back," she asked, turning over on her stomach as I pulled myself, panting, from the pool. "But make sure no one from the hotel is watching."

I picked up the plastic bottle and poured a puddle in the small of her back. It smelled of coconuts. Her skin was already hot from the sun and drank the oil quickly from my fingers. I rubbed and felt the muscles along each side of her spine, noticing a swirl of fine golden hair at the base of it.

"I always loved beaches when I was a girl," she murmured, head to the side, one cheek pressed against the chaise longue. "The smell of suntan oil, beer and sweating men."

Was she deliberately driving me mad, I wondered? In Delhi, before our departure, she had explained to me that since she was living in Varanasi as a student, we could not be seen together near her university. The security guards around her dormitory were very strict, and someone was always watching. She had to be in her room alone by 9:30 every night. If she was out too late or too often, it would ruin her reputation, which in India it was vital she preserve. Otherwise, she could be disgraced, or worse, hounded by every male on campus. I agreed to take a room in a tourist guest house near the university, and she promised that in three days we would travel together to

Patna, capital of neighbouring Bihar, a state rich in Buddhist treasures and precious little else. And then? Well, she did not exactly say what then.

I tasted coconut oil from my fingers as I crunched through my bacon-and-chicken clubhouse, and listened to her make plans for where we could meet for dinner the following day. The following day? I knew I had agreed to this, but I was so aroused after eighteen hours squashed on a single berth with her on the train and now all this rubbing and oiling that I could hardly stand it. She noticed my anxiety, and explained that Professor Strauss was also coming to Varanasi. He was a friend of her Indian adviser, she explained, and had offered to introduce her to various Buddhist scholars he knew in the city, all valuable contacts for her research. She did not dare risk his seeing the two of us together for fear he might recognize me from the conference.

"So Strauss is coming here, and I've got to stay hidden?" I looked at her, hard. The pudgy professor was offering her the academic equivalent of the keys to a Porsche.

"Yes, he's so sweet," she continued lightly but deliberately as she met my look, "and it's so kind of him to take an interest in my career. He was very angry with me at the conference for spending so much time with that American when I could have been making more contacts with Indologists."

This was a blatant but brilliant response. I decided I liked Strauss after all. Any enemy of Jerry's was bound to be a friend of mine. I didn't think Sabina would reciprocate favours with the chunky German. But she was clearly going to take advantage of whatever help he had to offer. At the same time, she was reminding me that I had already won her affections, at least to a degree, if I could just cool it for a little while longer. We agreed to meet next evening, in the courtyard of Ace's New Deal Restaurant, near the heart of old Varanasi.

I swam once more after lunch, trying to get cool. Then we changed back into our native clothes and re-entered India. She dropped me at the guest house. Alone in my sparse little room, I sat on my bed, drew my legs up into meditation posture, and contemplated the paradox of this woman who had made it clear she was sexually open but socially locked up tight. I pulled out my journal and wrote:

Really, the ache of desire is no different from the pain in my knees when I've meditated for too long. When I try to avoid the pain by shifting my weight, it only increases. But if I accept the pain without fleeing from it, just keep still, it's bearable, and soon recedes into the background of contemplation. Desire's of the same stuff. It torments me only when I'm racing towards ful- filment. I remember what Lama Philippe told me: "A monk doesn't look for results, he just does as his guru tells him." I can't force "results" with Sabina. For all I know, she'll decide to stay in Varanasi a month, just keep me hanging until I wither away. I guess either I can do as my new guru tells me, or else go my merry, solitary way.

Next morning I took a cycle rickshaw to the banks of the Ganges to visit the ghats—the great stone stairways that descend from the streets to the holy river's murky waters. Holiday-makers choked the market near the main steps, and I had to get off the three-wheeler several blocks from the water's edge. It would soon be *Diwali*, Festi- val of Lights, a three-day celebration in remembrance of the God- king Rama and his queen Sita's return from years of exile and separation back to their rightful throne. In Varanasi, India's holiest city, on the banks of its holiest river, the party had started early. Young boys lit firecrackers in the alleyways. Shops, homes and hotels were all draped top to bottom with strings of bright red, blue, yellow and green lights that shone day and night. Christmas lights, I thought with a laugh at my cultural baggage.

The riverside crematoriums just above the burning ghats were doing brisk business: there seemed no better time of year to die and have your ashes scattered in the sacred river. These rites, I was told, assured Hindus that Shiva, patron deity of the city, would place the word *Rama* in the mouth of the deceased; and to have the name of God in your mouth as you pass out of the present life is, for a believer, the surest way to enter a heavenly realm in the next. People from all across India came to Varanasi to die. Death hotels had prospered by the river's banks for centuries—no mean feat, considering that repeat customers came only once a lifetime. I sat for an hour in a rented rowboat with a young English teacher named Shankar who offered to be my guide. We watched the men at work at the top of the ghats. Bodies wrapped in white sheets were strapped to bamboo stretchers to prevent them from curling as they burned, each body on its own small bier. Since cremation was run by a special caste as a business, strict time limits were set for each burning; curling corpses slowed them down. Ashes and any leftovers were dumped into the river with the appropriate, if somewhat brief, ceremony.

At first the burning ghats and the attached waiting rooms seemed to me a gruesome tradition, though beyond a doubt an excellent source of revenue for the those who ran them. I saw nothing holy about the great river, half a mile wide, its waters swift and dark. From the boat I watched hundreds of bathers perform their purifications where the water met the ghats, and felt horrified as they ritually dunked themselves five times, then swished out their mouths with the water. Holy water, according to Shankar, who claimed no one had ever fallen ill from drinking from the Ganges.

"They ran scientific tests," the Hindu told me in earnest. "There were not bad germs, only good germs. If you are sick and you drink the water, these germs will make you well! If you bathe in it, covering yourself five times, you will wash away all the sins of your past lives."

I had my doubts. Shankar watched me intently, then ordered the boatman to row upriver. He stroked steadily against the current, past the last of the main ghats and the golden spires of countless temples to a huge cylindrical metal column connected by pipes to the shore. Near the column, the river bubbled and churned fiercely. I asked what it was, but Shankar paid no attention. His eyes scanned the turbulence.

"There!" he cried, clutching the sleeve of my kurta.

A smooth black shape rose in an arc from the midst of the river, glistened for a second, then slipped quietly back under the surface.

My skin went cold with fear. The creature surfaced again, barely five metres from the boat. This time I caught sight of its dorsal fin. A small jet of mist shot out from its back as it curved beneath the boiling water once again.

"Holy dolphins of the Ganges," Shankar told me, pressing his palms together reverently.

"But dolphins only live in salt water," I said, stunned.

The teacher wobbled his head at me, making a sideways figure eight with his nose. "You're a hard man to argue with, Mr. Tim."

Two arching backs broke the surface together.

"So you think about it. How can the Ganges be polluted with such creatures living here?"

When we returned to shore I said my thanks to Shankar and wandered back towards the bathing ghats, where white-robed believers sat on wooden pallets, preparing themselves for the ritual dunking. A priest manned each pallet, blessing each person and smearing each forehead with sandalwood paste and a bright red blotch of cinnabar. I watched one old man wearing a marigold garland, his shaven head covered with grey stubble. He rose from the pallet, removed his robe and, wearing only a loincloth, stepped with dignity down into the water. Coming up for the fifth time, he rinsed his mouth, then raised his pressed palms to the river in worship while the sun beat down overhead. For a flicker of a second, I saw the river as if through the old man's eyes: as the mother who embraced all who entered her, the living and the dead. She was the source of life for over a thousand miles, stretching herself across north India like a great grey-green python. From her glacial streams in the Himalayas to her fertile delta in the Bay of Bengal, her floods and droughts governed the course of history. The Ganges did not need the Hindu myths and Brahmin priests for her sanctity. Rather, it was the holiness of the waters that gave credence to the gods.

"And will you not take a bath?" said a rotund priest with a fleshy chin and dark pools for eyes.

I, the perpetual observer on the shore, had been observed. The priest motioned me to join him on his pallet under the shade of a large white umbrella fixed to the boards. To my surprise, I nodded. The sandalwood felt grainy and cool as he rubbed it across my forehead and then marked me with cinnabar. The priest refused to take a single rupee for the service, and indicated the final steps of the ghat. I stripped to my underwear, laid my clothes in a pile on the edge of the boards and made my way down the stone stairway to the water's edge. None of the other bathers took any notice of my pale, hairy flesh, intent as they were on their prayers.

My foot disappeared beneath the brown surface. The bottom felt muddy, but no slippery bones, no slime oozing between my toes. As I waded in, the water cooled my skin, soothed the heat in my crotch. I looked around for charred remains. None bobbed nearby, and I realized with some relief that the bathing ghats were strategically located upriver from the burning ghats. Still, I could not see my hand held just beneath the surface, and knew that millions of holy germs swarmed round my body, eager for an orifice. I held my breath, squeezed eyes shut tight, and dunked five times. But I could not bring myself to open my mouth and rinse, preferring the past sins of my tongue to the evils the sacred waters might work on my still unbelieving belly.

"It feels so maddeningly Indian to be near you and not be able to touch you."

"But don't you think it's good we've both had to hold back so much, go so slowly?" she replied, her eyes flickering up at me, playfully.

We sat in Ace's New Deal Restaurant, a tourist café set up in the courtyard of a decaying Hindu temple. Sabina leaned back in one of Ace's ancient, overstuffed armchairs, watching closely for my response.

"Wonderful. We've known each other two weeks, and the closest we've come to being alone is on the upper berth of a packed train."

"I told you, my reputation—oh, but you don't mind waiting, do you?"

"Waiting? No," I said stoically. "It's very good for meditation.

Watch desire rise and fall, rise and fall, rise and fall. Actually, I've been in a monastery so long I've probably forgotten what to do if ever we were out from the watchful eye of Mother India."

"Oh, I doubt that," she laughed. She held me in her eyes until I felt the blood pounding in my ears once more. How does she do this to me? I thought, helpless.

"I feel like I want to kiss you," she whispered.

"Let's take a walk around the temple."

I paid the bill and we strolled to the side of the aged holy place. It was classic Hindu Gothic, with dozens of spires shooting up towards the sky, and alcove-forming buttresses girding its base. Weeds and small trees grew in its crevices. I pulled Sabina into a dark corner, out of sight from Ace's tables.

"No, it's not safe."

"We're in shadow. No one can see us."

I brushed my lips against hers, felt the rush of pleasure as she kissed back, tentatively at first, then taking my lower lip between both of hers and gently sucking while she stroked my face with her fingers. Then suddenly she pulled back, out of the shadows.

"Too many people," she said, her face flushed.

"Too much India," I answered glumly, as we completed our circuit round the temple.

Before parting, she asked me to buy our train tickets to Patna for the day after tomorrow, and we agreed to meet again the following evening, back at Ace's. I dutifully spent four hours in line at the station next morning. Four hours was normal for such a task, but for the first time I was able to appreciate the languid pace of Indian ticket clerks. It helped the minutes tick by. Time no longer seemed the valuable commodity it was in North America. In India there was too much time, endless lifetimes of it. How much worse than the pain and suffering of reincarnation was the eternal boredom of it all, like season after season of television reruns.

For a couple of hours I watched the station's *pan* maker mix up his concoction for passing customers. For the first time, bored as I was, I decided to give it a try. Pan's a feel-good stimulant, more common than smoking in India, and available just about everywhere. You chew it, and the juice turns your mouth bright red. Over time it blackens and rots your teeth. I signalled the pan man. From the dozen or so tiny pots in front of him, he smeared and sprinkled colourful pastes and powders on a fresh green betel leaf, as if it were a miniature artist's palette, topping it off with a few chunks of betel nut. He expertly folded the leaf into a fat triangular package with all the goodies tucked inside, and brought it to me.

I popped it awkwardly into the side of my mouth and tentatively began to chew. The leaf bit into my cheek with the cool sting of menthol. As the wrapping broke apart, the coloured smears dissolved into pungent and sweetish tastes: cardamom, hot pepper, tumeric. The betel nut itself was hard as wood at first. It released a tingling sensation something like Novocaine, which gradually spread to my brain, making me giddy. Blood-red saliva sloshed between my teeth. But I couldn't bring myself to simply spit the excess out on the station floor like other betel chewers, who keep the platforms of most stations mottled with disgusting brown-red blotches. The polite thing to do, I thought, would be to spit it out in a toilet, or at least over the tracks. Yet I knew that once I left my place in line, I'd never get it back. So I swallowed, nearly retching as the juices burned my throat and worked their way towards my intestines. I held the mess inside my mouth another hour, gurgled my request for tickets, and then spat the remains out over the tracks.

I could still feel the burning in my belly and the tingling in my brain that evening as I sat alone at Ace's, eyes half closed in attempted meditation. Sabina arrived two hours late. She saw the tickets on the table.

"Oh, you bought the tickets," she said, her voice full of dismay.

"Yes, just as you asked me to." I knew what was coming and clenched my teeth.

"Well, it's just that Professor Strauss has made an appointment to introduce me to a scholar at Benares University tomorrow who is vital for my work . . ." her voice trailed off.

"But, it's almost Diwali! Soon the trains will be so crowded we won't be able to get seats out of here."

She shook her head, her German accent suddenly pronounced and grating on my ears. "No, during Diwali, families stay home. The trains will be empty." Suddenly she softened, but I dreaded hearing the words that followed. "I was thinking, maybe we should stay here until after Diwali. Varanasi is so beautiful during the festival."

"Stay?" I felt the last of my self-control vanish. The betel juice boiling in my belly shot a pain up my chest like heartburn. I swallowed down on it, hard, and spoke with gathering speed and heat. "But Diwali is still two nights away." (I now counted nights, not days.) "Won't that be a waste of your valuable research time? I think we ought to leave tomorrow. Do you know how long I spent in line for these tickets?" I felt my cheeks burn.

"I . . . I don't know if you'd want to," she replied, eyes down, voice subdued, "but I thought if we stayed for Diwali, we could find a room, away from my university. That would be all right, if you want."

"I want," I mumbled, my tongue made clumsy by anticipation, my anger washed away by shame, her kindness, and my own desire.

I spent the morning before Diwali searching for a secluded yet elegant place in the heart of the city, something several notches above the cheap rooms in which I usually passed my nights. I settled at last on the best room in the Maharajah Hotel. It held a wide, sturdy, maharajah-sized bed with two peacocks carved into the hardwood headboard and an ocean-blue bedspread. Bicycle bells and children's playful screams drifted in over the balcony from the narrow street below. A handwoven straw carpet covered the floor. Paint had begun to peel from one corner of the ceiling, which to me blended in well with the decrepit aura of Varanasi. Luxury hotels and swimming pools had no place in this sacred relic of a city.

The little black ants in the sink, however, were another matter. I called the manager.

"Can you get rid of these ants?"

"Oh, they don't hurt anything," said the manager, an agreeable, moon-faced man with a huge black moustache. "Just sprinkle a little water on them like this, see, and they run away into the cracks. I don't like to kill them."

I conceded. The ants, too, belonged. I shook my head at my in-bred preference for sterility over life. I scoured the bathroom clean, swept the mat, and ordered fresh sheets. It felt curiously feminine to prepare a room like this, for a lover. I slung a canvas shopping bag over my arm, then set off through the swelling holiday crowd to buy flowers and fruit in the market.

I picked up a pomegranate. As I handed the vendor a five-rupee note, he pulled out a bamboo stick and swung it fiercely at a woman standing next to me. The cane smacked hard against the side of her face. She stumbled and put her hand to her head, not uttering a sound.

"Thief, thief!" the vendor cried. The bamboo swished through the air again.

She didn't try to run or even dodge the blows. Instead she started screaming back at him. I froze, transfixed by the violence, so close I could feel the whistle of the stick through the air. A crowd gathered. Someone grabbed the bamboo from the vendor and began thrashing the woman viciously around the head and arms. She clutched her body and pulled two ragged children close to her. They huddled into her sari, terrified. She showed no sign of pain, just screamed with rage at the crowd as it closed in. Brown hands held her fast. The vendor yelled to me that the woman had reached inside my bag. He urged me to call the police. I shook my head. I had seen nothing. The bag at my side had been empty. I had no accusation to make. Not directed at her at least. But I had stood by and watched, done nothing to protect her, to shield her.

The right side of the woman's face was quickly swelling, blackening her dark and pock-marked cheek. She seemed numb to everything now: pain, the crowd, the threat of police, her children crying. She stopped yelling and looked around vacantly. Her eyes, flat and dull, floated past mine without making contact. She had sunken cheeks and dusty hair that looked as though it had never been combed or washed. The pattern on her sari was worn to a dull grey. It didn't really matter whether the police came or not. What could they possibly do to make her life worse? The vendor shrugged at me. The crowd released her. She stared at the fruit in the stall until the man with the bamboo prodded her with the stick, pushing her adrift a few metres into the throng.

I put the purchased pomegranate into my empty bag, then drew it out again. I had the sudden urge to give it to the outcast woman, but the futility of the gesture overwhelmed me. If I held it out to her, she might take it and run. I had already caused her one beating. I pictured myself grabbing the swinging bamboo, stopping the blows with my arms. Then what? Giving her money for a few days' food? Inviting her in to the Hotel Maharajah? No, detachment was the only way to survive the bloody karmic mess of India. And yet a cold knot lodged inside of me, the consequence of my inaction. What would Drukchen have done, I wondered? Or Philippe? I watched the woman fade into the crowd. It would have been easier if she were a cow, I thought. At least if a cow ate fruit from my bag, no one would beat it or call the police. A cow, at least, was sacred.

I wandered down to the ghats, bought guava and a passion fruit, a small bunch of red bananas and a lotus blossom. Next I bought candles and a small packet of multicoloured incense sticks. I peeled a banana and ate it, dropping the skin at the feet of a passing cow. She bent her large, gentle head. The great pink tongue licked up the peel in an instant. Still chewing, she turned to sniff expectantly at my sandal, moistening my foot with her breath.

I returned to the room and arranged the fruit in a bamboo wicker bowl, then gently pulled open the petals of the purple lotus. Careful not to bruise it, I set it floating in a dish of water. I lit a candle, tilted it, wick down, and let a few drops of molten wax fall on each night table, using it to fix two candles erect on either side of the bed. After pulling the curtains, I lit the rest of the candles and a stick of incense, then stood back to admire the scene created for this Diwali night. At last I felt the cold knot loosen in my belly.

Unable to bear staying in the room alone, I blew out the candles and retreated to our table at Ace's, where we were to meet for dinner. I decided to sketch the decrepit temple next door, where we had first kissed. Tracing the outline of the intricate latticework and thrusting spires proved thoroughly absorbing work. I barely noticed a ragged Hindu in a sloppy red turban who entered the courtyard carrying two large straw baskets on a shoulder-pole. The man seated himself in a corner of the outdoor café and pulled from one basket a large writhing cloth bag which caught my eye. He removed his reed pipe from the other basket, and drew from the moving sack a large grey-green cobra. He set it on the ground. The snake immediately slithered towards the tourist couple sitting nearest to it. The charmer grabbed the reptile by the tail and yanked it back into place. It twisted and bit his hand. The man cursed and clouted it with his knuckles. The snake, however, seemed intent on joining the diners, who were obviously having their doubts about this form of live entertainment. The woman wore shorts, and her sunburnt pink skin betrayed her recent arrival in India. When she first glimpsed the snake, she drew her feet up out of her sandals and onto her chair. The cobra slithered in her direction again. She gave a small shriek and froze. Her companion, a bearded man in a polo shirt, patted her arm in a patronizing way.

When the snake made a third lunge at her, she bolted, racing barefoot out Ace's front gate and onto the street. Her companion followed, waiter at his heels with the cheque. This left only two customers in the café: myself and a burnt-brown blond-headed Scandinavian who was writing a letter. Neither of us heeded the charmer's attempts to get his rebel cobra to dance. The snake alternately wriggled away and snapped at the charmer's hands. Disgusted, the man eventually grabbed it by the head and threw it back in its sack. Then he came around with the upturned lid of his wicker basket, expecting donations. The Scandinavian did not break from his letter, but ignored the man completely. I pointed to my sketchbook and asked him not to disturb me. The disgruntled charmer threw the writhing bag and pipe back in his baskets, hoisted his show back on his shoulders, spat on the spot where he had sat, and stomped out muttering. The tourists obviously had no appreciation for culture.

Through the long afternoon, a rough rendering of the temple gradually took shape in my sketchbook. I copied every groove in the stone, every leaf on the bushes that grew among the spires. She was late. Light faded in the courtyard. Eventually I closed my sketchbook and stared off into space, thinking of the empty room in the Maharajah, and what it would be like to climb the white staircase alone that night.

Sabina arrived at Ace's at seven o'clock. She put a tiny white clay elephant in front of me. A present, she said, and then told me she couldn't stay. Strauss had invited her to dinner to meet two more Buddhist scholars from the university. No way to get out of it.

"Fine," I agreed, tight lipped. "And so . . . what is your plan? I've got a room all ready." I was unable to meet her eyes.

She looked pained. She chewed at her lower lip.

"All right," she whispered, as if we could be overheard. "You come to my dormitory at eleven, and we'll go back together. Professor Strauss should bring me home in a taxi before then. Stay to the left through the main gates. There's a street lamp next to the dorm. If I'm not home when you come, there is a deserted house on the grounds nearby, next to the hedge. You can wait on the porch. No one will see you. But don't make any noise. If anyone knows you're waiting for me, I could be in big trouble. I have to stay here for the rest of my year, you know. If I lose my reputation . . ."

I nodded. "Eleven. I'll be there."

Sabina stood up. She placed her fingers lightly on my arm and leaned near to me so that the weight of her hair fell on my shoulder.

"You know, Strauss tells me I am unfaithful," she said with a smile. "'No,' I told him, 'in my own way, I am faithful.'"

"Are you?" I grabbed her arm as she started to get up, halting her.

"Let go. We're in public," she hissed low, and I released her. "He would love me if I let him," she continued with a strange and quiet intensity. "He says he's trapped in an unhappy marriage. But I'm not interested in rescuing him. So I mean it when I say, 'In my own way, I am faithful.'"

I read a mix of anger and excitement in her eyes. She smiled. Not the self-possessed smile I was used to: this was wild, almost fierce. Then she turned and walked briskly from the café without looking back. I watched the swing of her hips until she disappeared into the street. Life was much simpler in the mountains.

The evening passed slowly. I wandered up and down the market near Luxa Road, the main drag leading to the ghats, and eventually back to the Ganges. Workers had erected wooden stages and loud-speakers in preparation for Diwali. New stalls selling fresh flowers and candles had sprung up on the roadside. Even the beggars were working overtime, offering the opportunity for grace to the pilgrims that packed the waterfront. A few firecrackers exploded, startling the cows and me as well. I bought a pile of small change from a vendor and walked slowly up a stone stairway lined with lepers and cripples, some two hundred of them in all. Each displayed his or her particular deformities as if they were wares for sale. Into each raised cup or wooden bowl I dropped a few paise in return for blessings and a few cold stares.

By nine, the streets glittered with coloured lights. The entire city was out on the street, everyone streaming towards the Ganges. I found a rickshaw driver willing to pedal me to the university and back for six rupees. I promised him ten. The driver grinned. He was an old man, a veteran who pedalled his three-wheeler barefoot. He wore only an undershirt and a hiked-up grey sarong that revealed stick-like calves. As we set off, a power failure plunged the city into darkness. The drain of a million coloured lights had blown the main fuses. My driver deftly wove his way through the crowd in the blackness. A funeral parade passed us on its way to the burning ghats. Fireworks lit the dark streets like bolts of lightning and exploded like distant thunder in the humid night. I watched the driver's bare feet and scrawny black legs pumping up and down in smooth rhythm. Perspiration glistened on his skin and soaked a dark line down the back of his shirt.

When we arrived at the gate of the university, I assured the driver I would soon return, but paid him five rupees to ensure good faith, telling him to sleep in the back of the rickshaw. The campus was dark. A few ghostly square buildings loomed out of the moonlight. The lawns with their massive trees seemed like a jungle. Feeling safer off the path, I cut across the grounds in the direction of Sabina's dormitory, soon arriving at the deserted house she had told me about. It stood in a grove of trees, separated from the dorm by a wild hedge. I found a spot on the marble porch that allowed a clear view of the iron gate at the entrance of the dorm and the narrow road leading to it. Bats flew through the night, squeaking, black flits of movement in the darkness. I didn't dare rattle the bars of the dorm gate in case another resident answered, so I sat on the porch, folded my legs into meditation posture, and waited for Strauss's taxi to bring her to me.

After a while, a flashlight danced across the lawn, shone on the deserted house and held steady on my white face. A smiling guard approached and wished me good evening. I returned the Hindu's blessing casually, as if I regularly spent my evenings on this secluded porch. The guard asked politely where I was staying. The nearby tourist bungalow, I replied, adding that I only understood a little Hindi. The guard wobbled his head side to side and told me the gates lock at eleven and would I please be gone by then? I nodded. Before turning to go, he suddenly broke into singsong English: "Green grass, green grass, many cobra, many cobra."

With a gesture he pointed out the pathway, indicating, I supposed, that that was where visitors are supposed to walk. He carried a thin stick in one hand. As he strolled away, I noticed he kept the stick in front of him and the flashlight beam to the ground.

The marble floor felt cool and the night breeze turned cold as I sat and waited, eyes riveted to the road, searching for headlights, ears alert for the sound of an approaching car. At eleven o'clock a bell rang. I envisioned the ride back to the hotel and wondered how I would endure the night alone in the wide blue bed. Some action was needed. The guard would certainly be back to check on me. Whistling softly to warn the cobras, I slid my sandalled feet onto the wet grass and crept slowly towards the hedge. On the other side of it, a street lamp lit the entrance to the dorm.

"Hey, cobras, go away," I sang gently, pushing through the hedge.

I squatted by the lamp-post and tried to decide if the single light in the dorm came from Sabina's room. She was out too late. It would ruin her reputation. My heart alternately pounded and froze. A light flashed on in the porch. I cowered back in the bushes like a night creature, wondering if the cobras felt the same fear. I watched and held my breath as a shadow unlocked the gate from the inside. Whoever it was, was bound to see me under the light of the lamp. It was Sabina. I moved forward and waved, still crouching. She went back inside, leaving the gate open, and returned a minute later with a shoulder bag. She locked the gate behind her, then motioned me to join her.

"I don't know which of us is crazier," I whispered by her side. "You for suggesting this, or me for doing it."

"I thought you would never come," she said with a wild look. "I came back early and I've been waiting for you since nine-thirty."

She was dressed all in black, her hair pulled back into a ponytail and stuffed inside the back of her sweater. We walked like escaping convicts, slinking through the shadows without a flashlight. Keeping to the path, we would almost certainly be discovered by guards. But, cobras aside, creeping through the lawns would have been infinitely more difficult to explain if we were caught.

Ahead, a flashlight beam searched the grounds, found us both, and held. Two guards came to meet us on the path, then turned and walked alongside us like a police escort. Polite but surprised, they asked their foreign student just where did she think she was going at this hour of the night?

"Midnight prayers at the ghats, for Diwali," she told them in Hindi.

One man pointed to me with his stick and asked another question.

"Tim, I'm sorry," she said in a fast whisper. "They ask me what time I will be back. I think it is impossible that I go with you now."

"As you like," I replied, trying to mean it. "But if you turn back now, they'll know exactly what we're doing."

She thought about this in silence for several paces.

"What can I do?"

"Lie. Tell them—tell them you are staying with a family downtown near the Ganges."

She spoke in rapid Hindi to the guards, translating to me, "I tell them I'm staying with an English family, and that you are the son come to bring me safely to their house."

The guards explained this to the gatekeeper who reluctantly unbolted the front entrance. I roused the sleeping rickshaw driver outside. For some reason his presence and recognition of me seemed to quell the suspicions of the guards, who reluctantly released us. They watched sullenly as their foreign student and the stranger boarded the rickshaw and lurched off towards the centre of town. Sabina tugged the elastic from her ponytail and tossed her head so that her hair fell across her shoulders. Slipping her arm round my neck in the darkness, she laughed.

"Honestly, I didn't think we'd make it. Those guards asked so many questions. How good a liar I've become in India!"

"Me too," I said, still tingling with the thrill of our narrow escape. "You know, a guard found me at the house where I was waiting for you and gave me a real grilling, and—Oh oh, I told him I was staying at the tourist bungalow. I couldn't see his face, but if he was one of the ones we just left, then they know we were lying."

Sabina frowned a second, shook her hair again and laughed. "What are guards? I don't care any more."

A Roman candle whistled into the air and exploded over the city centre ahead of us. We watched the colours fall.

"And what will happen if I fall in love with you?" she asked, turning to face me in the seat.

"Why do you ask the question one-sidedly?" I tried to banter back.

I didn't know what to say. I had thrown myself at her far better prepared for rejection than anything else. I craved her wildness, her sensuality, her cool expertise at handling men. I wanted great sex and suddenly she was talking love. It scared me. For two years I'd been shackled to Tina, feeling perpetually inadequate and miserable, all because of love. It was so un-Buddhist, I told myself, desperately trying to subdue my rising panic.

"What is it?" she looked at me intently.

"So you answer my question with a question?" I feebly warded off her probing, fearing she had sensed my feelings. For all I knew, she might still stop the rickshaw, dismount and disappear into the crowd.

"Never mind," she said softly. "Diwali lights, they are so beautiful. I'll show you, tonight."

CHAPTER FOUR

FIRE BENEATH
THE SKIN

Patna

S MOKE hung over the city as we rode towards the ghats. In the
distance over the river, we saw fireworks flash, bringing the
jagged outlines of temples into dark relief, followed by thud-
ding like artillery shells. Our rickshaw driver tried to avoid the
crowds by following side roads. Off the main avenues, instead of
electric lights, dozens of small oil lamps and candles had been planted
in rows along the ledges of the homes. Strings of firecrackers burst
like machine-gun fire from the city centre. The explosions came with
greater and greater frequency as we neared the river. A young boy
stepped out from between two buildings and hurled a banger into
the middle of the road. It detonated in the path of our rickshaw,
frightening the driver. He swerved, rocked on two wheels, and nar-
rowly avoided a head-to-horn collision with a wandering cow.
Roman candles flared across the sky, fizzling gold above us. The sacred city could well have been at war.

"I *am* a *Dis*-co *Dan*-cer," the current hit song from a popular Hindi movie, blared out from loudspeakers set up along the main market
streets. Young men gyrated to the beat in front of garishly painted
plaster idols of the God-king Rama and Queen Sita, spotlit and
strung round with coloured lights. A mass of dancing worshippers,
all clapping hands above their heads, jammed the next intersection,

making further rickshaw travel impossible. I paid the driver and we dismounted into the crowd. Clutching each other's hands, Sabina and I pressed our way through the frenzy into the back streets at the centre of the city, trying to find a way to the river.

Wet, dung-filled paths, too narrow for cars or even ox carts, covered the heart of Varanasi like a skein of clogged veins. They twisted and turned, dead-ended and looped back upon themselves. Through one doorway, I spotted a flash of red and the glitter of candles; a rear window into a shrine room was filled with praying, white-robed devotees. In the next alleyway, a water buffalo munched softly on a pile of dried grass. All the shops were still open, their wares spilling out onto the street: silver bangles, pewter pots and water jars, row upon row of small golden idols. Candles and coloured lights covered every ledge. Young boys huddled in small groups, daring each other to hold the tips of red bangers in their hands. The explosions made Sabina jump, and her skittishness attracted the boys' attention. They threw their tiny bombs directly at her sandalled feet, laughing as she shrieked, and giving chase as we tried to escape through the winding alleyways.

The boys fell back when we joined a train of well-to-do women in white saris. The procession led through the inner-city maze to the shore of the holy river, just upstream from the burning ghats. We had inadvertently joined the final steps of a funeral march. The cremation fires seemed muted under a hundred bright electric lamps, each hanging on the end of a long bamboo pole. Lamps for the dead, Sabina explained.

A second power failure struck, dousing the city once more in darkness. But the momentary blackness soon gave way to the yellow glow of cremation fires. Orange embers flickered upwards to the sky. Looking over the Ganges, we saw hundreds of small oil lamps set afloat as offerings to Rama. Moisture rose up from the river and drifted inland, swirling warm and fishy around us. A dog barked near the water's edge, then growled. We stepped down the dark stairs of the ghats and heard a voice call to us from the river.

"Hello, Mister, you want go boat ride?"

We heard the gentle slap of oars. We could not see the hull against the black water, just the boatman's glowing white turban as he slid towards shore. He held out a near-invisible hand to steady us as we boarded. We sat close together on the wooden planks in the bow, and the boat surged slowly upstream away from shore, into the current of tiny river lamps. Sabina urged the oarsman to be careful not to overturn any of the fragile offerings. He allowed the current to take us farther out until a thousand dancing lights bobbed between us and the shore. Beyond the banks, the city's darkened profile was shot through with dots of candlelight.

"Oh, so beautiful," said Sabina. "It's as if the stars have settled on the city."

Where was the rational Indologist now? I thought with a grin. But it vanished the next moment as I felt her fingers touch my cheek, slide down my neck, press lightly against my chest and rest there. The sudden intimacy of her touch inflamed me. I placed my hand on her thigh, felt her muscles tighten and relax. After a minute she placed a hand over mine, holding it still.

"I have an idea," she whispered. "Another secret. I'll show you, back on shore."

When we reached the ghats she took me by the hand and led the way once more through the city's inner maze until we arrived at the gates of an ancient observatory. She quickly coaxed the watchman into opening the iron door for us, then drew me in after her through a confusing network of walkways and walls to a spiral staircase. It took us to an open platform where for centuries Hindu astrologers had charted the course of the sky. As we looked down on the city spread out beneath us, the power failure ended. Varanasi flashed out of the darkness with a million multicoloured lights. A spontaneous cry from thousands of voices rose up from the streets. "Disco Dancer" surged through the loudspeakers. A sudden volley of Roman candles filled the sky with luminous pinks and greens. The smoke that followed covered the city with a misty glow.

Sabina leaned against my side and put her arms around my waist. She pressed against my chest, her breasts warm beneath her kurta, her hair against my cheek.

"I give you Varanasi for Diwali, Tim," she said, holding me close.

It was past one by the time we made our way back through the combat zones of the old city and the still-crowded market streets to the Maharajah Hotel. The moon-faced manager sat outside on the steps, keys in hand. When we entered, he drew an iron gate shut behind us and locked it with a chain.

"Ah, Diwali!" he said dreamily as he climbed the stairs behind us. "Good night!"

Sabina's eyes slowly surveyed the room. She smiled at the sight of the pomegranate, guava and red bananas I had piled in a bowl in the centre of the wide blue bed. On one of the night tables the small white elephant she had given me raised its trunk playfully. I lit four candles around the bed, then turned off the light. Bicycle bells rang in the street below. A burst of firecrackers popped dully in the distance, and the occasional Roman candle sent bars of light in through the cracks in the shutters.

"This is our room," I said, glad for how she lingered over the small details I had prepared.

I left her briefly for the sink, quickly sprinkling droplets of water to scare away the ants. They scurried in panic all across the porcelain bowl and back into the cracked ridges in the plaster. I returned to the room and sat on the bed, legs crossed, eyes closed in a final moment of meditation, listening to her brushing her teeth, peeing, flushing the toilet. Even such earthy sounds filled me with bliss. I felt exhausted and exhilarated, drugged by Diwali, one corner of my mind still wondering if she was going to come back out and announce she had to leave for an important meeting with some Buddhist monks.

She returned and lay on the bed beside me, her head propped on one arm, looking straight into my face. I sank into her gaze. I couldn't speak. We didn't move. After a few minutes, she reached out and touched my cheek.

We caressed, easing each other out of our long Indian shirts. She touched me like an accomplished ballroom dancer leading a novice through his steps, sweeping me along in her grace. She guided my hands, my lips, to where she wanted me, pulled my head to her breast, drew my fingers between her thighs. I felt her muscles tense with pleasure. Her hands stroked my back, my neck, nails scratching lightly across my shoulder blades, her eyes watching me closely in the candlelight, as if learning how my body moved and taking delight in mastering it. Reaching down, she grasped the base of my penis and slowly drew her fingers towards the tip. Her touch felt cool and I trembled. I clutched at her shoulder, panting. She smiled, inscrutable, shifted her hips and pulled me from my side to lie on top of her.

I rolled between her legs, felt her wet heat and pressed into her, gasping for air, blood roaring in my ears. It was too intense, too fast. I wanted to thrust wildly, claw her flesh, but instead dug my fingers into the bedclothes. I froze, afraid to move in case I burst, and an old spectre of shame rose up. Her eyes tried to catch mine, but I averted them. She too was breathing heavily, but stilled her hips. We hung together motionless for a while. Then slowly she began to rock, sliding me in a little deeper with each gentle movement, and the intensity held, did not spill over prematurely as it had done all too often in the past. She wrapped her ankles around the insides of my calves and strained to pull me tighter into her, increasing her rhythm. I opened my eyes and this time met her gaze, the blue sparking dark, honey hair tumbled all about. She threw back her head and I kissed her neck, breathless with the quickening roll of our hips. Our breathing came together now, shorter, faster, her body quivering beneath me. She groaned, and I felt it through to my belly, triggering a shudder, a brief second of bliss, spasms of pleasure coursing outward as I rocked hard against her, and then lay still.

We made love once more in the late Diwali night, and again at dawn as the ringing of bicycle bells filled the alleyway below our room. Later she stroked me awake, taking my sex in her mouth until I grew hard and thrashed my head from side to side. Then, placing her feet on either side of my hips, she lowered herself onto me from a squatting position, still watching, still smiling, while I clutched the sheets. After we had made the great bed rattle one final time, she kissed my belly and slid off towards the bathroom.

"Where are you going?" I asked dreamily.

"Oh, I have a breakfast meeting with Strauss. He has—"

"I know, a Buddhist monk or scholar he wants you to meet for your research."

She grinned at me and closed the bathroom door.

"Ack—Ants!"

I hated to let her go, marvelled that she could separate herself so easily. I pitied Strauss, so infatuated with her, but denied the pleasure of her touch. Yet I felt no pride. Rather, a sense of awe that someone so beautiful, so sexually accomplished had chosen to be with me. It was almost religious. After she left, I lay in the blue bed, thoughtfully munched a guava and picked up my journal. My skin still tingled from her touch. A lazy, drugged warmth ran through my muscles, as if I was drunk on mulled wine.

"Technically," I wrote, "this has been the most intense, longest, most exhilarating night I have ever spent with a woman. I think I have a blister."

Technically.

I stared at the word in my notebook and pondered how it had flowed from my pen. Sabina was certainly a master in the arts of love, but I wondered if I and all men were for her just canvases on which she expressed her art. We had made love passionately and energetically, and I felt an acceptance of my sexuality—even desire for it— that I had never felt with previous lovers. Yet we hardly knew each other. This acceptance was exactly what I had longed for all my life; better, in fact, than I had ever imagined it to be. But somehow dissatisfaction was creeping in already. I picked up my pen again.

"Somehow it feels 'surface,'" I wrote. "Passion, but not real intimacy. I suppose that's not surprising on a first night. It just feels as if somewhere underneath there ought to be a lot more."

"If Strauss insists on coming to the station, can you just meet me on the platform?" she said after our second night in the blue bed.

She was on her way out for a final goodbye breakfast, and I had agreed to meet her at the ticket office for our trip to Patna later in the day.

"No, I'll jump up and kiss you."

She laughed nervously and bit her lower lip.

At the station, she was late. Ten minutes before departure, I decided to leave our meeting place for a minute to confirm that our train was on time. As I passed through the gate leading to the inquiry desk, a heavyset white man with a goatee came through the other way. He didn't recognize me, but the blonde woman at his side in the dark blue Punjabi-style pantsuit certainly did. She blanched, eyes pleading for silence. I brushed past her, not saying a word.

I inquired about the train, found that it was on time, and turned to see Sabina behind me.

"Meet me at the platform, please," she asked, out of breath from running.

I nodded. She turned and ran back through the gate.

"He wanted me to stay another day," she told me when we at last pulled out from the station, leaving the luckless professor behind. "But I told him I sacrifice myself for scholarship."

"Did he try to seduce you?" I asked.

The jealous tone of my own question annoyed me. I wasn't so much jealous as uncomfortable at the apparently lighthearted way she had used his desire to accomplish her own ends. Of course, Strauss seemed a willing enough volunteer. Still, I could all too easily picture myself in his shoes, and was glad I could not be used to further her career.

"No, he didn't try," she replied, "except in a very academic way. We were discussing Mara's daughters and he told me he didn't think their temptation of the Buddha was really about sex. He said he thought it symbolized the attraction of the world in general, and that it would be a misinterpretation to infer from the story that the Buddha was anti-sex."

"Quite a come-on. But it is a good question. What do you think about it? It seems pretty central to your work."

"I told you," she said, irritated, "my research is to catalogue and describe. It's science. You Western Buddhists, so concerned about whether or not Buddha thought sex was dirty! But I don't care."

"I'm not a Buddhist," I grumbled uneasily.

"Then tell me, what were you doing meditating in the mountains?"

"It's difficult to explain," I said awkwardly. "But let me try. When I became a Christian at eighteen, my perspective on the world changed radically. Suddenly God was everywhere. The devil, too. There were new spiritual meanings for things that I previously didn't think of questioning. Everything from events in the State of Israel to my sex life, or rather, sudden lack of one, had a place in God's plan. My non-religious friends thought I had lost my mind. Don't smile. Evangelical Christianity was just a different world, with its own quite consistent internal logic. After I started studying philosophy and travelling in Europe, it hit me there were lots of different worlds, each valid from its own particular point of view. By becoming Christian, I had changed viewpoints, but not necessarily come any closer to the truth. And the Western cultural background in which I grew up was still determining how I saw things. I wanted to experience something radically different in order to really shake up my perspective. I went to a monastery not to become Buddhist, nor get enlightened, but to see how the world looks to a Buddhist, and in doing so, loosen the grip my own culture has on my mind. Ideally, just to get more free."

"You would have liked my father," she replied, surprisingly softly, for I suppose I had expected her to dismiss my philosophizing with an impatient wave of the hand. "He was an atheist, but very drawn to Zen. I remember he used to tell a story about being captured by the Russians during the war. He was a doctor in the German army. They sent him to a prisoner-of-war camp. He thought he would never see anyone he knew again. When he arrived, they stripped him of everything, down to his skin. They left him with absolutely nothing. 'This was the happiest moment of my life,' my father used to say. But he said as soon as they put him in prison, he started searching for a pencil to write a letter to his family to tell them he was still alive."

We stayed in Patna for five days, wandering through its museums and ruins, sketching and photographing Buddha statues of Mara and his seductive daughters. In the third century B.C., Patna was the site of the imperial city of the Buddhist king Ashoka, and it remains the capital of modern Bihar State. Bihar comes from *vihar*, the word for a Buddhist temple. For some fifteen hundred years the region was the heartland of a thriving Buddhist culture, rich in monasteries, temples and universities, all of them wiped out by successive waves of invading Muslims who dispatched those unwilling to convert. It was now predominantly Hindu once again. For Sabina, Bihar was a treasure-house of research material, although by any economic standard, the state ranked among India's poorest.

One unique feature of the city made its most dismal streetside slums seem festive. Slum dwellers spray-painted their wandering goats and cows with bright Day-Glo patterns: hot pink, electric blue, lime green. Some streets looked like living, mooing, art exhibits. Presumably the markings identified the animals and kept them from being stolen; and in a land where the cow is sacred, paint struck me as a lot more humane than branding. The animals excited Sabina. Sometimes as we rode she would call to our rickshaw driver to stop just so she could take a picture of a passing neon cow.

"You should be doing your thesis on cow art," I teased her.

"Oh, wouldn't that be wonderful!" she replied in earnest. "I love the cows of India. They are so beautiful, so gentle. No wonder they are sacred to the people. They give only good things: milk, dung for cooking fuel, and urine, which used to be taken as a medicine for certain sicknesses. I have often thought about doing a photo book, you know, a coffee-table book, 'The Cows of India.'"

We stayed at the Patna Tourist Guest House through the hot and humid nights. Our bed was covered with a white cotton mosquito net, which looked to me like a silken desert tent, closing out India and the world, or so we hoped. The wooden bed frame squeaked. I

65

told Sabina I imagined the janitor sweeping one spot outside our door for fifteen minutes every morning, gradually being joined by other workers until the entire hotel staff congregated at our doorstep, hand brooms whisking in time to the rhythm of the bed, straining to hear the sounds coming from underneath the foreigners' door. We could shut India out, but could not prevent it listening in.

In Varanasi I had been forced to play the stranger for the sake of her reputation. In Patna, that same concession to Hindu morality demanded that we pretend to be husband and wife. Eyebrows were raised at front desk over our respective Austrian and Canadian passports, but provoked no objections. One elderly Brahmin, a visiting Congress party politician who spent his days chewing betel nut in a plush chair in the lobby, quizzed us thoroughly on our international marriage. For his sake we quickly created three young daughters and a family home near Vienna.

Sabina's public persona changed as radically as her marital status. She kept her hair pulled straight back, the blonde ponytail usually knotted into a bun, and carried not a single sari in her heavy duffle bag, just pantaloons and long-sleeved pullover kurtas. In Delhi and Varanasi she had always seemed soft and feminine, relying on her charms to get what she wanted. In Patna she displayed a hard edge I had never seen before in public. She was blunt, imperious, almost sneering towards rickshaw drivers, porters, even peons at the museums. She bestowed not a single smile, except to museum curators, and her instructions in Hindi to those required to serve her sounded harsh, even to my uncomprehending ears.

"You sound so sharp," I told her once after she had snapped out our destination to a rickshaw driver.

"Yes, I have become a real *memsahib* in India, like the wife of some British general," she said as the three-wheeler jerked us out into traffic. "If I show any softness at all, then they are cheating me and grabbing at me. Men here are not used to taking orders from a woman. Especially a blonde European. They see me, and all they think of is American movie sex scenes. But they understand a memsahib's voice, a memsahib's scorn. If I keep my head high, never look at them, and yell orders, then they don't bother me."

Until that moment I had not fully appreciated what it took for her to negotiate India. Her yellow hair was a candle for over two hundred million sexually repressed male moths. Beating them off would be an exhausting task for anybody, yet she managed not only to deflect them but to conduct research at the same time. I respected her for her daily battle, and had a new understanding of my role as her assistant. Having a "husband" along helped with much of the deflecting, and that, far more than lugging her bag or searching with her for statues, sped up her work. It felt good to be useful to her, after all, and quite wonderful to be the one man in all Bihar with whom, in the privacy of our room, she dropped her defences and smiled upon.

At dinner our fourth night in Patna we sat side by side at a table for four so that we could hold hands beneath the white tablecloth without attracting too much attention, although the waiters grinned widely with every visit to our table. Sabina asked if I had ever been in love. I told her about my years of celibacy, about trying to love Tina, my sense of inadequacy, both emotionally and sexually, and then leaving her to go to India. Sabina gazed at me.

"Is it such a long way to you?" she said.

"Yes. For you, maybe not so long. What you would find there, I don't know. Some of it scares me."

"I love you," she whispered to me as a waiter approached, then turned to him, "And now I would like the milk sweets for dessert."

I wanted to speak the words back to her, surprised at how quickly they were forming on my lips, but ordered a bowl of mango ice cream instead.

That night as we slid out of our clothing and under our gossamer netting, I caught something fragile in her mood, a sense of something slipping away. The way she held me when we embraced seemed almost mechanical, as if after several days of warming intimacy she had reverted once more to plain technique. It felt to me as if she was marking out a safe distance in the field of our loveplay. I wondered for the first time if she paid a price for her sexual freedom with men. I wondered if another kind of protective shield, far different from the memsahib act, had formed inside of her. Somehow it seemed her sexual expertise permitted her to embrace without being vulnerable enough to get hurt, as if she kept a divider between sex and love—almost like a man. Almost like me. Yet how quickly she seemed to have opened herself to loving me. Now the divider was sliding down once more, right in the midst of her caresses.

I thought I knew all too clearly what caused it. I had held back from her at the table. But not out of lack of loving, for now that the field was clear of rivals, I had abandoned my futile attempts at Buddhist detachment. Indeed, our sex was the best I had ever experienced, and she was a confident, informative and intriguing travelling companion. As far as watchful India was concerned, we were a happily married couple, and I found it rather to my liking. But to say the words was difficult, more so because if I was going to really love her, I felt first I had to confess something that I was afraid to say. She might conclude I was crazy and just leave. But if she was going to love me, it was only right that she should know. I held her firmly in my arms, stopped her stroking fingers, and put a stilling hand on her shoulder.

"There's something I have to tell you," I said, cursing the tremor in my voice. "It's going to sound strange, and I don't know what you are going to make of it."

"All right," she said, uncertainly propping herself up on her elbow, eyes intent.

"It's not like I'm about to confess a murder or anything. You can relax. It's something that happened to me during my meditation in Ladakh, perhaps the most revolting and disturbing experience of my life. It takes a little time to explain. Do you mind?"

She shook her head, encouraging me to go on.

"You see, the text I was working with started out with a section on freeing yourself from desire by meditating on the composite nature of all being. Basically, the instructions were to visualize a beautiful woman—or a man for a woman student—someone who fills you with desire, and then focus the meditation to find out where the desire is located. So, for example, say I feel desire for my lover's beautiful long hair. Then I examine the hair through each of the five senses: do I desire the sight of it, smell, touch, taste, or sound it makes maybe when she swishes it back and forth? Wherever you find desire, you look more closely, as if through a microscope with a zoom lens. If I desire the sight of my lover's head of hair, do I desire a lock of it? A strand? Well, perhaps a strand alone in the bed after she is gone. Do I feel desire over half a strand? A four-inch piece? Two inches? There comes a point where there's no more desire for the speck that remains. Then you build it back up, strand by strand, back to the lock, to the full head. If desire returns, you go back to where it disappears once more, until you realize no feature of a woman is desirable in itself. Desirableness is something the observer superimposes on the object of his desire. This may seem like a fancy way of saying beauty is in the eye of the beholder, but discovering it for myself, it no longer seemed a cliché."

"And you wonder why I have no time for this spiritual foolishness?" she said angrily. "So, you're telling me you have mastered desire?"

"Oh, God, you, better than anyone else, know that isn't so." I gripped her arm for a second to make sure she wouldn't leave. "In fact, it took me a few days just to get started on the exercise, because I didn't really want desire rooted out so viciously. The text said to look on the body as a 'dirty machine, a frothing scum or heap of sticks, stones and pus.' And I couldn't do it. It seemed to me intent on fostering aversion. I didn't want to do that, but I did want to get into the rest of the text. It was my whole purpose for being in Ladakh. So I decided to do the meditation without bias. If disgust arose, I would just accept it. And if desire stayed, I would just accept that, too. At least in the end, if desire persisted, I would have a much clearer idea of what turned me on.

"Slowly I worked my way down from hair, forehead, ears, eyes, nose, mouth, through chin, neck, shoulder blades, armpits, nipples, elbows, wrists, each finger and the navel. It was exhausting work. Each single part took at least an hour's meditation. Some parts much more than others. But feeling all this desire every time I sat down to meditate proved good incentive for the work. It was amazing how clear the image grew, as if I could really see a woman in front of me, and could then get close-ups almost to the cellular level. It was working, too. In most cases, I could observe how I was adding the component of desire to the image, and then watch it disappear, but with some exceptions. For example, no matter how much I analysed my imaginary lover's eyes, I couldn't shake the feeling that this was more than looking into little black holes. Even in certain photographs or paintings, it's just ingrained in me that there's someone in there, someone I desire.

"After about two weeks of meditating four or so hours per day, I made it to the waist. From there on down, it was really slow going. Cutting through desire was as much work as clearing a rain forest with a pocketknife. Fortunately, by this point the process was moving almost automatically. Focus. Zoom. Analyse for desire. Repeat. Finally I got past the mons Veneris. The genitalia were hell. They took forever to get through, and kept me in a pretty constant state of horniness that just wouldn't go away. In the next session I turned my attention to the buttocks.

"When I zoomed in close on the buttocks, I felt desire take on a new quality, something dark. I tried to focus on it and suddenly it ballooned in intensity. It was as if a carefully controlled experiment was going into meltdown. From inside my chest a creature sprang out with a yell, leapt into my meditation and grabbed violently at the imaginary buttocks with long, bushy arms. It thrust itself fiercely, sexually, into the image—a dirty, hairy, ape-like little creature, hunched over, furtive. It reminded me of Gollum, you know, the obsessed, repulsive cave creature from *The Lord of the Rings*.

"It realized it had been lured into the light, and the beast froze. It cowered like a thing long used to caves and subterranean passages. It appeared as distinct and real as if it was physically standing in front of me. I knew perfectly well it was a hallucination. But it was a *real* hallucination. It had come out of me. Luckily, I kept calm. I didn't break from my focused, meditative state, just noted the extreme aversion the vision aroused. It revolted me, this stinking, filthy animal. It chilled my flesh.

"'Stop,' I said, forbidding the beast from slinking back into my chest. It trembled, rooted to the spot by my voice, and obeyed. 'If you are my lust, my dark nature, whatever, all right,' I said out loud. 'I don't want to kill you. I won't deny you exist. Not any more. You are a part of me. I—I never knew—did I do this to you? Did you have to be this way? Now I know what you are, and I will accept you. You do not lunge in real life. You are under my control. I just want to look at you, see if those sick emotions can be lost without denying or repressing you.'

"The creature glared at me, frightened and malevolent, while I looked it over.

"'Now go,' I said.

"In a flicker, the beast leapt back inside my chest. I felt it lurking there, prowling, angry at being tricked into the light. I fell back on my cot, completely exhausted. I never dreamed this part of me existed, so twisted and ashamed. I almost quit the meditation, Sabina, because I wasn't sure how to guard against the beast returning. But I had come to Ladakh to study Buddhism. To break free of my culture, get another perspective—you remember what I told you? I had to laugh. What I had wanted was so abstract, so analytical; instead I hallucinated a personal demon that feels more real than any philosophical truth I've ever known. I couldn't deny it. So I continued with the meditation, staying on my guard, without incident, right down to the toes.

"What I need to tell you, Sabina, is that it's still in here, this creature. It's a part of me. But I think I feel him changing since I've met you. Maybe it's possible for it to grow into something healthy? I don't really know."

I looked at her, eyes barely visible in the darkness. She said nothing. I knew how she scorned metaphysics, and this one was right over the top. But I continued.

"You said to me at dinner that you loved me, and I didn't say anything back, and you must wonder: Did he hear it? Is it making him afraid? Does he love me too? Yes, yes, yes. I do love you, without even knowing what the words mean. Here and now, I do. Does any of this make sense to you at all?"

"No, it sounds pretty confused," she said gently, stretching her arms around my neck, and pressing her breasts against my side. "But it doesn't matter. The last part is sounding better. Keep talking."

She crouched over me and kissed my shoulders, my nipples, ran her fingers through the hair of my chest, then bit my stomach. Her hands ran down my legs, and she slid down to take me in her mouth. I stopped talking. The feeling of impending orgasm grew in the centre of my belly. But instead of driving outward towards her body, the energy began to burn within. Heat seared up and down my limbs from inside. My nerves tingled like pins and needles, as in a leg that has gone to sleep and when the feeling returns it's so painful at first you can't walk. I began breathing fast and deep, hyperventilating, trying to absorb the strange sensation so that it would pass quickly, but its intensity kept growing. Bursts of white light flashed behind my eyes. It scared me. I felt I was losing control of my body. I pulled Sabina up, then rolled over to lay on top of her, anxious to have an orgasm and get rid of the sensations. My head, hands, feet and belly felt on fire, the nerves incredibly sensitive to touch. The rush was weirdly ecstatic, electrifying, almost unbearable in its intensity. My body shuddered like paper before it ignites. The image of a curling corpse aflame in the burning ghats flickered through my mind. My hips thrust down at her, desperate for release. Suddenly I realized my erection was gone. My penis lay limply against her while the sensations inside my skin seared white hot. I felt I was losing consciousness. Beneath me, Sabina moaned and clutched. I could barely feel her, but held on, frightened and amazed as everything began to whirl around, and she was all that there was I could cling to.

I don't know how long it lasted, but gradually the burning ecstasy faded from my twitching nerves. It took perhaps another half-hour for me to slow my breathing. Exhausted, slick with sweat, I turned to her and stroked her hair. Her eyes met mine uncertainly.

"This has never happened to me before," she said, her voice quavering, "that I have orgasm without penetration, without you . . .

touching me." She felt my belly and the shaft of my penis. "You're still hot, but no sperm. It's very strange."

I nodded. For a while I could not speak. My mind searched for some frame of reference to connect this to, and an image surfaced from a visit to a remote mountain monastery in Ladakh. A lama friend had taken me to the special red chamber where the guardian deities dwelled. He permitted me to draw back the curtain to gaze on the wrathful aspect of the deity drawn on the temple wall. The ancient being radiated rings of flame. Its blue head was that of a snarling, fanged bull. Four of his arms bore tantric objects of power: a sword, a bell, a sceptre, a human skull filled with blood. The other two pair of hands caressed a green-skinned female goddess pressed against him in sexual embrace. She gripped him, standing, one leg wrapped around his waist. Their red tongues met, and in graphic detail the icon showed the thick blue shaft of the bull-god's penis entering her.

Such graphic sexual depictions of celestial and demonic beings were metaphors, so my Western commentaries on Tibetan Buddhism had said, for the spiritual union of the female and male poles of existence: yin and yang, darkness and light, potency and fertility. Yet I had also read that some tantric Buddhists and Hindus lived out their metaphor in their own secret practices, transforming sex into a spiritual force so blinding, so powerful, it consumes all pleasure, all lust, all personality in its purifying fire.

I shook my head and sat up in bed, wondering if we had inadvertently touched that power together. It scared the hell out of me. What if we had been sexually united, had carried it through to orgasm? It felt as if I would have exploded, unable to contain the energy. My body would have broken open and shattered like a shell. But from that shell what would have emerged? I wondered with a brief laugh if Sabina did this to all her lovers, like some goddess in disguise. God, she'd laugh at me for that, I thought. I'm enthralled enough with her as it is.

"You give me so much," Sabina murmured, placing a hand on my back.

The remark caught me totally by surprise, for in all honesty, I had hardly been aware of her. Her gaze, her stroking, her subtle movements and sounds of passion that usually delighted me in our lovemaking, they were all lost in the storm. All I remembered was gripping her and once hearing her groan. She reached up and clasped my waist from behind, drawing me back down into her embrace. I realized it must have been late into the night.

"Sabina, I think we may have touched something here," I said, reluctant to lie down, but unable to resist her arms, "some kind of tantric energy. What was it like for you?"

"You were wonderful."

"That's not what I mean!"

"Hush, let's sleep a bit."

She put her fingers over my mouth and curled against me, one leg sliding up on top of my stomach. Metaphysics loses another argument, I sighed, and, suddenly feeling very weary, went to sleep.

CHAPTER FIVE

THE DEVIL'S DAUGHTERS

Vaishali

ROM PATNA we travelled to Vaishali, ancient capital of a thriving republic during the time of the Buddha, twenty-five hundred years ago. There were no direct buses. We had to change twice and ride in the back of a sputtering, dust-spewing auto-rickshaw the last ten kilometres together with six Bihari villagers. By the time we arrived, a red coating the colour of the fields covered our bodies and baggage. The driver let us off at a quiet cluster of straw-and-mud houses surrounded by brilliant green rice paddies and groves of banana trees and palms. Not a trace of Vaishali's past grandeur remained except for a lone column erected by the Buddhist king Ashoka in the third century B.C. A small museum near the pillar housed a collection of Buddhist sculptures and pottery, dug from the red clay by archeologists. But for the most part, the remains of the city still lay buried under rice fields.

Sabina and I checked into one of the four rooms of the Vaishali Government Tourist Bungalow. The only other visitors were three Thai monks on a pilgrimage to holy sites of India. When evening came, the two of us walked along a narrow road leading into the fields to watch the pink sun swell and dip below the ragged horizon of palms. The air felt moist and heavy on my skin as we pushed our way through it. Grey smoke from family cooking fires curled up from mud houses and seeped across the rice paddies like a fog, scenting the air with burnt buffalo dung and curry. With the coming of dusk the houses and banana trees lost their colour and merged with the smoke, their features blurring in the darkness. I felt trapped in the thickness of the coming night like a fly embedded in honey. In the red earth beneath our feet, a giant corpse lay buried, and in the layers underneath, how many empires more? An irrational fear prickled over my skin that when darkness submerged the last glimmer of light, we too would disappear.

I turned to Sabina walking beside me, almost invisible in the twilight at my side. I could feel her more than see her, although we did not touch. It was as if the fluid motion of her body sent ripples through the heavy air that lapped against my skin. It tingled. The electricity that had filled my body the previous night in Patna had not entirely faded. I felt an invisible current pass between us, a sexual charge, making me suddenly hard and fully aroused.

That night beneath the mosquito netting, while a single candle flame kept back the darkness, our bodies meshed, and the strange energy returned. It began as before, deep in my belly, burning inside, gradually spreading out to my limbs. This time, before losing all control, I noticed that the painful pins-and-needles tingling had a fiercely sexual quality to it, as if every nerve ending was aroused: fingers, feet, neck, legs, back, as sensitive as the skin of the tip of my penis. The force of the energy jolted me spasmodically at times. My eyes rolled back in my head. I pushed against Sabina's flesh, scarcely aware of her, scarcely aware of myself, unable to see, knowing only the dark thrusting that guided me. And yet, my penis lay useless between us, soft, with only the faintest hint of an erection. There was no orgasm, just the struggle to contain the agonizing ecstasy, breathing deeply and rhythmically as the energy raced through my body, until the fire burned out and normal feeling gradually returned to my limbs. It left me gasping and shivering in her arms.

I looked down on Sabina, her gaze a mix of confusion and concern. She stroked my hair and we lay together in silence for a long time, slowly drifting towards sleep. Suddenly my shaft grew hard, the intensity of the arousal almost violent. I saw her eyes open in surprise and she spread her legs wide as I entered her, rocking wildly. Tears welled up in my eyes as we clutched each other and both shuddered swiftly to climax. Covered in sweat, I lay panting in her arms. A wave of unexpected emotion struck me and I rolled to the side, clenching my jaw to keep from crying out loud.

"Something inside of me can break against you, Sabina," I said after a few minutes. "I need it to break, want it to break."

"It's all right," she whispered, pulling me back to her.

"No, no, not break like *shatter*, but break open. Remember the sick beast in my chest? It feels as though when I break open, maybe something healthy and strong will emerge. I'm sorry this all sounds so crazy. Maybe you know more than I. Is this really unusual?"

"Tim—there are some things you just can't talk about. I like to make love to you. It makes me happy. What more than that matters? If sex is a problem, then talking about it can sometimes help. If it's not a problem, then talking about it—I don't know."

"As your countryman says: 'What we cannot speak about, we must pass over in silence.' Wittgenstein."

"Oh, if you must put it in the mouth of a philosopher," she said, shaking her head and smiling.

I never did like Wittgenstein's remark. But I thought I understood how Sabina felt; it was the difference between talking about art and experiencing it. She was an artist at love. The way she threw back her head, half closed her eyes, raked her nails with just the right amount of pressure—even her groans struck me sometimes as chosen for their effect, which was usually quite stimulating. It was as if she had a wide range of gestures, utterances and positions that constituted her artist's palette, and I was the canvas on which she painted. I certainly liked being the canvas, yet felt something illusory about the art of sexual love as she practised it on me. Her most intimate expression, sometimes coming just moments before orgasm, was "It's so beautiful," and it plunged me into ecstasy just to hear it from her lips. Her pleasure seemed so esthetic. Talking about it, perhaps analysing the deliberateness of elements of her work, would be bad taste. Perhaps, I wondered, this was what happened once one exhausted the physical possibilities of sex: one either transformed it into an art form, or else got bored.

Yet this electrical force that had invaded our lovemaking was of such a totally different nature. It came from so deep within me, felt so primordial, so overwhelming. It left me with little room for artistic appreciation. There was no romance in it, no excitation of the finer emotions, not even, when I came to think of it, desire, though I had felt tender and aroused once the sensations subsided. But this was not something I controlled. It took me over, strange and wonderfully terrifying, and though I talked of breaking to be made whole, I was speaking mainly to alleviate my own fear. I fell asleep still wanting to ask, "Was it frightening for you, too?"

"I had a dream," I told her next morning as we were getting dressed. "You were a temple courtesan, and I was the son of a Brahmin priest in ancient Vaishali. Actually, you had been born into a high-caste family, but you rejected your caste for the freedom of life in the temple. I fell in love with you. Though you remained strong willed and aloof from society, you consented to marry me, despite the outrage you felt from my own narrow-minded family. Somehow we ended up on a rickshaw riding through a Buddhist museum in search of Mara, who was hiding between the statues. The driver tried to overcharge us for the ride, then tried to kiss you. So I decided to strangle him."

She laughed. "So that's what you think of me? Temple prostitute?"

I reddened. To me, this was not the point of the dream.

"Hmmm. Maybe, in a sense. With the emphasis on 'temple.' For me, you make sex holy, and I have it in my mind that you must have been a blessing to every man you've gone to bed with. More like a goddess than a prostitute."

"Well, either way, that's all right. If it excites you. Sometimes I like to think of you as my Canadian woodcutter, too."

"What? A lumberjack?" I was totally confused.

"Yes. The hairy chest"—she reached under my shirt and dug in her fingers—"like fur."

We emerged late for breakfast. It consisted of grey flakes of flattened Bihari rice and fresh buffalo yogurt, brought to us on the porch by a small bird-like man with a wide moustache and glossy, curly black hair. Rajiv was the waiter/watchman of the tourist bungalow. He wore a dirty faded sarong and a grey undershirt, yet spoke to us with the full dignity of his Brahmin caste. He had thin, delicate arms and legs and precise, quick motions that made every gesture of serving the meal seem like parts of a ritual. He sat and chatted with us as we ate, polite, but not the least bit obsequious. That evening, he explained, the annual sun-worshipping prayer ceremony would be held in one of Vaishali's ancient ponds. We accepted his gracious invitation to join his family for the event, and promised to meet him at the guest house at three o'clock so he could be our guide. He smiled serenely, deftly swept away our cups and dishes, then waved us on our way to the Vaishali museum.

As we walked through the fields in the hot morning sun, children sprung from the mud-and-thatch houses along the way and ran after us, half playful, half fearful. Young boys riding water buffalo in the paddies whooped and waved greetings to us. Two women in bright yellow and red saris, one carrying a large earthen water pot on her head, the other with a jug propped against one outswung hip, eyed us with frank curiosity, and laughed at a whispered joke after we had passed. We followed the path to Ashoka's grey stone column, which soared like a limbless pine from a small excavation pit in the fields. A little farther and we reached the tiny, whitewashed museum.

Inside, in the midst of two rooms filled with broken pot shards and carvings of many-armed deities, we found a single statue of Mara and the Buddha. Sabina asked me to sketch the sculpture for her while she tried to persuade the curator to allow her inside his reserve collection. He refused at first. Sabina produced her sheaf of university documents and government certificates detailing the purpose of her research and her right to examine reserve collections. The curator took her into his office to read them all, leaving me alone with Mara and the Buddha.

The front half of the Buddha's face had been broken from the statue and his right shoulder was missing. But the Earth-Touching Gesture and the figures beneath it had remained intact. Under the lotus blossom on which the Buddha sat, the Earth Goddess rose out of the ground to bear witness to his attainment. To the left of her sat Mara, god of delusion, a round-bellied, bearded old dwarf with a sword at his side and something like a helmet on his head. He sat on the ground, resting on one leg with the other propped up beside him. To the far right of the Earth Goddess danced Mara's three daughters, ample breasts exposed, hips swaying voluptuously, long hair flowing down their naked shoulders. I could tell they were still trying to seduce the Buddha, for he had not yet looked at them and turned them into hags.

I pondered the daughters as I drew my pencil along the curves of their breasts, bringing them to shape on my page. They were neither young nor old. They were only illusions, as transitory as desire itself. Their father, Mara, was the "father of lies." Through his illusions of pleasure and pain, he bound all creatures to the wheel of life and death. It reminded me of Satan's temptation of Christ in the wilderness. And just like Christian monks, Buddhists who take to the robe are bound to celibacy by their vows. For what else pulls spirit into suffering flesh as powerfully as sex? I remembered Professor Strauss's interpretation of the daughters, as passed on by Sabina, that they symbolized not sex, but all that was alluring and desirable. Sex in itself was irrelevant to the greater metaphysical issue.

Sex metaphysically irrelevant? In my present highly charged state, I could hardly accept that. I shaded in the swaying hips, the penultimate temptation the Buddha faced. After Buddha turned the daughters into hags, Mara raged and, in his final lie, declared Buddha's meditation would be fruitless because there was no one to bear witness to his accomplishment. It was only then, in answer to Mara's charge, that Buddha touched the earth. The Earth Goddess, aroused by his touch, bore witness to his efforts, defeating Mara. The next instant, the Buddha was enlightened.

I turned my artist's gaze to the goddess rising directly beneath the

Buddha's fingers, traced the line from her upstretched arm down to the full spheres of her breasts. She too was woman: fertile, fruitful and very sexy, to judge from the artist's rendering. Although monks were not permitted to touch a woman, in touching the earth, Buddha was touching the ultimate feminine power. Suddenly the difference between the goddess and the daughters came clear to me: the Earth Goddess was real, Mara's daughters, a mirage.

I considered the myth in this light: Perhaps Mara had charged that in refusing to have sex with his daughters, the ascetic Buddha himself was fruitless. He had cut himself off from sex, from the cycle of birth and death. Hence his meditation would have no place on earth. Mara knew that Buddha would never fall for an outright lie. So it seemed to me that Mara's challenge must have held some truth if Buddha felt compelled to respond. Perhaps sexual desire, the desire personified by Mara's daughters, masked some deeper truth about sex?

Why such an ache and a longing associated with sex? I wondered. Just to master pleasure and desire, to linger in those feelings, extend them and seek to repeat them as frequently as possible until they degenerate into the mindless repetition of addiction that still never manages to fill the void: indeed, it seems so fruitless. Yet the strange experiences I was having with Sabina convinced me that something lay beyond desire, something of an entirely different nature that I could not yet grasp. Perhaps the truth Buddha recognized in Mara's charge was that in sex, a connectedness to the earth can take place, a kind of union that goes beyond two bodies. Mara implied that to deny sex was to cut oneself off, to deny connectedness with the earth, to be without a witness. But Mara's daughters were not sex: they were merely desire, the wrapping and trappings of sex. It seemed clear that for all my meditation on the subject, I had missed something crucial. Sex and desire are two separate things: reality and mirage. Though I had often experienced desire without sex, in the throes of this violent, blinding ecstasy, I was now experiencing sex without desire. The Buddha denied the illusion of desire, but touched the fertile earth.

Three details from the Buddha's story suddenly hit me. First, before taking his seat, the Buddha had accepted a drink of milk offered to him by a woman, rejecting the path of extreme asceticism, and taking the nourishment he needed for the task ahead. Second, for his great act of the spirit he chose to sit under a tree—symbol of the fertile energy of earth, and if I remembered rightly, associated with earth goddesses all over the world. And finally, in virtually all his representations, the Buddha sits upon a lotus blossom: symbol of unsullied compassion, and strongly identified with the feminine force. I looked at the stylized lotus petals on the statue in front of me and realized for the first time the Buddha was sitting on the sex organs of a plant. The tree above, the lotus below, milk in his belly and a milk moustache topping his serene smile, the most potent feminine imagery surrounded the Buddha at the moment of his great awakening.

Now I felt the power of his earth touching in an entirely new way. The fertile earth the Buddha touched was not delusion, not part of Mara's world, but something more primal, more powerful. The goddess, unlike the daughters, was not subject to Mara's rule. Once aroused, her words vanquished the father of all lies: a feat that the Buddha had not been able to accomplish on his own. By bearing witness, she legitimized his efforts, not just in front of Mara, but for the entire Buddhist world for whom the myth was told.

Was it not possible for sex, once freed of worldly desire, to be an earth-touching gesture: earth touching earth, sex, carrying within it the seed of creativity and potency that creates life? Like the earth, the bodies of men and women are fertile clay. Only through Mara do they build the walls of illusionary ego that lead to separation and then yearning for union once again. In the Buddha's gesture of touching, the earth bears witness. In sex, perhaps the earth of our flesh bears witness to the reality behind our illusions.

That feeling of deep, latent potency stirring within when Sabina and I lay locked together in this mysterious embrace—it felt as if something inside was awakening. And when fully aroused, it would break open through the shell in which Mara had me encased. The blinding flash of it would bear witness to whatever lay within that shell of self. Perhaps it would explode Sabina too, dissolve all walls between us. What, I wondered, would we find on the other side?

Sabina found me gazing at the tiny Earth Goddess rising beneath the Buddha's hand, my sketch half-finished in my lap. I jumped, startled, when she touched my shoulder from behind, and shook my head as if clearing away the effects of too much betel nut.

We hurried back to the tourist bungalow, arriving just before three o'clock. Rajiv stood waiting for us on the porch, ready to take us to the sun-worshipping ceremony. He had changed his faded, dirty sarong for a clean white kurta and *dhoti,* the white loincloth worn only by the Brahmin caste. His hair shone with fresh oil. With light, springing steps he led the way across a small pasture and along a raised path that seemed like the remnant of an ancient wall overgrown with grass. Here and there small patches of crumbling brick showed beneath the green carpet: fragments of red bone from the once-great city. As we walked, Rajiv explained that each year, at the end of October, Hindus thank the setting sun for providing light, warmth and energy for growing crops. The rising sun is welcomed the following morning and beseeched to continue its blessings for another year. The prayers were preceded by forty-eight hours of fasting. He and his family had not eaten for a day and a half. He invited us to join his household next morning to break the fast with them.

From across the paddies we could see dozens of families walking single file towards the pool. We fell in line with the converging crowds. The women, clad in their most elegant saris, carried handwoven baskets full of fruit and flower offerings on their heads. Already a hundred or so worshippers ringed the pond. They had laid out mats and set out their offerings as if they had come for a great community picnic by the waterside. Bananas, grapefruit, sugar candies, rice sweets wrapped in banana leaves and other gifts to the sun lay in little piles beside each family cluster.

The pond itself was about fifty metres square, gouged out of the surrounding pasture land centuries ago to provide water for buffalo and human bathers. It was a muddy, milky brown. Frogs and tadpoles bobbed in the midst of the green-grey weeds around the pond's edges. Farther into the centre, small fish splashed after insects. As we watched, dozens of women waded waist deep into the pond and dipped themselves three times in prayer. Their cotton saris clung to them like a sheen of winding seaweed, revealing their plentiful bellies, the curve of their breasts and the small, hard lumps of their nipples. Palms placed together in the attitude of reverence, all turned solemnly towards the red eye of the god who glowed down on them from the western horizon. It seemed as if the women had grown up out of the pond like delicate lotus flowers, their red, blue and yellow saris glowing in the pink light, fading into brown where the water swirled around their waists. Where did water cease and woman begin? I envisioned their feet rooted deep in the ooze at the bottom, minnows swimming around their submerged thighs, becoming entangled between the folds of their saris as if trapped in silken nets.

And at that moment of what I imagined to be profound and mystic union between water, sun and worshipping women, the local brass band struck up the chords of "I Am a Disco Dancer." Immediately the younger men, who until then had been sitting on the banks watching the womenfolk with mild boredom, began to boogie. They shook, rattled and rolled in what appeared to be a cross between the Dance of Destruction and the twist. The band consisted of half a dozen trumpets, a few baritone players, a flute, a clarinet and three drummers. They were dressed in their ceremonial best, with faded gold brocade fluttering across the shoulders of their scarlet jackets. They wore off-white bell-bottom trousers with an orange stripe sewn down the sides and navy blue plastic construction hats to which a crest of orange plastic bristles had been glued as if to look like the plume of a centurion's helmet.

Across the water someone set off a string of firecrackers, shattering the air and for a moment drowning out the frenetic toots and blats of the band. A Roman candle shot into the sky with a siren-like whistle so loud Sabina and I covered our ears. It exploded above the water, higher than the huge broad-leafed trees which loomed like weary sentinels around the back edge of the pond. In their branches, hundreds of bats were suddenly roused by the crack of fireworks and whizzing lights. Fluttering in confusion and circling wildly, the bats rose up into the purple sky, enormous creatures, each with a wingspan I guessed as close to a metre. Their high-pitched shrieking filled the night air between explosions. Like a black, swirling cloud, the creatures' silhouettes brought a premature darkness over the heads of the worshippers like a bad omen as the last drop of red glinted over the horizon. Then they scattered in all directions into the coming night.

The women emerged from the darkened water, dripping. I marvelled at their skilful modesty in changing out of their wet clothes and into dry saris without exposing their flesh to the surrounding crowd. Sabina pointed out to me several young girls, not yet in puberty, clad in saris and each wearing a ring through one nostril.

"The government says child marriages are no longer permitted in India, and yet look at these young girls! Wearing saris is the sign they have been promised already."

"But look at their mothers. It seemed to work for them."

"Oh, you're not going to be a stupid male, are you?" she said, suddenly quite angry. "For the lower castes, especially in the countryside, child marriage is slavery: trading a daughter for a bicycle and two goats, or something. A daughter is a liability, an extra mouth to feed. She goes to the new household at maybe age eleven, and in many cases becomes virtually the servant girl. Her husband is likely to be much older. Who knows how long he will wait before having sex with her? It certainly won't be up to her. And if her mother-in-law is not pleased with her obedience, she can send her back to her family. Then no other man will ever want to marry her. She's used goods."

"I'm sorry," I mumbled. I already knew that much of what she said was true. My remark had been stupid, yes, and I could see that for Sabina each girl's sari screamed out the physical and sexual slavery into which she was sold. Yet to me the beauty of the modest women who had so recently drenched themselves in worship overpowered her words.

"The system is horrible, I agree," I added. "But there seems something of the goddess in them still. Far more than the men, disco dancing."

"Such consolation," she said coldly.

We sat on the grass, not talking. I felt disconnected and hated it. As it grew dark, the village women set hundreds of small lamps afloat upon the pond, each one a leaf boat filled with oil and a wick. They drifted out into the dark water, a miniature Diwali. I felt her hand press mine briefly.

"I'm sorry," I said again.

"Me too."

Another group of young men armed with Roman candles fired one horizontally over the water into the crowd on the far shore. In retaliation, an incandescent fireball whizzed back at the offenders. Soon a full-scale fireworks war was under way across the ancient pool. Some crashed into the water fizzling like meteorites plunging into the sea. Others whizzed red hot right into the crowd. We decided to retreat to the safety of our room.

All through the night trumpets and baritones blared in the darkness and rockets thudded. Mara's daughters, the lotus-like women rising from the pond, the child brides, the bats, the heaviness of the air all merged in my dreams. Sabina rose. I listened to her footsteps in the bathroom. She had forgotten to take her birth control pill. She returned to my arms and held me, scarcely visible through filtered moonlight.

"It would be so good to make a child with you," I spoke my thoughts without thinking.

"What?" She half rose in surprise.

"No, no. I don't intend to do so at this time . . ."

She put a finger to my lips to prevent further explanations. "I know what you mean. Just as I was thinking now."

The frenzied ecstasy had come and gone earlier in the night, leaving me relaxed, able to last a long time when she pulled me round on top of her. She slid her legs up so that her ankles rested on my shoulders, and drew me deep inside her. We made the bed rattle until I was convinced we must have woken the Thai monks sleeping in the other room. I opened my eyes to see her staring at me. She smiled, but her gaze seemed clouded, and I had the sense of disconnection once more. It puzzled me, this smile like a mask, covering something. She closed her eyes as if in ecstasy, though now it seemed to me a way of avoiding contact.

She thinks I love her only for her sex, I thought, sure of my intuition, and she accepts this self-judgement, but it hurts her somehow, to have me rocking into her like this, as if the motion in our hips was all that mattered.

I allowed the motion to slow and then cease, and waited until she opened her eyes. I slid to the side of her.

"If you were a guy, Sabina, you know I'd want to be your friend."

"What crazy thing is this? I'm a woman—"

"Yes, thank God, but I mean, I'd still like you even if you were a guy, not in the same way, with our legs all tangled like this. You are a beautiful lover, but I also love your understanding of India, your ability to travel through it without being driven crazy by the pain of it, and most of all, for your appreciation of its beauty. You see it in places I don't even look."

"Oh, now you will make me cry," she said, surprising me by turning away. "I'm not particularly intelligent or of good character—"

"Now, your turn not to talk." I gently pulled her around, kissed her, stroked her between her breasts, just soothing, until we both fell back to sleep.

We shared mangoes, bananas and Bihari rice for breakfast with Rajiv's family, then returned to the tourist bungalow to pay our bill. On Rajiv's advice we visited the nearby Shiva *lingam*. According to our friend, it was more than fifteen hundred years old, the holiest Hindu object in Vaishali. To my surprise, the lingam was not enshrined in a temple, but stood in the centre of a small dirt clearing. Piles of fruit, flowers and a few coins were spread in front of it as offerings. It looked like a missile head, about half a metre in diameter, a little more than knee-high. The smooth, tapering stone rose up from the granite platform, curving slightly forward at the tip like a giant finger—or, far more accurately, a giant phallus. This was the ancient fertility symbol of God the Destroyer, husband of Kali. We raised our pressed palms to the holy object in the Hindu gesture of reverence. I wondered if perhaps, during my travels with Sabina, the ancient phallic god might have been a better teacher for me than the Buddha, with his trees and flowers. I offered a tattered purple rupee note to the lingam, unsure myself whether it was meant in supplication or in thanks.

The bus back to Patna—the only one for the day—was not due until two in the afternoon. Sabina and I sat on the banks of a small water hole near the narrow road and waited.

"Two more days, and I have to go back to Delhi to meet my girlfriend coming in from Austria," she said. "Then she and I will go back to Varanasi."

She didn't ask me to come with her, and I didn't say I wanted to. I remembered, dimly, that I had wanted to go to Nepal.

"I don't think I could handle secret meetings at Ace's again," I said, trying to joke, "not after being your husband for so long. Unless you think the guards would buy the dual passport marriage routine."

She feigned a laugh.

"I'll do my trek in Nepal. But that conference in Bodhgaya is not so far away. I'll come out of the mountains in time to meet you there, if you like. Do you have any plans after it's over?"

"Well, I was thinking it would be a good time to do more field research through the rest of Bihar, Calcutta and Orissa. A lot of work, actually."

"Then you'll still need a woodcutter to assist you?"

She smiled. The moment had been awkward, but we had gotten through it, made the next step. Now we could relax, return to the warmth of the present.

Three young boys arrived at the pool, riding on the grey backs of water buffalo. They led the beasts in up to their necks. The boys splashed and played, shrieking with laughter as the buffalo wallowed luxuriously. In deep water only their horns, eyes, noses and small isles of rump protruded from the muddy surface. The boys swam among them like otters, sliding over their backs, stopping occasionally to scrub the creatures' grey flanks. Sputterings of water and air shot out through the wide flared nostrils of the beasts as if they were sea elephants spouting in the ocean. For how many centuries had this play of boys and buffaloes gone on in Vaishali, exactly as we were witnessing it today? When the Shiva lingam was new? When Ashoka erected his own phallic column? When the Buddha walked through the streets of the thriving republic? Back into prehistory when the Hindu cosmos was first taking shape in the songs of the Aryan priests? The torpor of the sun and heavy Indian air drugged us as we sat on the bank, drew us back into its timelessness. Planning the future made no sense when there was only the present, stretching forever. When a bus pulled in at the roadside, neither of us moved. We watched it idle for five minutes or so.

"That's our bus," I murmured.

"Yes. We should hurry," Sabina replied dreamily, her eyes floating back to the buffalo.

We stood slowly, as if we had been sitting for twenty years, then walked with the same languor as the natives towards the iron monster rumbling by the roadside. We watched it pull away in a cloud of blue exhaust and wandered down the road after it, unperturbed as it vanished from our sight.

"I guess we missed it," I said, finally stopping my momentum a quarter of a mile later.

We flagged down a passing truck. The driver, a burly black-faced Sikh in a yellow turban, said he was heading straight through to Patna. We accepted this good fortune with the same trance-like bliss. My mind still full of snorting buffalo, naked boys, women standing waist deep in the water, I felt a conviction that these things would always exist, that time had little influence on the eternity that was India. I could not have been more ill prepared for the chaos that awaited us.

CHAPTER SIX

DEATH OF
THE MOTHER

Patna

T HE DRIVER kept his hand on the horn. He drove like a demon, careering at high speeds around cycle rickshaws, ox carts, bicycles, pedestrians, the occasional motor rickshaw or car. His assistant kept his head poked out the passenger window. His full-time job was to holler abuse at slower traffic in warning of the approaching juggernaut. In India, a truck is power. It stops for nothing, only veers to the side if a greater vehicle, say a packed bus, is bearing down on it, even then swerving only at the last second to avoid a head-on collision. We sped through the countryside back to Patna in an hour and a half, three hours less than the journey out to Vaishali had taken. Crossing over the kilometre-wide Ganges at the Patna bridge, the driver cursed and scowled as we found ourselves wedged into a traffic jam. We stopped moving altogether. After about fifteen minutes, Sabina and I decided it would be better for us to get out and walk. A concrete stairway from the side of the bridge led us down into an industrial section of the city.

The crowd seemed menacingly frenetic after the serenity of Vaishali. Thousands of people filled the streets, rushing in different directions, as if the communal heartbeat of the city had received a syringe full of adrenaline. Rickshaw drivers, their double seats empty, ignored our attempts to flag them down. When at last we cornered one, he told us he didn't know where the Patna Tourist Guest House was. Instead, he dropped us at the train station, but not the one we knew. For the first time we realized we were on the far eastern side of town, ten or so kilometres from our hotel. Dusk was coming. By this time, people should have been returning to their homes and hovels. Instead the streets grew more and more crowded. We saw a newspaper shop swarming with Biharis shouting and struggling for a paper as if they were starving men fighting for rice. Smoke filled the air. Not the acrid curry-and-buffalo-chip scented smoke of cooking fires: it had a chemical odour, like burning paint.

Our eyes filled with dust and stung from the smoke. We were exhausted and filthy. Sabina looked drained, her face coated with dirt from the harrowing truck ride. A dozen lepers sitting in a row at the front of the station began wailing for alms when they saw us. We fled, unable to deal with the artificial urgency of their chorus. Though it would be expensive, we decided to take a motor rickshaw back to the security of our guest house, but couldn't find a single one at the station. We ended up with another pedal-rickshaw driver who told us he could drop us at a motor-rickshaw stand. His eyes were bulging, his motions jerky and erratic as he pulled away from the station.

The area we cycled through seemed desperately poor. Shacks of tin sheeting and canvas lined the roadside. The few women we saw on the streets hurried by with pots and baskets balanced on their hips. Our driver pedalled madly as if afraid to stop, then jammed on the brakes and turned the vehicle around where a crowd had blocked the road ahead. A shop was on fire. Black smoke billowed from the windows and bright red flames licked upwards into the purple sky. The driver turned his head around and yelled something to us in Hindi.

"What does he say?" I tugged at Sabina's sleeve.

"I don't know, something about Indira Gandhi."

She shook her head at him.

The driver reached into the breast pocket of his tattered shirt and brought out a piece of folded newspaper, which he handed to her. It was written in Hindi. Sabina carefully pronounced the phonetic script, squinting at it in the half-light.

"Indira Gandhi . . . something . . . I don't know. Why is he giving me this?" She smiled at him and thanked him for showing it to her, offering it back.

The driver turned again, no longer watching where he was driving. He pointed his index finger at her, thumb raised in the air, and jabbed it at her.

"*Ki, ki!*" he said ferociously.

She gripped the paper again, pressed it close to her eyes.

"*Mein Gott!*" she whispered, the blood draining from her face. "They've killed Indira Gandhi. I can read it now. It says here, three Sikhs shot her."

The driver dropped us at an auto-rickshaw stand, where we were piled into the rear with six others heading for Gandhi Maidan near the western train station. It was dark now. The surging crowds had formed themselves into marching armies, chanting anti-Sikh slogans in unison. Again and again the driver had to turn his vehicle around in search of detours to avoid the angry mobs.

"Ah, Indira, I have lost my own mother!" the elderly man crammed next to me cried in his grief.

From the crest of a small hill, I looked back on the eastern half of the city and glimpsed three or four fires burning in the distance. The next day's papers revealed that forty-seven people had been killed in Bihar State, though unofficial estimates put the number above fifty in Patna alone. In Delhi, 115 had died during the night. Scooters and buses were set on fire. Shops of Sikhs had been looted and set ablaze. So easily marked by their long beards and turbans, Sikhs across the country became the victims of revenge. They were beaten, murdered, the women raped. Nine Sikhs were pulled off a train by gunmen and shot on their way to Delhi. From all across the country Sikhs abandoned their homes and struck out for the Punjab, fearing that Hindu and Sikh would never live together in peace again.

The driver seemed lost in the confusion. He turned down blind alleys and unlit back streets. One of the passengers shouted something towards the front.

"Stay on the main road. This is a bad area," Sabina translated for me.

It took another two hours to cross town to Gandhi Maidan, the wide circular park named in honour of Mahatma Gandhi. We found a rickshaw driver willing to take us the last three kilometres to the guest house. Sabina pumped the pedalling Bihari for more information on the assassination. He merely wobbled his head indifferently.

"What, your leader has been murdered, and you don't care?" she said.

"We are poor people here in Bihar," he replied. "What does it matter to us who lives and who dies at the top?"

The tourist guest house was located in the centre of a government office district. The streets were nearly deserted, in eerie contrast to the raging crowds in the east end of town. A shoot-on-sight curfew had been imposed on Patna, we later learned, and it seemed the government offices were the first places the police had moved in to protect. A mournful young man with dark circles under his eyes unlocked the front door of the guest house and told us he had no vacancies.

"But you must have a place for us," said Sabina, marching into the lobby and dropping her bag on the carpet. "Where else are we to go?"

"No room."

"Look, you can't be full," I said. "This place was almost deserted just three days ago. You have a single room?"

Shake of the head.

"Anything?"

Two waiters from the guest house restaurant came out. They had served us dinner every night of our stay and took apparent delight in our under-the-table hand-holding. I hailed them, making deliberately friendly conversation, just to prove to the front desk clerk we had indeed stayed in the guest house before. This would have made no difference had the rooms been full, but I had learned to discard logic in dealing with Indian paper shufflers.

"Well, there is a room," the clerk blurted out suddenly. "But it's got no bed sheets."

94

"I have a sheet in my bag. We'll take it," I said.

"And no pillowcases."

I marvelled that the man was prepared to turn us out into the insanity of the night rather than give us a room with no pillowcases. Most likely, he too was terrified by the assassination. Two more tourists in the hotel would only complicate a life that had already turned frighteningly unpredictable. The clerk simply wanted us to go away. But by proving we were old customers, I had, so it seemed, obliged him to accept us as if we were family. From a cabinet behind the front desk, he suddenly produced a pair of clean linen sheets and handed them across the counter to me without a word. An hour later, pillowcases were sent up to the room.

We spent the night in shock and exhaustion, unable even to touch or hold hands, and I grieved silently that all too soon I would lose her. In the morning the streets were deathly quiet. The hotel restaurant was out of everything but rice, sugar and butter, which made a strange breakfast. We scoured the morning papers for details of the assassination. The killers were Sikh members of Mrs. Gandhi's personal guards. It was betrayal as well as murder. A twenty-four-hour shoot-on-sight curfew was in force throughout Patna in an effort to control mob violence and the torching of Sikh shops and homes. Sikh families had gathered in their community temples for protection, surrounded by police patrols. The iron gates of the hotel remained locked. The desk clerks requested that we not go outside the building. Several guests of the hotel told us we would not be permitted to ride the trains even if we were able to make it to the station.

"But are the trains still running?" Sabina asked, her memsahib voice sharp.

"Yes, of course. But why take a chance?" advised the betel-chewing politician, still ensconced in his plush seat in the lobby. He was perhaps the sole aspect of Patna that remained unchanged. "You want to risk your life for what? To rush to New Delhi where the violence is worse? No." He turned to me. "Sir, you should not permit your wife to make such a dangerous journey!"

I nodded grimly. "But she's not an Indian wife. I can't tell her what to do."

The politician scowled. Sabina vacillated and at length decided to wait another day. She could catch a very early train and still make it to the airport in time to meet her friend. Through the afternoon we wrote letters and embraced lightly.

Rested, we were able to begin to say goodbye. We went to the roof to watch the sunset. Cooking fires smouldered in the alleyways near the hotel. The families who lived in canvas shelters on the streets had no way to abide by the curfew order, so the armed soldiers at the nearby intersection ignored them. Cows and goats still wandered freely across the main thoroughfares. The gaudy pink, orange and purple Day-Glo paint sprayed across their bony flanks seemed incongruously festive. The blaze of the setting sun appeared equally indifferent to the nation's loss. The god continued to bestow its blessings just as the Vaishali villagers had beseeched of it only forty-eight hours previously. The pink ellipse widened as it sank through the haze of cooking fires. We followed its stately decline until it hid behind a huge government complex in the next block. A moment later Venus emerged, a single white light in the fading sky.

"Let's lie naked together," said Sabina, touching my arm.

Back in our room, curled together like spoons, only half-undressed, we rocked slightly on our bed until I gently climaxed. Then we stripped away the rest of our clothes. She kissed me and pulled me down on top of her. The strange energy began rising within me once again. Now aware of its course, I began at once to breathe deeply, moving with its flow and giving myself over to it.

"Christ, let it break me now," I prayed silently.

Yet the image that arose was that of the great stone lingam thrusting up out of the earth, and then of Shiva dancing on burning corpses. It was Shiva I yielded to, and I felt the god's blessing blow through me like wind rattling through a half-open window. It tore like a whirlwind. I struggled to keep my breath slow, afraid that if all control was lost, I'd be destroyed. Arms, legs, hands and feet filled with electric fire. My head burned with it. I hyperventilated, then passed through into a calm and tingling awareness, an eye in the centre of the storm. Dimly I sensed Sabina next to me, breathing with the same rapid rhythm. She held my limp penis tightly between her legs. The energy had not yet reached it, but was moving. Her arms caressed my back, stroking me as if to guide the power downward past my belly to my loins. She groaned. Spasms shook her hips. She grabbed the hair of my head and pulled my face hard against her cheek. I quickened, then fought for control of the rhythm.

Sweat drenched us both. How long had it been? An hour? Two? I had no way to measure. Sabina climaxed a second time and sent a jolt through me that triggered my own orgasm. I came without ejaculating, my penis barely stiff. Instead a current shot inside through my body, shaking it violently. My legs arched high behind my back like a scorpion. I reared and became the motion, the rhythm itself. Still the power burned and gathered within, the charge building like lightning, ready to crack me open as it shot inside her. Slowly it forged itself while we rocked faster and faster. Energy throbbed between my thighs. I could feel myself stretching, growing hard against Sabina's skin. My shaft felt like a mould being filled with incandescent metal. Consciousness flickered briefly, rose like a whale surfacing for air before a dive to the black ocean floor. I released a silent prayer.

"O God, split me open, destroy me. This very act, now, I give to you."

From the midst of the heat and fire and pounding of blood came a familiar cool voice inside my head that said, "Then stop."

"What are you saying?"

"Stop."

Shiva, Christ, Buddha, Mara, my own delusion, I didn't know the source of the voice, but I felt afraid of it, for a second hated it and what it was saying. I tried to lose myself again in the fire. But the voice held me.

"Stop."

It drew me back to full consciousness, gave me clear-headed

97

choice. Slowly I eased back on the rhythm, let the current gradually dissolve between us. Some twenty minutes later I lifted my head shakily from her shoulder and looked into the blue of her eyes.

"Can you read my mind?" I asked.

"I don't know."

"But do you know what happened?"

"I think I feel something is changing . . . Tell me."

"I hope you feel it. Because I think if we continue this to where it could go, to whatever sex is at the end of this, it will bond us deeply. Too deeply for what either of us want or need right now. It would have dissolved us. So . . ."

"I'm afraid."

"Don't. There's no reason. Oh, Sabina, it's good to be alive with you."

"I had two orgasms. Without contact, without touching, with you limp between my legs. How is it possible?"

"I had an orgasm without an ejaculation or an erection. How is *that* possible?"

"I felt my breasts fill with milk—no, how could it?"

"I know. I feel you would have gotten pregnant no matter how many pills you'd taken, if we had continued to the end."

I rolled on my side as if to get up, then looked down on her wet, open body. Quickly I rolled back and embraced her again.

"I know," she said, holding me. "It seems so empty."

I cried a bit. She stroked my hair.

At four in the morning we rose. Sabina packed and I carried her bag downstairs. We walked undisturbed through the cool night to the train station. The sleeping bodies of passengers and station beggars covered the floor of the dark waiting room. Their white clothing gave off a ghostly glow. They lay motionless, as if victims of some deadly sleeping gas. The train was two hours late. Standing in the midst of the bodies, like archeologists in a giant communal tomb, Sabina and I went through the painful banalities of exchanging addresses, in case our rendezvous in Bodhgaya did not work out. I laughed feebly at the thought that I should have no expectations for the future. My heart was dead set on meeting her again. The train came. I boarded with her.

"Take good care of you in Nepal," she said like an elder sister.

"Nepal's a lot less dangerous than New Delhi these days. I'll be glad to get out of India. Crazy days ahead."

She nodded. A whistle blew. The train lurched. I leaned forward to kiss her goodbye. Mindful of the two dark-skinned men eyeing us across the compartment, Sabina offered me her cheek.

CHAPTER SEVEN

THE GENTLE GRINDING OF THE MILLSTONE

Nepal

November 2, Patna, Bihar State

Dear Wendy,

Patna is not the best place to be trapped in a shoot-on-site curfew. India is mad with grief at the assassination of Indira Gandhi. Sikhs have sought refuge in their local temples, while their homes and businesses are being torched. Even the curfew hasn't brought the violence under control. Sabina escaped to New Delhi yesterday. I tried to persuade her not to go, as much out of longing for her to stay as out of concern for her safety on the train. We had planned this nice and rationally of course, that she would go back to Delhi, and I would climb mountains in Nepal. The assassination has made everything seem like such a crisis.

It was hard to watch her go, harder than I imagined. Forgive the metaphor, but I felt like a plug that had found its perfect socket. Not chemistry: electricity. We got close to something, Wendy, and I feel I backed off at a crucial moment. I don't know, at the time it felt like God wanted me to stop. I heard His voice—at least the voice I have attributed to God since I became

Christian. Funny, first time I heard it, I thought He wanted me to be celibate, and I listened to it for four years. This time it turned me away from something so sexually intense—a kind of breaking open—that I have to wonder, was it in fact the voice of God? If it wasn't, then whose voice was it? If I apply Occam's razor, the simplest explanation is that it was my own voice, and blaming God just a way of escaping responsibility. It sounded so other, so spiritually authoritative. But then I have experienced parts of myself that seem pretty "other" before. Once I spoke to my darkest, most sexual self, and—you know, it suddenly hits me that my own voice, speaking to that repressed sexual part of me, sounded very much like the voice of God that told me to stop. Yesterday I felt so goddamn virtuous by pulling back. I didn't want to hurt her, I told myself. Today I feel that I was just too weak for it. Now that she's gone, I feel unplugged, wretched, as if I turned away from something that maybe can never be re-captured. We're due to meet up again in December at a small Buddhist conference in Bodhgaya, and I wonder, will I get a second chance?

My skin still feels her skin. When I wake, I feel her arms around me. It's like a phantom limb. I still feel the space next to me where she ought to be. It aches like hell.

November 9

I'm sitting in my hotel room in Kathmandu, cold bottle of pasteurized milk at my elbow, a chunk of dark bread and wedge of yak cheese on the table for breakfast. I awoke at dawn to a flute playing somewhere in the alley below. I went out to buy breakfast and in the lobby found the desk clerk and two Swedish guests sniffing powdered heroin through a tiny tinfoil tube. They had been up all night.

"You don't get addicted this way," said the Nepali. "You just have to remember to stop after a month or so and eat. You know, to get your strength back."

Since I have returned to my room, my neighbours have

awakened. I've not seen the couple, but every morning I hear the woman rhythmically moan and crescendo, and again I feel the ache in my phantom limb. That's one of the reasons I'm beginning my trek as soon as possible, to keep my mind in the present moment, my focus on where to put my feet on the trail. For a while, I don't want to think about the past or the future. Frankly, the mountain air will be a welcome chance to clear my head. I've decided to hike the old trade route between Kathmandu and Nepal's second city, Pokhara. The route has fallen into disuse since the highway went through farther south, so it's about two hundred kilometres of mostly quiet trails that serve the local villages. Once I reach Pokhara, I'll travel south to Lumbini, birthplace of the Buddha, and then cross the border back into India again, in time for the conference.

Oh, and bad news: the Indian Embassy in Kathmandu was only handing out two-week transit visas to tourists re-entering India. Three-month extensions are as rare as yeti. It took all my finesse and good karma just to get my previous visa date, December 26, to stand. Suddenly, there seems very little time left for me on the subcontinent. I'm not giving up, though. Travellers here tell me Gaya has always been a great place for illicit extensions. I'll give it a try when I'm back in Bihar.

Love you, Wendy, your brother,
   Tim

Three days into my trek I was lying naked in a stony riverbed when I met a Nepali lawyer. A thin young man in a dusty grey suit, he carried an old leather briefcase as his only burden. Unfazed at discovering a naked Canadian on the rocks, he hailed me with a hearty "Good day to you, sir!"

I had recently fallen down the side of a ravine. Dazed and hurt, I had rinsed off the blood, sweat and burrs in the glacial stream at the bottom, and was drying myself in the sun when he happened along. I pulled on my shorts and returned the greeting.

He politely introduced himself as Dhunbar, and said he was on his way home from his office in Kathmandu to visit his family in Be-sali. When I told him that his village was my current destination, he was delighted, and invited me to his home for the night. In the morning, he brought a friend of his to my bedside, a young farmer named Gophal who had gone blind in one eye. Did I have any medicine for it, Dhunbar inquired? The whites of the eye had gone completely red with inflamed blood vessels, and the pupil stayed di-lated when I shone my flashlight in it. I said I had no medicine, but would take him to the nearest clinic, a three-hour walk to the south. The idea apparently had not occurred to him on his own, and it took some coaxing to get him to go.

One-eyed and barefoot, Gophal walked ahead of me along the mountain trails at a pace I strained to match. For a while I tried walking with one-eye closed, and found the loss of depth perspective dangerous on the muddy slopes. The medical attendant at the clinic said Gophal had conjunctivitis; untreated, he would go permanently blind in one eye and it would inevitably spread to the other. But if he could make it to Kathmandu, he could get an operation for free. Gophal said he had a brother-in-law a few hours farther along the trail. The family was well off and could help him. He invited me to come along.

They owned a steep slope of terraced rice fields, and were in mid-harvest when Gophal and I arrived at their mud-and-thatch house. His request for help could not have been more ill-timed. Gophal ges-tured towards me, as if arguing that his case was so serious, a *foreigner* had gotten himself involved. I thought Gophal's speech was a little slurred. His lower lip protruded and he seemed on the verge of drooling. His right eye was half closed from the swelling. Brother-in-law listened quietly, then returned to the fields for another load of fresh-cut bundles of rice. It was impossible to gauge his response. Gophal put his head on his knee and gazed at his young niece play-ing with her baby brother.

The toddler was peeing merrily on the mat I was later asked to sit on during dinner. His sister, about five years old, was the most beau-tiful, radiant child I had seen in all Nepal. She had black hair that ran wild down the back of her neck like the tendrils of some exotic jungle plant. Her skin was tanned deep brown and a healthy protruding belly stuck out from the bottom of her grey rag of a shirt. She showed a constant flow of smiles, eyes full of mirth and good-natured mischief. She played coy with me, keeping her distance while grinning and laughing whenever she looked in my direction. Where on this isolated hillside was the source of so much happiness? I wondered. Her thirteen-year-old brother, Shankar, spoke polite schoolbook English, and I encouraged him to talk. The wild-haired beauty giggled at the tremendous joke of her brother babbling with the stranger. She hefted her baby brother high so we could all see his tiny nakedness. Dangling in mid-air, he kicked with his legs like a frog, squealing with laughter.

Mother moved in and out from hearth room to porch. She wore a purple patterned sarong and a crimson vest, stitched with elaborate designs. I had never seen anything more elegant in all Nepal. She looked surprisingly young, her waist slender, her long hair wound in a thick cord down her back, her bare arms smooth, well muscled from the endless round of household chores. She said little more than a greeting to her brother. Taking the toddler from the mirthful daughter's arms, mother knelt on the porch and tugged up her vest to offer her breast to the boy. He lunged at it, smacking into her, lips first. He grabbed her breast in both hands and suckled noisily. The force of him rocked her back on her knees. She balanced against the assault, then hollered something to her eldest daughter inside the house, and carried on a noisy conversation over the slurping. She seemed at ease and unperturbed by the white stranger, barely two metres away on the porch, who was trying to pretend he was not looking at her.

She was exquisite. She had borne four children, the eldest thirteen, so she must have been in her late twenties. Sabina's age, I could not help but think. Yet her face was unlined, marred only by two dark windburn patches on each of her high cheekbones. The bright red of her vest and the dancing pattern of her sarong blended with the dark hue of her skin. Her eyes looked clear, yet somehow faraway.

Sitting this close to her, I sensed her love for her children like the radiant warmth of a cooking fire. She rocked slightly to the rhythm of her son's feeding. When her husband returned at dusk with his final load, I noticed her eyes followed him with a glowing intensity.

The toddler, satiated, rolled his eye upwards and dropped off to sleep in her arms. She pulled down her vest again. Gophal crossed the porch and spoke to her. I saw her eyes fill with concern. From the few words I grasped, I guessed that it was not yet decided if brother-in-law could go with Gophal to the city. One spoiled crop on the hillside could devastate a family that ate most of what it produced.

They served me a standard Nepali rice and lentil dinner, with chillied greens and a bowl of hot buffalo milk, which I consumed alone on the porch, sitting on the pee-stained mat. After I had finished, the family gathered inside to eat, leaving me to wonder uncertainly if I had been fed separately as an honoured guest or unclean outsider. Looking out from the porch, I watched stars appear in the twilight, crisp and clear. Below, orange flecks of cooking fires studded the black hills.

After dinner the adults came out and sat on the porch with me. Brother-in-law pulled out his bamboo pipe, lit it, then passed it around to grandfather, Gophal and Shankar. Next mother took a long, thoughtful drag on its bamboo stem. They talked, presumably about Gophal and how to help him. I felt an easy equality between sexes and generations, perhaps borne of the hard rice farming life. They depended on one another. They were companions.

The old man brought me the pipe, then sat down at my side. The offered tobacco made me feel like one of the family, and I was grateful, even though I coughed as the hot smoke dusted my throat. Grandfather was skinny as a leather-coated skeleton, though earlier I had seen him, clad in only a loincloth, carry a huge bundle of rice in from the fields. Now he wore a coarse white blanket to protect him from the evening chill. His head was shaven, a few stiff white hairs sticking up in a fuzz around his huge wrinkled ears. He looked me in the eye and began speaking an incomprehensible dialect that gurgled out of him like water boiling in a large pot. I struggled to guess at his questions and tried to answer. The old man grinned wide and nodded his head, obviously understanding not a word. When I dropped the Nepali and responded in English, he smacked me on the knee and laughed. Then I spoke my heart, words spilling out into the dark air, blending with his, just patterns of sound playing out strange rhythms in my ears that tickled and delighted. I told him I admired his family, felt honoured to be allowed to share the evening with them, and what it was like to be alone, travelling without family or fields of my own. Grandfather picked up my soft hand and examined it, tracing my lines with his earth-blackened bone-and-leather finger. His eyes danced. He clapped again, held my hand between his own, then smiled, stood stiffly and walked into the house to sleep.

The rest soon followed, except for mother, once more suckling her youngest in her arms. Shankar had indicated I was to set up my sleeping bag on the earthen porch, but for the moment I felt no rush. I settled back with my journal, staring at it in the dim light of a kerosene wick, while watching her out of the corner of my eye. She rose slowly to her feet, keeping her back bent so as not to pull her nipple from the child's mouth as she carried him towards a rough burlap sack strung into a makeshift hammock between posts of the porch. Slowly she lowered him, then dropped him down into it. A loud "pop" rang across the porch as her nipple slipped out, followed by a quick cry of anguish from the hammock. She rocked him gently, whispering musical sounds. In seconds the wail faded unwillingly to a whimper, then silence.

She pulled her vest back down over her breast, picked up a small sack of rice, crossed in front of me to the corner of the porch and sat on the floor in front of a small hand mill. It had a stone base, flat and smooth with a slightly raised circle in the centre. The round millstone which she placed over the base had a wooden handle on top. To turn the heavy stone, she had to use both arms, and braced herself against the wall with one leg, while the other was tucked under her so she could sit as close to the mill as possible. She poured a handful of rice in a hole in the centre of the stone and began a slow rhythmic grinding, swinging the stone round and round over the base. Soon white rice flour spilled out over the rim. The rubbing of stone on rice filled the air with a warm throbbing noise. It conjured domestic sounds from another lifetime, sounds that made me feel drowsy and secure when I was a child: my mother's vacuum cleaner, clothes tumbling in the dryer.

Shankar came out of the house to speak to her for a second, and I asked the boy, pointing, what a millstone was called in his language. She answered instead, turning to look at me directly for the first time. She rested her faraway gaze on me for an instant and smiled, answering what must have seemed an awfully stupid question.

"Millstone," she said in Nepali. It was the only word she ever spoke to me, and I forgot it instantly.

After a while she swept up the rice flour using the same hand broom she had used earlier to sweep off the porch. Then, before rising, she suddenly stopped, as if breaking the flow of her own rhythm, and stared at the red-earth floor near my hand. In the dim light of the lantern, I noticed she looked tired. Her family may have been prosperous by Nepali standards, she had four lovable children and a strong husband, hard-working, but still it was a hard existence. Her eyes wandered near to my fingers. I imagined I could read her thoughts. She was wondering, perhaps for the only moment in her life, what it must be like to belong to that other world where this white hand had come from, free of husband and children and the endless round of cooking, winnowing, cleaning and milling rice.

"Take me with you, to the cities and the land of smooth hands, where I can dance, and there are no millstones that slowly grind away my beauty."

As if on a boat, we slowly pull away from the house and its half-harvested fields. Her family looks on silently from the porch, which becomes a dock. Her eyes fix on the glowing light past the horizon, on freedom she has never known, freedom to be other than mother, cook, grinder of grain. She looks back and sees them, unable to separate themselves from each other and their land, uncomprehending. They are frozen as if in amber, fossilized. It is as if their hearts have stopped beating. But it is she who is entering time, speeding up. Suddenly, in one fluid gesture, she stretches out a departing hand, touches a post on the red-earth porch, and halts the boat. Her chest heaves. The pulse of it, like a heartbeat, shatters the amber. The family moves. Her husband reaches out a strong brown arm, helps her onto the dock. There is rhythm once more to this life she has chosen, a dance outside of time that I will never know. The boat sails on with me in it, alone. I watch the red vest moving rapidly, her lungs sucking great gulps of air as if she has been deprived of oxygen. My last glimpse, as the vision vanishes, is of her reaching down to touch the earth.

Her gaze changed, uncluttered by idle daydreams now. She brushed her hair back into place behind her ears with her fingers, then carried the new-ground flour into the mud-walled house.

After breakfast, I found Gophal crouched on the far corner of the porch, smoking. I wanted him to confirm that brother-in-law was definitely going with him to Kathmandu that day. He shook his head. They had reached a compromise. Gophal would stay with the family two more days to help bring in the harvest. Then they would go to the capital for the operation. Shankar would be allowed to accompany them. It would be the boy's first trip to that different world of the city. I breathed a sigh of relief. Gophal would be two days closer to blindness, but he would get his operation in time. In time. I forced some money on him to pay for his bus fare, which he accepted once he realized I would never relent. Then he departed to join the others in the fields. I hefted my pack and looked around, but the house was deserted except for grandfather, back in his G-string, washing the family goats. He turned to me, pressed his palms together at his chest, and grinned broadly. I felt humbled by his cheerful dignity, returned the gesture and the grin, and set off once more towards Pokhara.

I arrived in Nepal's second city ten days later, feet and lips blistered, my skin burnt the colour of copper. My body had grown hard and thin from near constant walking and diarrhea. I rested a few days, swimming in the warm lake and dining on delicacies like *aubergine au gratin* and apple pie at the Hungry Eye Restaurant in

Pokhara's tourist ghetto. Once recovered, I took a bus south back towards India, with a stop at Lumbini, birthplace of the Buddha.

Lumbini had seen better days. It contained two temples, one Tibetan style, for the mountain-dwelling Buddhists, and one Theravadan, for the lowland Buddhist castes and the recent Nepali converts from Hinduism. A few dilapidated structures were connected to the temples, including a guest house. Otherwise, little remained other than ruins. King Ashoka had been here long ago, leaving his signature stone column with an inscription authorizing a tax break for the sacred ground:

"King Piyadasi [Ashoka] the Beloved of Devas in the twentieth year of the coronation, himself made a royal visit, Sakyamuni [Buddha] having been born here. A stone resiling was built and a stone pillar erected. The Bhagavan [Buddha] having been born here, Lumbini was tax reduced and entitled to the eighthpart."

The pillar had been re-erected recently, and was held upright by iron bands, ten metres up off the ground. Inside the temple was an old stone relief carving, the only ancient icon of the birth. It showed the Holy Mother holding the branches of a tree while the baby Buddha leapt from her side, above the hip, landing on his feet on a lotus blossom.

According to the ancient texts, the Sakya court astrologer interpreted the unusual birth and other mysterious signs to mean that the newborn prince would be either one of the world's greatest monarchs, or else one of the world's greatest spiritual teachers. The king, like so many fathers, had his own preference for his son's career, and wanted him to be a great king. He decreed that his young son would live forever inside the palace walls, and that no sickness, suffering or death would be permitted to enter in at the gate. He reasoned that if he could keep the prince from ever discovering the true condition of the world, his son would be successfully deterred from the spiritual path.

The prince grew into a strong and handsome man. He had a large harem and also took a princess for his bride. Soon she produced an heir. But the prince was always curious about the outside world, and so one day shortly after the birth of his son, he mounted his horse in secret and passed beyond the palace walls. In the course of his journey he came across a sick man, an old man, a corpse and an ascetic wanderer. Immediately the prince knew his true vocation: to find a way to free all beings from the endless round of suffering. He returned to the palace in order to see his son sleeping at his mother's breast; then he cut off his long and beautiful hair with his sword and went out into the world alone.

He studied with various yoga teachers, quickly mastering every technique. Next he joined a community of ascetics bent on attaining wisdom through mortification of the flesh. For six years the prince starved himself and wore only rags. One day, reduced to skin and bones, he realized that following this extremist path he would soon die, and miss accomplishing his goal. So he left the ascetics and accepted milk from a village woman. He soon regained his strength. Then, finding a bo tree, he settled under it in meditation posture, determined not to arise again until he had penetrated the source of suffering and found its cure . . .

Or so the story goes. The earliest written biographies date to the first century A.D., although moral teachings drawing from incidents in his life were written down somewhat earlier. Buddha himself would probably advise not worrying over past events. "Test the words *attributed* to me," he might say. "If they prove true and useful to your life, then follow them accordingly." He would be no help at all to a frustrated historian.

Beside the Theravada temple lay the foundation walls of ancient ruins, the edges rough and jagged. The excavated brickwork itself was exposed about a foot above the neatly kept grass. It appeared remarkably well preserved: the outline of perhaps a great hall or temple here, small rooms like monks' cloisters there. A sign on the fence read simply: "These buildings are generally attached with sentiments surrounding Lord Buddha's birth." Perhaps nothing more would ever be known about them.

Walking farther, I discovered additional excavations were in process. About thirty sarong-clad workers laboured with pickaxes and shovels, digging up the underground brickwork and dumping the rubble into piles. Where the walls' hollowed-out foundations lay, string markers had been put in place. A little farther along, workers were rebuilding the walls by stacking two parallel rows of new brick and then shovelling the original materials into the trough between the rows. The edges were finished with special bricks with the outward ends broken off, to add to the ancient-ruins look I had admired in the completed section.

I collared the lone Nepali in a pressed white shirt, obviously the foreman. He explained that the goal was to rebuild the ruins with mixed new and old brick in exactly the same spot. He pointed to the elegant, park-like features of the earlier section I had seen. I had to admit, it looked authentic. The jagged cornerstones were the perfect touch. I realized the Buddhist archeological sites I had seen in India had all been preserved in the same esthetically pleasing manner, which was very appealing to the tourist eye. Constructing historic sites had reached a high level of accomplishment on the Indus Plains.

But I felt duped, as if I had bought an ancient artifact in a market bazaar that turned out to be mass-produced at a local factory. I retreated to the Tibetan temple to sulk. It was a sturdy, wooden building, far newer than most Tibetan temples I had visited in Ladakh. I noticed modern touches on the artwork that must have dated to the Second World War. In a giant wall painting of the Tibetan Wheel of Existence, the realm of the warring titans showed them aiming artillery pieces at the kingdom of the gods. At the back of the hall, where paintings of the Buddha were surrounded by heralds of Buddhist divinities and Bodhisattvas, I recognized in among the celestial clouds the images of Nepal's Hindu king, and the king, his father, before him. I wondered if King Ashoka would have rebuilt Lumbini's walls as a tourist attraction, and adorned himself as a celestial divinity?

I found a pile of cushions against one wall, and wrapped my legs up in meditation posture in a funk. I hated the compromises the past, even the mythological past, was making with the present. History seemed as insubstantial as Jell-O. Suddenly, I felt desperately alone. I wanted to talk with someone, just to settle the jiggling. Easy enough, in this land of illusions, to conjure your own conversation partner. I decided to call up Lama Philippe. I felt he would understand. Closing my eyes, I returned to the high winds of the peak the day we planted prayer flags. I saw him sitting on the boulder in front of me, the barren red mountains all around us. He raised an eyebrow and, as usual, cut right to the heart of the matter.

"So, you are lonely? And now you are rushing back to India, to Bodhgaya, the place of Buddha's enlightenment. And why? For wisdom? To penetrate the core of your loneliness? No—because now you are in love. You long for her touch, her embrace, but most of all, her attention."

"Most of all, I just want to tell her about Nepal, what I've been through in the past month. Just to watch her eyes. When I think of seeing her again, I feel like a little kid."

"Tim, if we are going to have this conversation, you must get past this grossest layer of your self-deception."

"I admit, sex has a lot to do with it. Something very strange was happening with Sabina—"

Philippe held up his bony hand to cut me off. "Still you are getting sex and excitement mixed up with love and attachment!" He wobbled his head at me like an Indian, making a sideways figure eight with his nose. "Sex and excitement are mere sensations, however extraordinary they may seem: they arise, they pass, we let them go. Remember, significance is what you attach to sensation, nothing more."

"But a kind of spiritual energy was being generated. I turned my back on it. I thought God wanted it that way. Now I wonder."

Philippe stared out across the mountaintops. "Your problem, Tim, is that sex for you is a moral battleground, with lust and love all mired in the muck of good and evil. Sex can't simply be sex; love can't simply be love. It's all got to mean something grander. This is the delusion of the ego, that you can't crawl into bed with a woman without bringing Jesus and Buddha and all the archangels with you."

"Well, what do you think, then?"

"I think your longing for Sabina is an attempt to unite the opposite poles of your cravings for sex and God. You think you found something mystical with her. But you fail to see that lust for sex and lust for spirit amount to the same thing. Both drive you blindly. Sabina merely serves a purpose for your ego, as does your fascination with the Buddha. And what did you really find in Nepal that you are so anxious to tell her about? A romanticized vision of domestic bliss, something new to crave. Oh, don't look surprised. I can barely tell the difference between your lust for Sabina and your longing for the woman in the red vest."

"You are becoming a damn irritating imaginary companion," I said. "I should just push you off the cliff."

Philippe stood up, unbidden, and did a backwards somersault over the edge. He floated in space, level with me, and then glided back down in meditation posture.

"Just because I am a figment of your imagination, don't think you own me," he said haughtily. "The truth of my words speaks for itself. Sabina and I are no different in your mind. You use us equally for your fantasies, though in different ways. Ask yourself to what purpose, to what end?"

"Sometimes I need a friend."

"Pathetic. It is the horror of being alone—"

"Stop it."

"The horror of being all alone with your dirty little secret. Take a close look at yourself. There's no saint behind the would-be-Buddhist on his perpetual quests and treks and trysts. Why does this confused mess of craving mean so much to you?"

"Stop it, stop it. You are an illusion!"

"No, my friend, I am your imagination. Not for a moment, even this highly dramatic one, are you deluded that I am real. *You* are the illusion to yourself. You can't bear to face the filth and chaos in your heart—as if it was only your personal beast, and not also Kaliyuga, bursting forth. Desperately you seek something to attach yourself to—God, a woman, a mission—something meaningful, divine, comforting, that you can belong to. But you can't escape what's inside.

Wasn't it your Jesus who called religious hypocrites 'whitewashed tombs'?"

"What can I do?" I said wretchedly.

"Phhh, it's your problem. Now I'm sorry I got involved."

"I'll listen, I promise."

"You come to India to live like a monk, but won't give up desire; you pursue Sabina, but turn back because you think God speaks to you. Back and forth you go like a badminton shuttlecock. But wherever you go, you can't escape what's inside of you. You must face it without distraction."

"How?"

Philippe smiled, maddeningly silent.

Gradually, an idea took root in my mind: Sabina's story about her father, stripped of everything by the Russians. Possessing nothing, he was truly happy. I knew that this was what I wanted, to be shorn of everything I had. All at once it was clear that not only lovers and God, but passport, credit card, sketchbook, even spare underwear, created the shell. I would do it. I would go back to Sabina for a while and then when the time came to leave, I would become a wandering ascetic, blown by the winds. There would be no better place than India, where there are many thousands of such wanderers, called *sadhus*. My heartbeat quickened at the thought. I could leave my documents some place safe, perhaps just to try it out for a month or so.

I looked at Philippe. He was scowling. He opened his mouth wide, I could see his long teeth, all the way back to the molars, and he let out a terrible loud honking sound.

It was so startling that I opened my eyes, and saw through the open doors of the Lumbini temple that the sound was coming from the horn of a black minibus. The panel door opened and out streamed a dozen or so Japanese Zen monks wearing billowing black robes. Around each neck hung a camera. They fluttered into the temple hall like a flock of crows, clicking their lenses at everything that glittered: the statues, the banners, the frescoes, pillars, butter offerings. One of them discovered me, flashed a bulb and brought the others, black robes flapping, as if I were carrion. For a moment, I dwelt at the centre of a lightning storm. Then, as one, they flew out of the temple to rob the sparse images of the Theravada hall as well. With equal thoroughness they photographed the pillar and every reconstructed wall of the pseudo-site. In forty minutes, start to finish, they were back in their minibus and roaring down the road. Like good Zen monks, they had grasped the essence of Lumbini far more profoundly than I: it is empty of all meaning; that is why one venerates it.

I plunged back into India. Bus, train, bus, train, bus: thirty-six hours non-stop to travel about three hundred kilometres from Lumbini to Bodhgaya. The closer I came to my destination, the crazier my imaginary conversation with Philippe seemed. Becoming a sadhu was just another fantasy, another distraction. For the present, I had the impending Buddhist conference to think about and, more importantly, meeting Sabina again. No more time for fantasies, I told myself.

I slept for two hours in Hajipur train station's second-class waiting room, waiting for my next ride. At dawn I woke, washed and shaved in the sink. Two young men in cotton pantaloons and kurtas approached me, offering apricots and calling a coolie to bring us tea.

"Please, let us exchange a song," the Indians requested with great courtesy. One thrummed a tabletop like a tabla while the other sang both parts of a love duet in Hindi, and then translated for me.

He sings: *The moon is half, the night is half, Our love is half—ah, that it were complete!*

And she responds: *Your eyes are half, your smile is half, All love is half—oh, it never is complete!*

Late afternoon I reached the town of Gaya. Pressed into the back of a three-wheel motor-rickshaw loaded down with nine other passengers, I sped through the final fifteen kilometres to Bodhgaya, centre of the Buddhist universe. It was a dusty little town, with temples built or under construction from just about every Buddhist sect on earth. I registered for the conference, and discovered each participant was expected to hand in a paper on Buddhism and World Peace to be read and discussed by the group. With three days to go before opening ceremonies, I started making notes.

The organizers also directed me to a Tibetan temple that had cheap dormitory rooms for pilgrims. Three young Tibetan novices quickly adopted me. I gave them the last of my Canada-flag souvenir pins, and they in turn toured me through the Mahabodhi *stupa* that marks the site of the Buddha's enlightenment. A stupa is a Buddhist memorial monument, usually pyramidal or dome-like in shape. Bodhgaya's original stupa was erected by—who else—King Ashoka in the third century B.C., and has been rebuilt and restored several times since then. The present monument is a massive, intricately carved stone monolith like a stretched pyramid which soars about fifty metres into the sky, in a phallic fashion of which Ashoka, with his column fetish, would certainly have approved.

At the rear of the stupa stood a gnarled bo tree, the grandchild of the original tree under which the Buddha attained enlightenment. Ashoka's son, a Buddhist monk and missionary, took a shoot from the Bodhi Tree to the island of Ceylon. The tree still lives today, in Anuradhapura. At a much later date, a sapling from this tree was returned to Bodhgaya and planted where the original once stood. Tibetan prayer flags and small white blessing streamers cover the lower branches of the world's most sacred tree. I noticed spiders sent their own streamers out between its holy twigs, catching and mummifying flies for dinner.

At the front of the stupa, dozens of people, mostly Tibetan pilgrims and monks, performed grand prostrations. From a standing position they crouched and slid flat out on their fronts, arms stretched along the ground, foreheads touching the dust. One hundred thousand repetitions is minimum for the initiation into the Tibetan tantric path. To ease the physical wear and tear, most initiates wore leather aprons and mitts with blocks of smooth wood attached to the palms for smooth sliding. I had known a German woman from Ladakh who told me that after completing her 100,000 repetitions, she went to see her teacher. He took one look at her and told her she had better do them again. "And you know," she told me, "the second time was much better."

Now I could see what she meant. One Westerner, his hair cut monkishly short, like mine, was bobbing up and down at a great pace, his body rigid, muscles tense, his face straining as if in pain. There were also three or four old Tibetan women who slid slowly through the motions with a fluidity that was relaxing just to watch. The guy seemed to be trying so hard to get somewhere. The women just seemed to be enjoying the trip. I registered for the conference, and then waited for the second round of my own initiation to begin.

CHAPTER EIGHT

SPIDERS IN
THE BODHI TREE
Bodhgaya

S EEING HER AGAIN at the conference opening ceremony, I
felt a mixture of fear and excitement that shattered all pretext
of serenity. Inside the tent, erected especially for the conference, about two hundred monks had gathered for the opening devotions. We sat cross-legged on the floor, wedged together before an
altar consisting of several Buddha statues which the various sects'
temples had donated for the day. I sat surrounded by Thai and
Burmese monks in Day-Glo orange robes, chanting the sutras.

Sabina and her Indian adviser arrived late. I watched them take a
seat together on the floor on the far side of the tent. She looked
around. It was all I could do not to wave. When she saw me, she gave
me a brief smile, as if I was one of many old acquaintances, and then
turned her eyes to the altar. Have to remember, I told myself, this is
public. My impulse was to leap up, race across the crowded tent and
embrace her. Got to pull back, I thought, struggling to sit still, these
monks will probably sniff out this burst of sexual energy like a fart.

I mumbled along, sweating, trying not to stare at her. I had to
keep my hands over my crotch, because my little lingam was rising in
a most unmonk-like fashion, and my thin cotton pants provided little cover. We chanted, reminding ourselves of the infinite round of
death and rebirth, of the Buddha's promise that by following the

eightfold path of restraint and moderate living, then over however many lifetimes, impure karma, the clinging to that which we desire, will drop way and we can be free.

I wanted her. I wanted her now. I imagined standing up and deliberately walking towards her, the monks drawing back in surprise. I pull her up to her feet next to the makeshift altar and set her on the edge. She's wearing a sari, and I wrestle the folds aside to find her hips. She protests and I shush her. The monks are still chanting, but now all eyes have fixed upon us, waves of energy surging into us like the surf. There is a ritual here, I'm rocking back and forth with it, a purpose for we two lovers to attend such a gathering at the place of Buddha's enlightenment. The monks intone, drone, eyes half-closed. My hands slide around her hips and grasp each cheek. Her flesh is moving, moving with the buzzing rhythm of the chants. I press myself against the silken folds, my flesh finding her flesh, and enter her, thrusting us both back against the central brass Buddha on the altar, her head thrown back resting in its lap. I feel the familiar lock of her legs against the backs of my thighs. She grasps the edge of the stage with her arms and leans back, pushing her pelvis towards me. The heat from our bodies burns. My face is on fire, glowing, igniting with a red light that leaps like a lightning bolt from my mouth into hers, fusing us with a stream of fire that races down her throat and torso, her crotch, and coils round my penis, up my belly and throat, then out again. Her arms wave with the waves, the ecstasy. My hands are raised, slowly we become the tantric deities, and will, in the course of the ritual, fuse and then tear each other asunder . . .

The fantasy is getting out of control. I'm chanting and sweating in my seat, hips pumping slightly, but noticeably enough that the Burman next to me gives a funny look. I've got to pull out or I will seriously embarrass myself and make getting up impossible. But the chanting draws me back into it, back to becoming the ritual. In the vision, the monks are not repulsed. No, they are using us for their own meditation, for the essential unity of male and female elements, drawing our combined sexual energy into themselves, their metaphor for spiritual perfection, the fusion of all opposites, whatever. Jesus, I can't even fantasy fuck the woman I love without turning into the headliner at a prayer ceremony. I exhale suddenly, half blurt out a laugh. The monk next to me widens his eyes for an instant, which from a Burmese monk is more shocking than getting the finger. I chuckle out loud and I'm grinning like a nut. But the brief laugh broke the spell. I'm still crazy with hormones, but less likely to explode.

The chanting ended abruptly. The conference organizer, a Tibetan exile named Professor Tulku, made a few concluding announcements and gave out directions to the lunch buffet. The monks all stood and began padding out of the tent. I sat still, waiting, without much success, for my phallus to relax. I watched the brown sea of feet and ankles, swishing saffron, ochre and maroon robes. Gradually they cleared, leaving not a trace of her. My spirits drooped. Far more than disappointed, I was hurt, confused. A few laggard monks chatted outside the tent. The rest of the conference participants had headed off towards the luncheon hall. A sick feeling entered my stomach. I had been heading in her direction for, well, it suddenly seemed like every swift step of my trek had been a step towards her. Now she was trying to avoid me. Or playing coy? Had she perhaps found another man? Jerry's jeering face flashed like one of Mara's demons in my mind's eye. No, certainly it was her sense of Indian propriety. She always remembers her reputation, I thought wryly, while I envisage ravishing her before the assembled monks of Bodhgaya.

I headed towards the guest house where lunch was being served. The room was simple, but the tables had been covered with white tablecloths that made it look elegant. I found her there, talking to her adviser on the far side of the room. I stared at the back of her neck, reproaching her silently for leaving me. She turned and her eyes caught mine for a fraction of a second. They spoke as if pleading, "Please, my professor . . ." I turned away to the vegetarian buffet, and sat near Professor Tulku to congratulate him on the turnout.

About forty participants had shown up, not counting the local monks who attended the opening ceremony. Sabina and I were the only Westerners. Most were Indian academics, but several non-resident monks and a few visiting scholars had also made the pilgrimage, perhaps attracted by the conference theme of world peace. Two monks I had not noticed earlier sat side by side at a corner table. Their faces looked old, incredibly old, with thick creases and dusky skin, darker than Tibetans, yet with oriental eyes and the reddish tinge of the Tibeto-Burman race. Their dark hands mashed saffron rice on their plates. Their robes were dull yellow and made of heavy cloth, worn and dusty, and on their heads they each wore a yellow hat like a bishop's mitre, topped with a brass *vajra*, the Buddhist crown-shaped symbol for the lightning-bolt energy of tantric power. Lightning bolt? I had seen it in Tibetan-Buddhist symbols all over Ladakh, but only now connected its meaning with my own experience with internal electrical storms.

"Who are they?" I asked Tulku.

"I do not know," he shrugged. "They came from some monastery in the hills of Assam."

"Not Tibetan?"

"Oh, no."

"Well, what does their registration form say?"

"They didn't fill one out. I don't even think they speak Hindi."

I felt reluctant to press the busy professor any further, and so after finishing my lunch, I went over to greet the Assamese. I pressed my palms together and greeted them in Hindi. They returned the gesture, but it looked stiff and formal, as if it were something they were mimicking, rather than a part of their daily life. They smiled slightly, bowing their heads a fraction. They were old. Old like giant, gnarled trees. They were solid though, not withered. Every gesture slow, deliberate. They did not appear to understand a word I was saying, which could well have had as much to do with my Nepali-adulterated pronunciation as with their supposed lack of Hindi. I pressed my palms once more in the parting gesture and retreated, feeling awkward and insubstantial in their presence.

As I turned, I saw Sabina leaving. Her professor was still seated, embroiled in discussion with a frail, balding Indian in a dull black suit. She did not look back on her way out. It took effort not to race as I walked towards the door. She was halfway down the carpeted hallway when I caught up to her. I reached out and grabbed her arm to turn her.

"Sttt," she hissed, sharp and low.

I let go with a jerk, as if she were red hot. I felt stupid, touching her in public. I was starting off on the wrong foot before I had even spoken a word. My hands were shaking. For all I knew, she might want nothing to do with me. She saw my pained look and softened. I drank in the look of her like a man lost in the desert, not bothering, for the moment, to question whether or not I was gulping oasis water or sand from a mirage. But her eyes did not rest. They flitted over my shoulder, back down the hallway.

"Someone's coming," she whispered. She started walking again, turned down a corridor. "No, you can't come this way. It's for women guests only. You're not staying here?"

"The Tibetan monastery, just down the road."

"Of course."

"When can we talk?" I whispered.

"My professor is here. I really don't think—"

"Look," I said sharply. Her eyes darted back down the hall. I took a deep breath. I was angry that my presence made her so uncomfortable. "Let's go for a walk."

"I can't. My professor delivers his address in the afternoon session. I can't see you like this, here." She moved away from me once more.

"Stay still or I'll grab your arm again."

She drew herself up. "What are you trying to do? Blackmail?" Her eyes flashed at me, angry, now.

"After the session, then," I said quietly. "By the Mahabodhi stupa. I prepared a picnic for us."

"A picnic?"

I nodded. She nodded too, perhaps just to get rid of me. I pressed my palms together, then left her for my monk's cell, to meditate before the afternoon session began.

The conference participants sat along the sides of a long and narrow table, with the speakers taking turns at the head. The table was low to the ground, Indian fashion, and we sat on cushions. Despite my temple training, my knees could not endure so much pretzelled sitting, and I ended up sticking them straight out, surreptitiously, beneath the table, trying not to jab whoever was sitting opposite me. Sabina sat next to her adviser, studiously avoiding looking at me. I felt like a grade-school kid trying not to look at my sweetheart in class so the children wouldn't sing songs and shame us.

I feigned interest and tried not to doodle on the scraps of paper I had brought. Despite wall fans, the room grew stiflingly hot. When Sabina's professor delivered his paper in Hindi, it was all I could do to keep my head from drifting downward and then jerking up, hovering on the lip of waking consciousness. When the session finally ended, I carefully avoided looking at her. I returned to my room and gathered up my picnic supplies. I was sweating. Once more I sat on my cot and meditated, watching the stream of emotions gush through me like an open fire hydrant on a hot summer day. Then I wrote in my journal:

Jesus, I want this woman so much I could cry. I want my blood to boil over and my eyeballs to roll back in my skull and just dunk myself in her Ganges, lose myself in its sweet purifying bliss. I want to ravish her, clutch her, rock into her. Want, want, want: the desire is driving me crazy. How can I want with such passion someone I've had so many times? What is to want but the repetition of the past? That's suffering, to want what is past. You can't enter the same river twice. And here I sit, as delirious for her as the first night together. Can you enter the same woman twice? I'm steaming out, losing control, and now I've got to walk through this holy city to the world's most sacred monument to the great renouncer of desire, and do my damnedest to seduce her again from scratch. I'm furious that she can be so cool to me when I'm erupting all over the place. Sometimes I feel as if this woman's sole purpose in my life is to teach me some self-restraint. Yeah, easy to practise restraint on a mountaintop. But how to do it sitting next to the woman you lust after?

I packed up my goodies and left, stiff-legged, for our rendezvous at the stupa. It was a five-minute walk. I forced myself to walk slowly and practise walking meditation along the route. She was waiting.

"I thought maybe you weren't coming," she said as I reached her.

Although most of the town was dust, I had scouted out a grassy park not too far from the temple. It was surrounded by trees, with a few gardens in the shade where flowers would not fry. I led her to a quiet, secluded patch of grass. From my pack I pulled out my freshly washed head cloth, which had served as turban, sweat-rag and first-aid bandage on my trek. I laid it out as a groundsheet, then dug in my bag again for some mangoes and oranges bought at the local market, and my treasures from Nepal.

I had shopped for this picnic in Pokhara a week ago, and had kept the contents well insulated and protected throughout the long journey south. I brought out a thick wedge of yak cheese, a loaf of crusty bread and a bottle of Italian wine. All these items were virtually unobtainable in India. Perhaps it is hard to imagine bread and cheese producing ecstasy, but when I first tasted them in Nepal, after several months' deprivation, I almost swooned, and my first thought was to bring some back for her. For a European stuck in India, I figured there would be no better aphrodisiac.

Part of the bread had gone mouldy, but most was still edible; blue fungus covered the surface of the yak cheese, which was easily cut away and fortunately did not affect the tart and buttery interior. I broke the dry cork off with my Swiss Army knife corkscrew. Deprived as we were, the wine still tasted like thin strawberry jam, and proved virtually undrinkable. I fussed about the provisions, but she smiled and thanked me for the trouble I had taken.

We talked about our adventures in the aftermath of the assassination. She had travelled safely to New Delhi, which she described as a city under siege. Her girlfriend, acting on government advisory notices at home, had cancelled her trip to the violence-stricken nation, and so Sabina returned to the museum stacks, searching for more statues of the Earth-Touching Gesture. She had attended Indira's funeral, and watched with the multitudes as Rajiv Gandhi, Indira's son and political heir, set the funeral bier on fire. A dark twist on passing the torch. And then India, purged of grief through the funeral and the bloody retribution exacted on the Sikhs, returned suddenly to normal. The elections were postponed until early January, but the pundits all agreed Rajiv Gandhi was assured a majority win in a vote that would be a national testimony to the memory of his mother. That is, if he survived.

Sabina had returned to Varanasi and then travelled with her adviser to Bodhgaya, just in time for the opening ceremony.

"And when it's over?" I asked.

"Then I continue my research here in Bihar, then to West Bengal, Calcutta and Orissa."

"Alone or with your trusty research assistant?"

She avoided my eyes. "I think you wouldn't want to go with me to these places, so remote. It is not very safe in the backward regions I am going to."

"Yeah, I'll be much better off in the slums of Calcutta or hanging out on tourist-filled beaches in Goa. Why would I want to go to remote villages filled with Buddhist ruins, just to be with the woman I love? I mean, I'll think about you in these dangerous places while I'm sipping coconut milk in Madras and wonder if you're okay all alone with the bandits in Bihar. In fact, the Indian Embassy in Kathmandu refused to extend my visa, so I've only got until December 26, by the books. I think I can bribe someone to get it extended. I've been told Gaya's a good place to try. But if two weeks is all I've got left of India, I want to spend it with you. In the service of scholarship, you know."

She had begun smiling at me as I rambled. She glanced around to see that no one was watching, then brushed her hand along my cheek. I exhaled deeply, felt the tension release from my body.

"I have missed you, you know," she said. "I was angry at you for a while. But now—thank you for the picnic. You are such a good research assistant. They are so hard to find."

"Angry? Why angry?" I was confused: happy and feeling vaguely guilty at the same time.

She looked into my face, this time studying it, then shook her head.

"It doesn't matter. You want to travel together for a while. Yes, that's good. After the conference. Until then, my professor, we can't—"

"I know, I know."

We wrapped up the rest of the cheese and bread and poured out the wine on the grass. I shook out my cloth, and we rose to return to our separate quarters. It felt so strange, walking next to her through the heat and dust, just chatting about the conference as if we had never been lovers, never touched that burning ecstasy together. Angry? Why? For pulling back? For not abandoning my plans for Nepal and going with her? I wanted to know, but didn't want to risk further damaging the fragile second start we had just made. We would be travelling together again soon enough. If it was important, she would tell me, I reassured myself, only half believing it. In the meantime, there was the conference, and the matter of my visa to attend to.

I spent the next afternoon back in Gaya, where I failed abysmally at attempting to bribe two officers into giving me an extension. They explained most kindly that new government orders were strict on the matter, and no exceptions could be made. I told Sabina about it that evening, and she suggested I try Calcutta, where the Communist party held state power, and the bureaucrats might be less inclined to follow the policies of the national ruling party.

We met each evening under the cover of darkness for a walk together around the Mahabodhi stupa, which was illuminated by the candles of devoted meditators who in their stillness looked like human miniatures of the great tower. Once in the moonlight, in a rare moment when we were alone at the side of the monument, she whispered to me, urgently:

"Quick, put me up on your shoulders."

"What?" I said, suddenly excited, but very confused by her instructions.

"I want to look up here on this ledge. There is a relief statue of the

Earth-Touching Gesture up here, and I have been looking for Mara. I think maybe if you lift me, I can get a better look."

I let her scramble up my back. "It's good to be between your legs again," I told her.

She shushed me, but I laughed, and it was all I could do, with her swaying on my shoulders, just to keep my balance.

On the second last afternoon of the conference, my paper was due to be read. Most of the presenters either read current research papers on Buddhist Indology (most bearing little reference to the main conference theme), or else generally extolled Buddhist peace as the best hope for a cold-war world bent on mutually assured destruction. I thought my perspective as both a Westerner and a Christian (a much adulterated one, true) might be interesting for other participants, and so I wrote how I felt my own life had been altered by exposure to Buddhism. Sabina rolled her eyes at my chutzpah. She had not prepared a paper of her own; she was attending the conference as the student of her adviser, as a disciple and observer. And as her adviser had to leave that afternoon, she would have to go with him to Gaya to see him off at the station, rather than sit through my reading.

Mine was the fourteenth paper of the day, and yet received surprisingly warm debate. The lone Chinese scholar in attendance informed me Asia was still suffering from the white man's burden, and that Buddhists shouldn't come crawling to the West for help. An elderly Sri Lankan monk asked what the bloodthirsty God Jehovah had to do with the Buddhist vision of peace. But other participants quelled these objections as misconceptions of my main points. After the group dismissed, two Indian Theravadan monks cornered me outside. They asked to discuss with me the immorality of Christianity, which, judging from my paper, I obviously had not grasped. We walked together to the Mahabodhi stupa, and sat in the shade of the Bodhi Tree. They were calm, gracious men with smooth chocolate skin, perhaps in their mid-forties. The one with glasses spoke eloquent English, while his companion, though comprehending well enough, spoke brokenly at best.

"You see, my dear fellow," said the bespectacled monk, "Christianity is immoral because it teaches forgiveness of sins. A very, very dangerous doctrine. You cannot but agree that karma is the law of the universe. Every one of your actions, good or bad, will come back to you in kind, if not in this life, then in some future rebirth. Therefore, to proclaim that past evil deeds can be washed away by the grace of God is harmful both to those who believe it, and to those around such persons. If a Christian believes he will be forgiven, he'll be less restrained than a Buddhist or even a Hindu about inflicting harm on others, less inclined to count the cost. For example, you see how seldom it is that Christians are vegetarians? They kill animals for food, or even for sport. To a Buddhist, all animals, including insects and worms, are fellow beings who deserve compassion for their lowly rebirths."

"But a Christian also hurts his own self," the other monk chimed in, "because he is not aware that his evil acts will return to him in the future. Every act draws like to itself. Act out of generosity, you draw to yourself wealth. Act out of anger, you draw to yourself violence. Not knowing this, a Christian may be reborn as an animal, or perhaps in the hell realms. There is no escape."

I pondered their words. "So when we think Jesus is giving heaven by grace, actually, he's sending us to hell?"

They nodded, seeming pleased I had understood so well.

"But what about the tantric path? I've been told you can attain Nirvana in as little as three years. I guess it comes down to much the same thing as forgiveness of sins, though 100,000 prostrations would be a big penance by Catholic standards." I nodded towards the old Tibetan women, sliding gracefully up and down on the far side of the stupa.

"Beastly! Let's not call all this superstitious magic Buddhism," said the bespectacled monk. "Just to clear the mind to where it can receive the dharma takes many lifetimes. No shortcuts."

"But imagine if it worked!"

He shook his head. It was like asking an astronomer to imagine orbits without the law of gravity.

"Anyway," I continued, "I don't think most people become Christians as an easy way to escape hell. For myself, when I became Christian I believed my sin, my bad karma, separated me from God, and that through Christ we were made clean before God in order to be reunited with Him. It was the uniting that mattered, not escaping hell. I guess I don't really believe it any more. These days, I think the Christian God just loves us dirty, and lets us work out the consequences of our karma pretty much on our own."

"Is this Christian?" said the bespectacled monk suspiciously.

"I don't know. I've got to admit, I don't have a very clear sense of the Christian God right now. I used to be pretty sure about these things, but maybe I've misunderstood it all. I remember about six years ago I was trying to convert a young Dutch woman to my idea of Christianity, and she told me she thought Jesus' message didn't have anything to do with sin or forgiveness. 'Then what was it?' I asked her. 'I think Jesus just came to tell us to be free,' she said to me. Liberation. Isn't that the Buddhist goal, too?"

The monks looked at each other. They had tried their best.

"This is very different," the bespectacled one said non-committally, and we all rose to circumambulate the stupa together.

CHAPTER NINE

BACKROADS OF THE DHARMA TRAIL

Eastern Bihar

T HE MORNING after the conference we eloped. That is, Sabina left the women's wing of her guest house a single woman, and I left the Tibetan dormitory a single man, but by the time we presented ourselves to the director of the little yellow museum in Nawada that afternoon, Sabina was introducing us as husband and wife. Although it was a second marriage of social convenience, I took delight in the thought of the wedding night ahead.

Nawada had a sparse collection of carvings and crockery, housed in two modest rooms. The curator refused to let Sabina see the reserve collection, relenting only after she showed him all her red-stamped authorization papers and made it clear she was prepared to stay and argue. She had long ago learned that getting her way in India sometimes meant blocking the path of resistance like a belligerent water buffalo. The curator finally yielded. He opened a closet door and flipped on a light. The reserve collection was a heap of broken statues and other trash piled waist deep, stuck together by cobwebs. Their condition explained his reluctance. He was embarrassed.

"We have to look through all this." Sabina gritted her teeth. "There might be something. Tim, could you lift up that tiger, so we can see what's behind it?"

I picked my way through the shards and cobwebs towards the mangy carcass of a stuffed tiger cub. I grasped the underside of its head and belly. The fur felt cold and clay-like. Heaving it up, I saw the entire bottom was covered with a white mould. The skin flapped in places. A giant spider, with a leg span the size of a Frisbee and a body the size of an Oreo cookie, crawled out of one of the holes and scurried across my knuckles. I yelled and pushed the tiger aside. It fell away from the rest of the heap. The spider disappeared back into the rubble.

"Gee, lucky I didn't break anything," I said, my hands shaking.

"It's all fragments," said Sabina grimly. "Let's go."

One more grimy bus ride, a brief haggle for a good price at a cheap hotel, a quick dinner discussing the next day's travel plans, and then we were alone. We took turns in the bathroom. She took her pill. We got into bed. She turned out the light.

"Kiss my breasts," she instructed.

I did, and then she pulled me on top of her. The movements of her hips were so familiar, yet I felt like a stranger. Sexually aroused, yes, after six weeks of longing, but the fire in my belly was gone. She held my head close to hers so I could not look into her eyes as we rubbed against each other until we climaxed. At least, she acted as if she had climaxed. I doubted everything. Soon afterwards I heard her steady breathing. She was either asleep or wanted me to think so.

I lay awake, stunned. Where was the passion, the burning ecstasy? Instead I felt locked out where once she had let me in. Should I wake her up and talk about it? No, I reminded myself, this was just the sort of thing she explicitly did not want to talk about. Talking would just make things worse. Truth was, I didn't want to talk about it myself. It would sound like whining, as if the only reason I had come back was to recapture the mystical sexual sensations. I tried to accept our mechanical lovemaking with appropriate Buddhist detachment. After all, in two weeks I might have to leave the country, so why make a fuss? It was a pathetic attempt, and left me with an ache in my chest. Woefully, I hoped the ecstasy would return on its own.

Sabina had set us on a heavy schedule with little time for talk except on public vehicles. I shook off my melancholy in the morning, and raced with her to catch the next bus. We visited the great ruins of the ancient Buddhist university of Nalanda that had been excavated from beneath the green fields of this poor, remote corner of this poor, remote state. Once, Nalanda was one of the greatest centres of learning in the world, drawing zealous students from Japan, Indonesia, Korea and Tibet. By the seventh century A.D., it held more than ten thousand resident monks and students. Then in 1199 a different brand of religious zealots arrived: Afghan invaders. They killed all those who would not convert to Islam, virtually eradicating Buddhism from most of India.

I was beginning to realize why Indians viewed the cosmos as cyclic. It seemed that everywhere we went, beneath each rice paddy, a grand relic of some once-mighty kingdom lay buried, often with a layer of blood and corpses mixed in. Empires arose from the dust and returned to it. Kali's Dance of Destruction was not a horrible break in continuity, but an indispensable piece of the natural cycle. Death was a way of clearing out old growth to make way for something new. But did the Nalanda monks welcome Kali as an indispensable part of the cycle when she appeared in the form of Afghan soldiers? Would our generation welcome her when she appeared as, say, nuclear war or a viral epidemic?

I was clearly getting depressed. Sabina's memsahib voice grew shrill as she bullied a loutish rickshaw driver and a ticket clerk. I wondered what I had seen in her that made her seem so attractive. When her sharp tongue snapped at me, I found myself sliding into old habits: apologizing for things that were not my fault, or else getting defensive and bickering. There was so much I wanted to say, yet our conversations were mired in urgent details of bus schedules, museums, restaurants, hotels, and how to avoid the beggars and hawkers who clamoured after us along the way.

We caught a train to Rajgir, meaning "Royal Palace," a tiny town that was the capital of the Magadha Empire during the time of the Buddha. Prior to his enlightenment, the ascetic meditator had visited the city and impressed King Bimbisara so much that when, newly enlightened, the Buddha returned with a thousand disciples, the king built a monastery for the new order of monks. Buddha spent many years in the area, teaching and giving sermons, and after his death, his followers held the first great Buddhist council near the city.

At the Rajgir museum a peon informed us that the curator, "the man with the key," had gone home to his remote village and would not be back for two weeks. Sabina bit her lip in frustration, her face turning red.

"Oh well, we can still visit Buddha's cave on Vulture Peak," I said, trying to cheer her up.

"You don't understand," she said, her Germanic accent becoming more pronounced as it often did when she was angry. "For me, this is not sightseeing. It means I have to come all the way back here. My research has to be comprehensive. For my thesis defence, I can't just say, 'I couldn't find the man with the key.' Now it's going to take extra time, extra money. I think maybe I have wasted a lot of time already."

I wanted badly to break her black mood, and suggested we take a soak in the town's famous hot springs, which proved tepid and stank of sulphur. Then I coaxed her into a visit to the Buddha's cave anyway, which was a long walk out into the hot and dusty countryside. I found myself walking unintentionally close to her, several times bumping into her and accidentally treading on the sides of her sandals.

Buddha had passed several rainy seasons on Vulture Peak. It was the closest thing to a home he had had after abandoning his palace. I had lived in a cave in Ladakh for five days as part of my meditation retreat, and suddenly felt like an authority on cave dwelling. I extolled to Sabina the Buddha's fine choice of real estate. The cave was high enough to stand up in, with a narrow mouth that opened up inside, and was actually quite spacious. I pointed out how it was formed of fallen boulders, which meant good ventilation, for air could probably circulate through the cracks. From the entrance there was a commanding view of the surrounding brushland below.

"Strange, isn't it," I concluded as we sat in the cave's cool shelter, "to think the Buddha sat here, year after year, meditated, taught his disciples, and just plain enjoyed the scenery."

Sabina had on her sunglasses, her hair pulled back in a ponytail. Perspiration ran down the sides of her face from the walk. She turned and looked at me for a minute in silence. I could not see her eyes.

"What's wrong?"

"I'm tired, and I am accomplishing nothing," she snapped.

"Well, at least you can be sure there're no Buddha statues up here," I replied sunnily.

Cheerfulness was a knee-jerk response of mine towards an angry woman. Unfortunately it seldom worked. In fact, it generally produced exactly what a knee-jerk is supposed to prevent. I knew what would happen next if this relationship deteriorated according to my old patterns: my tendency to feel responsible for whatever went wrong would grow. I would apologize constantly and profusely while she would get more and more bitchy. Eventually I would want to get away from her, and she would say, "You don't really love me," and I would say, "Of course I do," and then go on apologizing as if that would cover up my growing resentment while she grew to despise me. Unfortunately, I could not avoid her by going off on a spiritual quest to India, because I was already on one, supposedly. I felt a familiar sense of failure stretch out its ugly hand from the past, and squeeze me by the balls.

That evening before bed, I massaged her back to make her feel better. (Making her feel better was becoming the main point to my existence, I grumbled to myself.) Her muscles were knotted and tense. Gently kneading her flesh, I felt wretched. The long walk in the heat had exhausted us. She had snapped at me again during dinner because, sitting as close to her as I could, I had sat upon the long flaps of her Indian blouse and wrinkled them. I told myself we just weren't used to each other yet, hadn't meshed back into bliss. But these were feeble excuses. I let my hands drop and just rest on her back. I had been treating her so gingerly, as if one false step and she would get up and walk out on me: even my fingers rubbed at her as if she might break. There was something wrong here, and I had no idea how to fix it.

Without thinking, my hands started up again. I made two fists and began pounding harder along the muscles that ran up her spine. The knots could never be teased out. They had to be released with a thump.

"Ouch," she said. "You are hurting me."

"You're like a board. It's what you need," I replied, surprised at the anger that tightened my voice.

"So you pound in some nails?"

I dug in my fingers and tugged roughly at the muscles of her shoulders, making it hurt. I didn't know exactly why I was doing this, but I noticed it was working. She was relaxing, softening. Her hips began to move beneath me. I grabbed one arm and turned her firmly towards me. She kept her eyes closed and her head away to one side. I reached for her breast, felt the nipple harden, sucked hard on it for a while, until she moaned. Her loose cotton pants slid off in my hands, but then she drew her legs together and twisted her hips to one side as if to avoid me. My craving for her dropped. She was withdrawing. Distraught, I tried to formulate the words that would make things right once more. Instead, a flickering sensation of a dark, hairy limb moved across my mind with rapid violence.

"No fucking way," I said.

I grasped her knees and wrenched them apart. She looked up at me, blue eyes wide in sudden surprise. Then she closed them, slowly, relaxing her legs, parting her mouth, and I fell inside her. I closed my eyes and moved in the darkness, slowly, finding her pulse. So different from the night before, now I could feel her pulling at my sex with the tightening muscles of her vagina. I stayed slow, refusing to surrender control as she tried to quicken the pace. I wanted this to last.

It was so unlike our previous lovemaking, when I felt the energy washing over and through me, pummelling me senseless. Instead my senses felt alert, acutely aware of the movements of her flesh beneath me—the shuddering of her thighs, ribs swelling and falling as she panted, her breath coming quick and sweet. When I opened my eyes, I noticed her hands wringing the corners of the sheets, and the pink coloration of her face, how the flush of it ran down her neck between her breasts. Her eyes remained closed tight, her brow furrowed. The sweat between us felt slick and hot. She was on the verge, as was I, but with the control to ease back, cling to that edge so we would not go over into the froth, but wait for that dark impulse to gather once more in my belly like a wild thing rattling the bars of its cage. She opened her mouth wide and gasped, a deep, throaty moan, and I rocked hard, streaming into her, shaking. Her calves locked around the inside of my legs and held me tight to her until our spasms subsided.

She stroked my hair, eyes on me now, and mumbled, "Never before like this."

I rolled to the side and she held me, her head pressed against my neck. A moment later she was asleep.

"Do you remember what you said, just before you went to sleep last night?" I asked over yogurt, crushed rice flakes and honey the following morning.

"No, what?" she shook her head.

"I don't think I caught it all. Something about 'never before.'"

She shrugged. We ate in silence.

"Why are you here?" she asked suddenly. "Why did you come back?"

"You're good for me."

"How?"

"I don't know how to say it. These last few days on our own, I've just felt out of touch with you, as if I've forgotten how to listen, how to be around you. My intuition gets lazy, I don't know what to think. I feel like I'm stumbling, but then, somehow I catch myself, as I've never done before. I've felt so far from you. I guess I expected we would just pick up where we left off when we started travelling again. But I felt something had changed between us. Then last night, suddenly I felt reconnected. I guess I want to know if you felt it too."

"Yes, you were good."

"That's not what I mean," I said, annoyed. "I don't want my ego stroked like, like one of your *men*. I want to do better by you than the ones who just take what they want and then leave."

"But maybe I don't want them to stay," she said coolly. "It's not that I don't like them around, but most men, they don't leave me to myself. I even remember one man I used to go jogging with. He told me to take shorter steps! I said to him, 'No. I take them long so I can rest in the air. If possible, I would take steps like a kangaroo.' In India, everywhere I go, I feel blocked. The men have all the keys, and I have to be charming or fight just to get what they would give to another man without hesitation. It is wearing me down."

"So you probably don't need a sidekick kicking you in the side all the time?"

"No, that's not it, Tim. You make it so much easier for me, I can't say. I know why I want you to stay with me. But I don't know why you want to."

"Just tell me, did you think I would be there in Bodhgaya, waiting for you?"

"In Bodhgaya, yes. I know how you love these conferences. Waiting for me . . . I didn't think so. Now, you are making us late for the bus! Let's go."

On the ride to Bhagalpur we sat near the front. It was one of those peculiar buses with a sideways seat just past the driver. On it sat a hefty middle-aged woman in a sari with her young daughter. The girl looked about eight years old and wore a pink Western dress. She looked surprisingly clean, in stark contrast to the mother's dark appearance. The mother's hand rested casually on the girl's knee. It was wide, with thick blunt fingers and a large wrist. The arm that led up to the sari's folds was burly and covered with hair. I looked at her face, which had a black stubble over the cheeks. The hair was pulled neatly back into a bun, and the red dot of a Hindu woman was emblazoned on the forehead.

"He's a *hirja*," Sabina told me in a low voice. "A special caste of transvestites, mostly eunuchs. They are shunned by Indian society and perpetuate their caste by stealing and 'adopting' young boys, raising them as their own girl children."

"They steal boys? You mean the child in the dress . . ."

"Yes."

"And they castrate them?"

She nodded.

"I'm surprised they aren't stoned in public."

"No one molests them. Their curse is considered very powerful. It's believed they have a kind of black magic, part of the hirja religious sect. They worship the goddess Bahuchara, in the shape of a vulva, a form of the Mother Goddess, naturally enough. In fact, I think it is this connection that explains their one important role in traditional society, next to prostitution: they play as singers and dancers at weddings and religious festivals, and especially the celebration that marks the birth of a boy. They are supposed to bring good luck. Ironic, no?"

I fixed my eyes on the thick hand on the child's thigh, and tried to measure whether it was protective or possessive. The boy in the dress stared vacantly ahead. His mother was his kidnapper, and had mutilated him so that he was made over in the image of the goddess they both worshipped.

"This is legal?"

"Oh no, highly illegal. Just like child brides. I read an article that said about forty thousand illegal castrations take place each year, if I remember correctly. Of course, it must be just a guess."

"Of course. A guess."

"You look pale. Funny how much more the hirja seems to upset you than child brides."

Bhagalpur was one of the poorest towns I had ever seen. The inhabitants were gaunt, the near-naked rickshaw drivers looked like stick men on wheels. As we rode towards the depot through slow traffic, we passed one man on the roadside, limping. He looked to be in his early twenties. His shirt was grey and torn, and he dragged his left leg as if it was numb, as if he had just been hit by a vehicle and was in shock. Blood ran down the side of the leg, leaving a trail as he dragged himself along, ignored by the crowd, a fixed, cold stare in his eyes. It put a sudden fear in me, realizing just how close to death these people lived.

In the depot we found a motor-rickshaw driver willing to take us to Vishram Sheela, site of another monastic university ruin almost as large as Nalanda. He extorted Sabina for the price, informing her that the road was rife with "dacoits and bandits," and that he would wait for us only until an hour before dusk. If we were not ready, he would travel back alone rather than risk being outside town after dark.

The site was a vast stretch of grey and red ruins surrounded by empty green fields. Palm trees rustled in the hot afternoon breeze, and water buffalo turned their lazy heads to look at the two tourists. A lone Indian archeologist was at work. Sabina explained our mission, and he offered to guide us around. Earlier excavations had exposed many buried stone relief sculptures, now badly eroded by the salt that leached through the soil with each rain and trickled down the carvings. He winced at every picture Sabina took. He steadfastly denied that the sod-covered brick walls were recent reconstructions until I pointed out places where the bricks were bright red, as if straight from the kiln, and told him what I had seen in Nepal. Between the two of us, we made him very uncomfortable, despite his genteel manner. He was quick to confirm what our driver had said about dacoits on the road at night, and urged us to make haste back to the city well before bandit hour.

On the return trip our driver missed a turn, and we had to backtrack fifteen minutes. Half an hour later, the engine began sputtering. The sun hung red and low in the sky. In the back seat, Sabina and I clutched each other's hands. The engine coughed and died. There was not a building in sight along the straight, flat asphalt. The driver got off the rickshaw and walked around to the back. I had a sudden vision of throwing myself at the moonlit circle of bandits, going down in fury, protecting her honour. The fantasy lasted about ten seconds until I realized the driver was topping up his tank with an emergency soft-drink bottle filled with gasoline.

At the depot we retrieved our bags from left luggage and caught the night train to Calcutta. There, Sabina assured me, we would take a few days off to celebrate Christmas. We had been travelling non-stop between sites, often ending up checking into dirty hotels late at night, too exhausted even for sex. We needed a holiday. I had never spent a Christmas away from home. This year we would be all the family each other had. Calcutta was a good place to be for the holiday, she explained. Once the Second City of the British Empire, the city still had churches and cathedrals and a large native Christian population, not counting the many missionary groups that flocked to the city like buzzards to a corpse. Sabina said that with any luck there might be a festival program on at the Goethe Institute, and her enthusiasm for the celebration seemed not the least bit diminished by her atheism.

Many Indian treasures had been excavated and moved to Calcutta (and abroad) during British rule. Sabina estimated it would take her at least a week to run through the city's museums and speak with the relevant scholars and curators about her thesis. She had written in advance to the Mahabodhi Society, a Buddhist organization in the centre of town that ran a guest house for Buddhist pilgrims and scholars, and secured a room. We were all set to settle down and enjoy a brief season of holiday cheer in the city that bore Kali's name.

CHAPTER TEN

THE BOY
WITH NO ARMS
Calcutta

"So tell me about Kali," I said to Sabina on the train to Calcutta.

"Oh, I don't know if that would be wise," she replied. "If I do, you will probably want to go sacrifice goats at her temples."

"Blood sacrifice? I thought most religious Hindus were vegetarians."

"That's so. But Kali worship is associated with many frightening taboos. She is fearsome to look at, black with long dishevelled hair. She has fangs, a lolling tongue and bloody mouth, claw-like hands, and she wears a wreath of severed heads and girdle of severed arms. She is the wild, destructive aspect of the wife of Shiva, and she is usually depicted dancing on his outstretched body, his lingam rising towards her. When they dance together, the universe is destroyed. But in many places, she stands on her own, without connection to any male god. In Bengal especially, she is worshipped by the Tantrists, who deliberately break religious taboos in practising her rituals, which in the past included human sacrifice. Now they settle for goats. But there are also many Indian devotees who worship her as the Great Mother Goddess in very orthodox Hindu ways."

"What do the scriptures say about her?"

"Well, she appears fairly late in the Vedic sutras, around 600 A.D. The earliest texts invoke her powers as a warrior to crush enemies' bones and drink their blood. But she also appears in two different myths. Kali, which means 'black,' was the nickname of Shiva's bride, Parvati, the Great Goddess and *yogini* whose skin was dark, because Night had enveloped her mother's womb. Once Shiva teased her about her colour. In India, blackness is associated with ugliness, so he was annoying her. They quarrelled. She left him to perform her yogic austerities high in the mountains until she had transformed her skin to a beautiful gold. When she returned, they had yogic sex for a thousand years."

"Happily ever after."

"No. Shiva betrayed her. You see, all the gods had wanted Shiva to marry Parvati so that the couple would produce a son capable of defeating the terrible demon Taraka. But when the gods saw the power of her yoga, they became afraid that she and Shiva would produce an heir too powerful for them to control. All this time Shiva, being a great yogi, was having perpetual sex with Parvati without releasing his sperm. The gods were in a dilemma now. They still wanted Shiva to have a son, but not from Parvati. Finally they sent Agni, god of fire, to Shiva's bedroom. Agni convinced Shiva to go out and meet the rest of the gods. He did, and after hearing their request, he, well, he masturbated and ejaculated for them. Agni caught the seed in his mouth. But just after Agni left, Parvati came out and discovered what had happened. After all her austerities and lovemaking, she had been cheated out of a son! Childlessness is considered a curse for a woman in India, and Parvati's anger was so great she cursed the gods back, that they too would be childless. However, Agni had already left and escaped the curse. He took the seed to the Ganges. The river carried it like a mother and later brought the embryo to a mountain, where it was nursed and grew into Shiva's son.

"But this is getting away from Kali. The other important myth about her is that, much later, when the gods were weak and losing their battle with the demons, they combined all their energies and created the warrior-goddess Durga. At one point she was fighting two very fierce demons who were trying to capture her and bring her to the demon king—he had heard of her beauty and wanted to rape her. Durga grew very angry, her forehead grew black and from it sprang Kali. She was an emaciated old woman with fangs and red eyes, carrying a sword and a noose. She roared and laughed and devoured the two demons and their army, crunching up elephants and chariots with her teeth. She also defeated the last and most monstrous of the demons, who had a unique power: if he was wounded, his special seed-blood turned into thousands of replicas of himself. But Kali lifted him in the air and drank the blood as it fell from his wounds, until she had sucked him dry, killing him."

"That sounds like one hell of a sexual metaphor."

"Exactly. It is interpreted to mean that Kali overpowers the destructive element of phallic power. But she wasn't satisfied. Filled with blood lust, Kali continued tearing up the corpses of her enemies. Her wild frenzy terrified the gods. They feared she was going to destroy the whole world, including them. Finally Shiva slipped onto the battlefield and lay still until Kali in her wild fury stepped on him. Looking down, she recognized her husband, and came back to her senses."

"I can understand why the Tantrists adore her," I said. "But why on earth is she worshipped as the Great Mother? She doesn't seem much like the nurturing kind."

"Well, Parvati was actually an incarnation of Shiva's first wife, Sati, who was also dark. She was the original embodiment of female energy, *shakti*, which Hindus believe is life-force energy. This gets back to the problem of childlessness. You see, although the gods could create, they couldn't create life that would keep creating itself. They needed shakti, the feminine creative force to do this. At first, Shiva created Shakti as a goddess within him, separating himself into male and female aspects. You see some statues of him with one breast and a phallus with only one ball in this half-and-half state. This energy took independent shape in the form of Sati, and later in Parvati. In this sense, all Hindu goddesses can be considered different manifestations of Shakti, even, and in some ways especially, Kali—because she embodies these destructive and wild aspects of life-force energy too. The feminine is not always a nurturing mother with big breasts, you know," she concluded with an ironic smile.

"I know that."

"Really? I'm not sure you do. You are in many ways very naive, Tim. It surprises me sometimes."

"Naive?" I was stung. "Sure, I was naive when I met you. But haven't I learned a lot?"

"About sex, yes. About women? Well, it's more complicated. Most men never have a clue."

The train arrived at daybreak. We walked out of the station through a crowd of whining, clutching beggars and straight into a taxi. Crossing the Howrah Bridge over the Hooghly River, we caught our first sight of the city. Vapours from the grey-brown river mingled with the blue haze of dung-chip cooking fires, so that the city seemed wrapped in a gauzy shroud. Through it, I saw the shining dome of a church, turrets of a mosque, temple spires, a monument in a grassy plain. For a moment, as we crossed the water, the city looked grand and serene. Then we entered the crumbling heart of it. The pitted, broken-down roads and dilapidated stone buildings looked all the worse for the mirage of grandeur we had just seen. Taxis, streetcars, buses, trucks and motor rickshaws vied for space with donkey carts and sacred cows. I watched a foot-powered rickshaw roll along: an old man dressed in grey rags running, pulling a fat, well-to-do woman in a white sari ensconced implacably in the double-wheeled seat behind him.

I thought I had become inured to poverty in Bihar; but I felt repulsed at the sight of the rich woman and her rickshaw man. He ran hard, sucking in the morning smog as his feet picked their way over the rutted street like a human donkey. Tin and cloth shanties huddled all along alleyways between the great decaying buildings, and beggars clustered on every busy corner. In Bihar, it seemed no one had much of anything. In Calcutta, both wealth and poverty were plentiful, pressed together in the city streets with little space between them.

The Mahabodhi Society was next to the university, on College Street, just across from the campus swimming pool. A polite and gentle Singhalese Sri Lankan monk named Reverend Bandula led us to our room on the sixth floor. Out our window we had a fine view of the pool. It was Olympic-sized, complete with concrete high-diving boards, the water a murky grey. Along the rim, men and women stooped, lathering and rinsing their sarongs and saris and wading in waist deep to bathe. I didn't see anyone swimming. Apparently the pool functioned as a village pond for those living on the streets.

We fell immediately into an exhausted sleep, then rose and rinsed ourselves in the washrooms down the hall. They were white tiled, clean and free of the stench that permeated every lavatory we had visited between here and Bodhgaya. Sabina wanted to check her contacts at the Indian Museum as quickly as possible, while I made haste to the Foreigners' Registration Office (the FRO) to plead my case once more for extending my visa, which was due to expire in a week.

A waist-high wooden divider separated bureaucrats from petitioners on the first floor of the FRO. I joined a queue of half a dozen people that led to the only one of three wickets being operated. Behind the divider, twenty-five or so functionaries sat behind their desks, sipping tea, chatting with each other, reading newspapers, scanning slips of yellow paper or wandering in and out a door which led to a secluded back lawn.

The individual who manned the wicket, however, took each applicant's paperwork with him back to a desk, where he pored over the details and scribbled on a yellow pad. He was a small, hunched man with close-cropped grey hair and silver-rimmed reading glasses. The nameplate on his desk said "Mr. Besares." At times, Mr. Besares abandoned his piles of paper, or simply walked away from the wicket to shuffle forms on another desk. A silver-haired Armenian with olive skin in line ahead of me nodded towards the bureaucrat and muttered in slow, buttery English: "You see that man doing all the work? That means he's the least intelligent one in the office."

"A monkey could probably do the job faster," I commented.

"Ah, my friend, in truth, this is because most of the foreigners you see in line do not understand how to grease that monkey! Twenty rupees, no more, and the simplest procedure becomes just that. Without it, well, we stand in line all day."

The Armenian said he had escaped from Iran during the fall of the Shah. He was technically a refugee, but had prospered in Calcutta with the support of the native Armenians, the oldest foreign community in the city. They had come to Bengal in the sixteenth century, where they prospered primarily as bankers. When the British East India Company wanted to build a fort on the *Kalishetra*, the "Field of Kali," which included a temple called Kalighat, the Armenians loaned them the money with which to purchase land rights. Thus financed, in 1698 the British began to build. The name of Kalighat their British ears corrupted to "Calcutta."

More useful than the history lesson, the Armenian showed me how to slip money inside my passport. He told me to watch closely. When the Armenian reached the front of the queue, I noticed just the tiniest rim of colour peeking out from his passport. The old man squinted, walked over to his desk as if searching for something. He looked through his stacks, then opened his drawer. Leaving it open, he then brushed his hand over the passport, opening it at the same time and with one fluid movement slipping the bill inside the open drawer. He leaned forward, neatly shutting it, found the appropriate stamp, banged the passport and put the white form the Armenian had filled on top of his desk. In less than ten minutes, the Armenian had his passport back.

"Merry Christmas!" He gave me a wink as he left.

Suddenly, the official was glaring at me. I didn't have time to slip in a bill. I figured I could do it once I got my forms. I handed him my passport and told him I wanted a three-month extension.

The little man took one quick look at it and said, "You are here too soon for such a simple procedure. Come back in three days."

"Could I have some forms please to fill out before I return?"

He glared at me as if I had asked him to loan me his wife for the night. Rather than answering, he simply walked away from the wicket and sat down at his desk until I had left my position in line.

The news filled me with qualified joy: after such absolute rejection in Kathmandu and Gaya, I would be able to waltz in and snap up a new visa in no time. Feeling quite buoyant, I decided to stroll in the direction of the Mahabodhi Society, just wandering the streets. A rickshaw puller soon got on my tail, hollering after me, "Mister, where you go? Where you go?" I told him I didn't need a rickshaw, but he followed me for blocks, calling after me until I stopped, turned around and explained I was just wandering.

"Well, have a seat, and let's chat," he said in surprisingly good English.

His name was Gumrhu. Like most rickshaw drivers in the city, he was a migrant worker from Bihar. He told me about his life, how he would spend four months in the city, then four months with his wife and five children back home. As we talked, he hailed a fellow Bihari, an old man with good English who told me in his first breath that he had lost his business, his wife had died and his baby daughter had had to be put into one of Mother Teresa's orphanages, "since her father is a beggar out on the streets." A third man, who called himself R.C., joined in to talk about his two recent suicide attempts. He said he could not bear to be all alone in the city.

"But it is my friend I really feel sorry for," R.C. continued. "He is so sad. Like me he is a Catholic. Christmas is coming, you see, and he has no money. There will be no food, no clothing, no toys for his children, nothing to celebrate the birth of Christ. But I told him, 'God is good, perhaps he will provide a miracle.'"

All eyes fixed on me. Goddamn it, I thought, everybody angles for cash, as if I was a walking rupee dispenser.

"Yeah, maybe God will provide a miracle," I said, getting up off the seat. But it ain't gonna be me.

"Hey, mister, before you go," said the driver, "could you give me some baksheesh? I haven't eaten all day."

"You just told me you send money home to your village," I retorted coldly.

"But you sat on my rickshaw."

"You invited me. I guess I should have just kept walking."

I turned my back and left them. He followed after me for a few blocks, hollering that he still wanted to take me some place. I ignored him and eventually he gave up. The only one who hadn't asked for money was the old beggar. Perhaps he was off duty.

Encounters like this happened several times a day when I wandered the city streets. They filled me with hatred. Hatred for poverty, hatred for baksheesh, hatred of the smiles and offers of conversation that were so often set-ups for a tug at the walking money dispenser's pocket. Something in me hardened, refused to appease my conscience with a little petty cash, to fool myself into thinking it would do any good. Long ago I had found my own rule of thumb for giving to beggars in India. I looked at it as the national social security system—a tax for the healthy to pay on the spot to the elderly, crippled, and for destitute women with children. To these I gave my change, and when I ran out, I simply said no. Young men, however ragged, I habitually denied, and felt swindled when a friendly conversation turned out to be a con.

I crossed through a market square on the way home and saw coming through it a young boy, perhaps eight, barefooted, in filthy clothes. He had no arms. His eyes were hollow, empty, as if whatever childish joy there might have been had been dug out of them with a spiritual paring knife. A string was tied around his waist, and clutching the other end of it, an old hag dressed in rags, with wild white hair, toothless. Even from a safe distance, I could see that she was blind. He was her human seeing-eye dog. The woman squatted, called the boy to her, and put a topless tin can on a string around his neck. She cried out for alms, and sent the boy to the end of his tether like an organ-grinder's monkey. Hers was a stroke of entrepreneurial innovation. Simple blindness would earn little on a Calcutta street. The competition is too tough. But a boy with no arms, bound to her by such cruel karma: ah, that is worth baksheesh from even the most hardened Bengali.

Hatred flushed through me again. Had the boy been born that

way, I wondered, or had his arms been lopped off for her purposes? I pulled back so that he would not find my white face in the crowd. I could not stop staring at him, and I felt myself trembling. Pity: it had been a while since I had experienced this emotion. Now I despised myself for it. What was I going to do? Rescue the dead-eyed boy? Make a donation to reward his keeper? Pity in Calcutta could only be a means to alleviating one's own suffering: the suffering of the rich, come so unpleasantly face to face with human misery, mass-produced in the squalid streets.

Yet this was what I came to India for, to find out how poverty and spirituality coexisted. To penetrate the paradox, as I had explained so earnestly to my church and university friends in Canada. But unlike Sabina, I was not enough of a sahib to accept humanity beneath me, toss it an aluminum coin and step right over it. The sight of the armless boy ripped away my calm, my compassion, and my analytical rule of thumb for giving. Instead I felt mean and selfish and greedy. I still had over two thousand dollars in the bank, and every five represented a day I could spend in Asia. Money was time, and I wanted to keep it, keep it all for myself. I hated the beggars, hated the poor, hated the Indian rich, the British, and blamed them for it. I hated my own people and global injustice and economic tyranny. But most of all, I hated myself. At the honest core, I just didn't want this armless boy to brush his need up against my white and well-fed skin. The thought of contact made my flesh shudder.

I was learning too much in this city, all at once. Jesus, Buddha, Shiva I could learn from, but here, one day in Kali's city, one quick glance at her playground, and I was ready to return to the Mahabodhi Society, lock myself in its whitewashed rooms, plant my dick in Sabina and surrender.

"You win, bitch goddess," I said to the dust as I walked back to my room. "Your necklace of severed heads and skulls got to me, your tongue covered with blood. Or was that you holding the string back there, like a real organ-grinder, grinding those organs, making your music on the city streets. Are you Calcutta's street-corner Santa? Ho, ho, ho, Mother Kali, Merry Christmas. Merry Christmas and a Happy Yuga of Destruction."

Two days later, on the evening of December 20, we found a restaurant that served chicken cutlets and chips; it seemed the most exquisite of fine dining to our curry-soaked palates. Afterwards we strolled through the evening crush to Saint John's Church. The Calcutta Chamber Orchestra and Choir was singing carols and performing Handel's *Messiah*. I mouthed the familiar choruses in the stuffy heat of the sanctuary, yet every mention of Mother and Child brought back not the Nativity, but the blind hag and her armless boy.

We sat beside two chatty old women, Alma and Jellie. They were members of a caste of Anglo-Indians, half-breeds deliberately created and cultivated by the British Raj, which paid its soldiers to marry Indian women. The resultant children were then sent to Britain for education and returned to India as reliable servants, petty bureaucrats and officials. They were ingrained, if Alma and Jellie were any indication, with an ineradicable devotion to the empire.

"Oh, how India has come down since you people left!" Jellie moaned to us, though we had already told her we weren't British. She was a rotund lady in her sixties, her skin a rich chocolate colour, but her face structure, jawline, hairstyle, dress, earrings and pursed lips so perfectly British she looked like a well-tanned caricature. She spoke with a sharp British accent, making exaggerated *ah*'s out of all her *a*'s. As a young woman, she had worked in the house of a chief justice, she informed us with pride. Her companion was a bent, grey willow of a woman who offered no information about herself; Alma mostly murmured, clucked and nodded her head at all of Jellie's lamentations.

"We used to have such parties and cakes and, oh my dears, you would not believe it! Now everything's a ruin. Look at the streets: cracks and rubble. The economy—just the same. And it's so hard on the natives. Why, my poor servant, he gets pittance: five pounds a

month! Can you believe it? The poor soul. And you cannot walk anywhere, *my dears!* It used to be the police kept the streets clear. Now,
they sleep and eat and beg and do the most squalid things, right out
in public! *You* people never permitted this sort of thing, at least not
near decent folks' quarters. These pariahs, they should all be shot!"
she finished vehemently, while Alma clucked and shook her head.

Jellie told us Saint John's was almost two hundred years old, and
that the churchyard was the first burial ground in the city, used for
governors, chief justices and employees of the East India Company.
To Jellie and Alma, it seemed to be the greatest shrine in the city, for
its buried past was all the future either of them possessed. Tears
welled up in Jellie's eyes as we extricated our hands from her old
woman's grip and said farewell. She dabbed at her face with a hand-
kerchief. We hailed a cab. It had a broken meter, the driver said. Jellie cursed him. She said cabbies are required by law to have working
meters.

"They are filthy refugees from East Bengal. They haven't a shred
of decency and will cheat you people every time."

We found a working meter in the fifth cab that stopped, by which
time Jellie was inconsolable, more for the decline of the empire than
our vulnerability to taxi rip-offs, and Alma was clucking as if she was
about to lay an egg. Their handkerchiefs fluttered after us as we disappeared into traffic. Well warned by the women, we watched the
road closely, and halted each of several attempts the driver made to
veer off on lengthy detours from the route home. Still the fare
seemed high, almost double what we had calculated. Only after the
cab had gone did we realize we had fallen for the most elementary
taxi scam: he had left the meter running from the previous fare.

"I feel blocked," Sabina confessed miserably the next morning. I
knew she had been having trouble at the museum. The director had
agreed to let her search the reserve collection, but not until after January 16. She said he had offered no intelligible reason, but there was
no higher office to which she could appeal. She was tense and furious, requiring a succession of massages to bring any relief at all.

"You're doing your best," I said comfortingly, rubbing a hand along her back.

"No. I'm stuffed."

"What?"

"*Mein Gott.* What I'm saying is I can't breathe through my nose and my throat is sore."

"Oh." I readjusted my arsenal of sympathies.

We had pushed too hard through Bihar, and hit the crowds at full speed in Calcutta. It is one of the cardinal rules of travelling in India that going too fast for too long will bring you to a full stop.

"Let's take the day off and just rest."

"I can't," she said miserably. "I have a meeting with a scholar at ten. You are always finding a way to keep me from my work."

"That's not true! I'm here to help you with your work."

She reached for a bag of milk sweets she had purchased in the Muslim market a short walk away. I noticed that when depressed, she ate sweets and then that made her feel fat, and then that made her feel more depressed.

"You'll make yourself sicker if you don't take it easy."

She glared at me.

"That's how you operate, isn't it?" I continued. "If it's not working smoothly, let's really fuck it up."

"Okay, I'm going now." She got up and pulled on her street clothes.

"Wait." I pushed myself up from the mattress.

"What?"

"I'm going with you."

She turned and grabbed my arm, and in an incredibly deft manoeuvre, swung herself underneath me on the bed and pulled me down on top of her. She sighed, not resignation, but contentment.

"I'll meet the scholar another day."

On Friday the 22nd I returned to the FRO and took my place in the line-up. When I reached the front, Mr. Besares squinted at me and curled his lip. I smiled.

"Good afternoon," I said. "You asked me to return here today for my visa extension."

He picked up my passport and flipped it open. The twenty-rupee note fluttered like an autumn leaf from the pages, down onto the counter between us, for all to see.

"And what is this?" he glared menacingly.

"Oh, ah, it must have gotten stuck in there by accident," I blurted, face red as betel-nut juice. I reached out and pocketed the note.

"Your visa expires on December 26," Besares announced. "Extension, impossible! You arrived in April. Six months maximum for tourist visa. Next!"

I started to argue. I didn't know exactly what I was saying, but I decided to try the belligerent water buffalo approach. I could hear murmurs and shuffling feet in the long line-up behind me. I envisioned myself leading the charge over the divider, the petitioners cheering as we hurtled the barricades and pillaged the office, squirting red ink everywhere, upsetting coffee cups, toppling the stacks. But Besares met my gaze and, perhaps unaware of the impending revolution, remained unruffled.

"You will have to take it up with Mr. Singh, then," he said.

A peon escorted me from the rickety furniture, stacks of yellow paper and drab functionaries of the main floor, up to the second floor and a spacious office dominated by a wide, empty mahogany desk. The carpet was plush, the walls of rich, oiled wood. Mr. Singh wore a dark three-piece suit and a sky-blue turban. His beard was well groomed. I knew at once that it was his job to say no. I began fabricating a lie so white it shone. I told him I was doing research in India on Buddhist philosophy for an M.A. program in Canada. I told him about my summer in Ladakh, the two Buddhist conferences I had attended. I pulled out my old student card and my casual reader's permit at the Asiatic Society in Calcutta. After an hour of discussion, Mr. Singh sat back in his chair and sighed. He said he had no authority in this matter, but if I wished, I could file a report with the local branch authorities, although it would doubtless be denied. I thanked him profusely and asked him to give me the paper-work.

The peon led me back downstairs, where I dictated a report that was then turned back over to Mr. Besares's desk. He made a sour face as he read it.

"So you think you can just come into our country and do re-search on Buddhist philosophy, just like that! With no permit or spe-cial permission? Do you think we Indians can just go to Canada and do research?"

I bit down on my tongue. "This is already authorized. Can you please just tell me, sir, when shall I return to your office?"

"January," he sneered. "The second is a holiday. Come back on the third."

I pulled a sad, downcast face, sighed and scraped back my chair to stand. I turned around and grinned broadly at the rest of the line-up of supplicants. The revolution was cancelled. At the last minute I had won a full eight-day reprieve.

CHAPTER ELEVEN

TANTRIC SEX
Calcutta

Y STORY to Mr. Singh was not a total lie. I was doing my
own research in Calcutta, which was the reason that I
obtained a casual reader's card at the Asiatic Society
Library. I wanted to find out if the weird, burning, energy-charged
sex I had experienced with Sabina in Patna and Vaishali was in fact
that same kind of energy the Tantrists manipulated in their rituals.
If so, then perhaps I could determine what it was in our lovemaking
that had evoked these states, and what, if anything, could bring
them back.

Although I had acquired some second-hand knowledge about the
Buddhist tantric path in Ladakh, virtually everything I had heard
and read emphasized the use of mantras and other non-sexual rites.
Teachers and texts were quite explicit that the bizarre couplings of
gods and demons on temple wall hangings were not to be taken literally. Sexual union was only a metaphor for uniting masculine and
feminine energies in the practitioner. It occurred to me this was just
the inverse of Shiva, who, beginning with a state of absolute union,
separated the male and female energies within himself so that the
first goddess could be split off from his divine nature, and the creative process begun. Instead, celibate Buddhist tantric mediators
sought to recombine the energies so that they could re-enter the state
of absolute union. Shiva practised fission; monks practised fusion.
Both generated energy.

More advanced Buddhist yogis actually created mental images of spirit women called *dakinis,* and engaged in elaborate inner rituals to achieve union with them. However, there were hints that actual tantric sexual practices still existed. Books written by Westerners sometimes alluded to them, and once a young monk from a puritanical order in Ladakh told me disdainfully that monks of a different sect sometimes kept "secret wives." Properly understood, ritual sexual practices supposedly could bring one swiftly to enlightenment. But without a capable teacher, their misuse could destroy the experimenter and send him to hell for many incarnations to come.

But if Buddhist esoteric schools still practised union in the flesh, they were silent about it. What direct excerpts of texts I had previously run across were either poetically vague or deliberately cryptic; for example, this verse by a tenth-century Buddhist tantric guru:

In the lotus mandala of your partner,
A superior, skillful consort,
Mingle your white seed
With her ocean of red seed.
Then absorb, raise and diffuse the elixir,
And your ecstasy will never end.
Then raise the pleasure beyond pleasure—
Visualize it inseparable from emptiness.[1]

I had a hunch, though, that the florid Hindu branch of tantrism might be more forthcoming with its secrets than the tight-lipped Buddhists, especially here in Kali's city, where the blood stayed fresh on her altars. Accosting priests in the temples did not seem like the wisest place to start; certainly I wasn't looking for an invitation to a tantric orgy, not that this was very likely. So I began instead by searching the society's musty shelves for a clue, and soon found the

---

[1] K. Dowman, *Masters of Mahamudra* (Albany, New York: State University of New York Press, 1985), 216.

autobiographical writings of Gopi Krishna, an experienced Hindu meditator.

During Christmas 1937, while meditating, Krishna began having rushes of intense inner energy from the base of his spine up to his head:

> Sometimes it seemed as if a jet of molten copper, mounting up through the spine, dashed against my crown and fell in a scintillating shower of vast dimensions all around me. I gazed at it, fascinated, with fear gripping my heart. Occasionally it resembled a fireworks display of great magnitude. As far as I could look inwardly with my mental eye, I saw only a brilliant shower or a glowing pool of light. I seemed to shrink in size when compared to the gigantic halo that surrounded me, stretching out on every side in undulating waves of a copper color distinctly perceptible in the surrounding darkness, as if the optic center in the brain was now in direct contact with an extremely subtle, luminous substance in perpetual motion, flooding the brain and nervous system, without the intervention of the intermediary channels of the retina and the optic nerve.
>
> I seemed to have touched accidentally the lever of an unknown mechanism, hidden in the extremely intricate and yet unexplored nervous structure in the body, releasing a hitherto pent-up torrent which, impinging upon the auditory and optic regions, created the sensation of roaring sounds and weirdly moving lights, introducing an entirely new and unexpected feature into the normal working of the mind that gave all my thoughts and actions the semblance of unreality and abnormality.[2]

The power seemed to come of its own, and Krishna could do nothing to stop it. When the fire began to burn, Krishna's experience turned deadly:

---

[2] Gopi Krishna, *Living with Kundalini*, quoted from Shambala Dragon Edition (Boston, Mass.: 1993), 145-146.

The heat grew every moment, causing such unbearable pain that
I writhed and twisted from side to side while streams of cold perspiration poured down my face and limbs. But still the heat in-
creased and soon it seemed as if innumerable red-hot pins were
coursing through my body, scorching and blistering the organs
and tissues like flying sparks. Suffering the most excruciating
torture, I clenched my hands and bit my lips to stop myself from
leaping out of bed and crying at the top of my voice. The throbbing in my heart grew more and more terrific, acquiring such
spasmodic violence that I thought it must either stop beating or
burst. Flesh and blood could not stand such strain without giving way any moment.[3]

Krishna's ordeal continued until he remembered a warning that if
energy passes up the wrong energy channel of the spine, the one
which regulates heat, it can cause virtual self-combustion. Through
intense concentration, he found the cooling channel instead, and
was able to neutralize the burning effect.[4] (This seemed rather incredible on its own, but I recalled from my Tibetan readings that one
of the most common yogic powers cultivated by monks is raising internal body heat. Normally Tibetans eschew flashy paranormal powers, but this practice was deemed useful for nights meditating in
caves in the wintery mountains. Graduates of this technique were required to sit naked by a riverbank throughout a night, while assis-
tants covered them with cloths dipped in the icy water. The
meditators used their internal body heat to dry them.) Krishna's experiences, with diligent training and good luck, resulted in incredible, extended periods of bliss, to the point where he visibly glowed
and developed psychic powers.

Several features of his description of the energy seemed distinctly
similar to my own experience: molten metal, incandescent light, undulating waves (though my wave sensations were more a physical

---

[3] Ibid., 160-161.
[4] Ibid., 162.

feeling than visual waves), the releasing of a pent-up torrent, roaring sounds, and, when the energy got out of control, unbearable pain, perspiration, red-hot pins, scorching and blistering sensations like flying sparks, and spasmodic violence. It happened to Krishna in solitary meditation. In my case, what set it off during sex? My three months meditating in Ladakh may have opened up something, but surely Sabina had a lot to do with it. It wasn't just a byproduct of good sex, for we had been making love for well over a week before it began, and then after we had reunited in Bodhgaya, it had never returned. What had triggered it?

Gopi Krishna's writings named the energy *shakti,* or cosmic vital energy, the same energy Sabina had mentioned as the distinctly female life-force energy that infuses everything in the universe. Krishna wrote: "Nothing can convey my condition more graphically than the representation of the God Shiva and his female power Shakti . . . in which the former is shown lying helpless and supine while the latter in an absolutely reckless mood dances gleefully on his prostrate frame."[5] It still jarred me, this idea that the goddess of destruction could also symbolize the force that gave everything life.

On my next visit to the library I found some books on the life of Ramakrishna, a Brahmin priest at a Kali temple in north Calcutta during the last half of the nineteenth century. His devotion to Mother Kali was legendary, and gave birth to a worldwide spiritual movement. Ramakrishna, filled with yearning, sought a divine vision of the goddess, which finally came to him while he worshipped at her altar:

It was as if houses, doors, temples, and all other things vanished altogether; as if there was nothing anywhere. And what I saw was a boundless, infinite conscious sea of light. However far and in whatever direction I looked, I found a continuous succession of effulgent waves coming forward, raging and storming from all

---

[5] Ibid., 237-238.

sides with great speed. Very soon, they fell on me and made me sink to the unknown bottom. I panted, struggled and fell unconscious.[6]

Ramakrishna could not get enough of Kali. He decided to follow the paths of all major religions, one by one, becoming a Christian, a Muslim, a Buddhist, and so on, so that he could apprehend the Divine from every possible aspect. Although I never was inclined towards worshipping the Divine Mother, I felt a lot of empathy for the saint, for his approach to gaining different perspectives on God was pretty much what I had set out to do when I came to India.

Ramakrishna also was visited by a female tantric teacher, Bhairavi Brahmani. He described to her his experiences and visions, which people told him were symptoms of madness. She said to him:

"My son, everything in this world is mad. Some are mad for money, some for creature comforts, some for name and fame; and you are mad for God." She assured him that he was passing through the almost unknown spiritual experience described in the scriptures as mahabhava, the most exalted rapture of divine love. She told him that this extreme exaltation had been described as manifesting itself through nineteen physical symptoms, including the shedding of tears, a tremor of the body, horripilation [gooseflesh], perspiration, and a burning sensation.[7]

Once again I recognized the symptoms, although in my case the "divine rapture" was for Sabina. Maybe I was not so far from a goddess worshipper after all. In fact, in my case, the mysterious "lever" was pressed the night I confessed my secret and said I loved her. On

---

[6] Swami Saradananda, *Shri Ramakrishna, The Great Master* (Mylapore, Madras, Sri Ramakrishna Math, 1952), 141.

[7] *The Gospel of Sri Ramakrishna*, tr. Swami Nikhilananda (New York: Ramakrishna-Vivekananda Center, 1969), 18-19.

thinking back on it, that whole experience had been one of intense, almost obsessional focus on her and my yearning for her. Hadn't I set up our first night together as a ritual, and at one point thought of the whole encounter as "almost religious"?

I read on. The teacher Bhairavi Brahmani offered to instruct Ramakrishna in the ways of Tantra. Under his new guru's instruction, Ramakrishna was required to undertake certain tantric sexual/meditative practices although the holy man maintained that throughout his life, even his married life, he never had sex, not even in a dream.[8] On one occasion, his teacher brought a beautiful young woman to him at night, naked. Bhairavi instructed him to worship her as the Goddess, and when he had finished his devotions, she said, "Sit on her lap, my child, and perform *japa*"(repetition of the name of God).

"I trembled and wept," recounted Ramakrishna, "calling to the Mother, 'O Mother, Mother of the universe, what is this command Thou givest to one who has taken absolute refuge in Thee? Has thy weak child the power to be so impudently daring?' But as soon as I had called on her, I felt as if I was possessed by some unknown power and extraordinary strength filled my heart. And no sooner had I, uttering the Mantras, sat on the lap of the woman, like one hypnotized, unaware of what I was doing, than I merged completely into *samadhi*. When I regained consciousness, I saw the Brahmani waiting on me and assiduously trying to bring me back to normal consciousness."[9]

Here, worship of the Divine Feminine and being seated on her proxy's lap brought Ramakrishna to the "unknown power and extraordinary strength" that filled his heart and altered his consciousness. Vividly I recalled how this mystical contact with Sabina felt: searing, painful, yet somehow healing, as if the twisted part of me

---

[8] Saradananda, 198-199.
[9] Ibid., 195-196.

was opening, changing. I found myself longing for that touch once more. We had been so prematurely interrupted. I had had just a taste of this elixir, and grieved now that I could no longer find the lever to pull a second draught.

I found most definitions of shakti from Hindu texts quite obscure, with the clearest account on the library's shelves coming from a book written by a Westerner, Omar Garrison. In the introduction to *Tantra: The Yoga of Sex,* he writes:

The universe and everything in it is permeated by a secret energy or power, emanating from the single Source of all being.

This power, although singular in essence, manifests in three ways, namely, as static inertia, dynamic inertia or mental energy, and as harmonious union of these reacting opposites.

The universe, or macrocosm through which these modalities of cosmic force function, is exactly duplicated by the human form as a microcosm.

The Tantrik seeks, therefore, by mystic formularies, rites, and symbols, to identify the corresponding centers of his own body with those of the macrocosm. Ultimately, he seeks union with God himself.

The importance of the female consort in Tantrik practices stems from the fact that, according to Shastra, every woman is a *shakti*; that is, she embodies the secret, fundamental forces that control the universe.

By correctly joining himself to this line of force, pouring forth the supreme Absolute, the yogi experiences the ineffable bliss of divine union.

Tantrik scriptures state emphatically that spiritual liberation can come only through experience. States of consciousness cannot be controlled and transcended until and unless they are lived—rapturously, freely, and in all the fullness of their power.[10]

---

[10] Omar Garrison, *Tantra: The Yoga of Sex* (New York: Harmony Books, 1964, 1983), xxi-xxii.

This was exactly what I was searching for. It also brought back to me the words of Philippe on the mountaintop: that the tantric practitioner sees his or her body as a mirror of the cosmos, the macrocosm. But rather than passively reflecting the Age of Destruction, tantric practice, by tapping into shakti, seemingly allows the body to reflect bliss and divine union. This made perfect sense until I recalled again that both the Age of Destruction and shakti emanated from Kali. I was back to the paradox once more: what was the difference between opening to the healing life-force energy or to destruction?

I put the question aside for the present, for time was running out in Calcutta, and I wanted to make notes as best I could on Garrison's text. The first chapters described warm-up meditations to be undertaken over several weeks prior to engaging in tantric sex. Although Garrison obviously went to great lengths to simplify wherever possible, the ritual still seemed terribly ornate, involving specific articles of dress, certain foods to be eaten, symbolic colours to be worn by the partners, mantras to be uttered, muscles to be flexed and relaxed, and how the breath was to be regulated to flow through the appropriate nostril. The ritual was to be performed only once a month, on the fifth day after the woman's menstrual bleeding has ceased. I scanned through to the heart of the ritual, which I paraphrased:

After eating and drinking the ritual foods, the partners leave the table. The woman disrobes (except for any jewels she wants to wear) and sits on the edge of the bed. A violet lamp shines on her, and the man, viewing her as an incarnation of the Sapphire Goddess, gazes upon her with adoration and awe, pondering the mysteries of creation and the unfathomable secrets of Being, for she is "the awakener of pure knowledge, the embodiment of all bliss." Again he contemplates her as "the unsullied treasure house, the shining protoplast, the begetter of all that is, becomes, dies and is born again." Unless the man can envision the woman in this light, he should stop the ritual, otherwise it becomes no different than ordinary sex.

After thus worshipping the goddess, the man puts his hand over his heart and recites, "*Shiva hum, So'hum,*" which means, "I am Shiva; I am She," thus identifying himself with the cosmic union of

Shiva and Shakti. With the tips of his right index and middle finger, he touches the woman's heart area; the crown of her head; eyes and centre of her forehead (where the invisible "third eye" is located); hollow of her throat, left and right earlobes, breasts, upper arms, navel, thighs, knees, feet and genitals. The intention here is to awaken the vital energy that lies dormant in these regions of the body. As he touches, he recites the mantra: *"Hling . . . kling . . . kandarpa . . . svaha."*

Next she lies flat on her back and he lies beside her on his left side, facing her (lying on the left side brings the flow of air through the right nostril, which is important for balancing the man's energy). Once the energy is flowing thus, they assume the position for *maithuna* (ritual sex).

The woman bends her knees, pulling both her legs up to her chest. The man swings the top of his body away from her, so that his hips move towards her hips, and his penis comes into contact with her vulva. She then lowers her legs and he lifts his right leg and places it so that it rests between her legs. This should result in a position that keeps the sex organs in close contact without any physical strain or discomfort. The man then parts the woman's labia and partially inserts his penis. Deep penetration is not desirable, close contact is what is important.

For the next thirty-two minutes, the pair lie motionless and relaxed, visualizing the flow of energy currents between them. According to Garrison's source, among Western students practising this ritual, between the twenty-eight and thirty-two minutes, an abrupt excitement "unlike anything ever experienced before" takes place, resulting in the "orgiastic and involuntary contraction of the body's total musculature," . . . "unlike anything experienced before."

"A clearly perceived decrease in tension follows," as the direction of the energy currents is reversed, now flowing inward, rather than outward, "entering the subtle body and energizing the entire organism." It is a nirvanic state of blissful unity, which is why the rite has such an important place in tantric texts: "By means of this inversion, this flowing back of pranic [energy] currents, reabsorption of the cosmos occurs. Time and eternity become one, Shiva and Shakti are wed within the [man's] own being, and he knows the totalization that preceded the creation of the universe."

Unless this inflowing of energy occurs together with the rapture, the meditation has failed. Additionally, ejaculation is not permitted at any point. Garrison says this rule "obviously calls for great self-control and previous training on the part of the male partner," and at the same time places the rite beyond the reach of "the libertine, the voluptuary, and the idly curious."[11]

The explicit details in common with my encounters with Sabina amazed me: sexual contact without deep penetration (or in my case, with close contact but no penetration at all); the "abrupt and total orgiastic contraction of the body's total musculature, unlike anything experienced before"—and all without ejaculation; and finally, the mysterious, quiet bliss that usually followed. To me, the most convincing concrete detail that my experience was indeed what the Tantrists were talking about was male orgasm without ejaculation. It just did not seem physically possible, yet I had definitely and repeatedly experienced it. Now here was verification in print, that it was not only possible but required for the release of cosmic energy.

At the time, of course, I had thought this strange sex was driving towards some kind of sublime ejaculation. It occurred to me now that the voice telling me to stop was a wise instruction, wherever it came from. The calmness that came afterwards was the true completing phase. I didn't quite buy this interpretation, though. It seemed too convenient. There was, no denying it, a pulling back, perhaps from something other than this guidebook for Westerners was going to reveal.

The other element of the rite in common with both my experience and Ramakrishna's was, once again, the adoration of one's partner as a goddess. I had thought of Sabina in pretty much these terms, "O shining protoplast" that she was, and had felt embarrassingly adolescent about it. She wasn't even nice to me sometimes, let alone

---

[11] Ibid., III-155.

divine, yet touching her had seemed so sacred. What had happened, since seeing her again, that had tarnished this element between us, turned the gold into brass? The sex was good again, after a rough start. But good sex was so much less than we once had. Perhaps it had to do with the heightening of all our senses in Varanasi, Patna and Vaishali: the fireworks, river smells, painted cows, the press of humid night air. All India conspired with us for a time, and now we were stuck grinding our way through poverty and grit. My image of the goddess had come down to earth.

We had not spoken of this ecstasy since reuniting in Bodhgaya. It was, I thought, the sort of thing she wanted to pass over in silence. I assumed it had been unusual for her too, because she said she had never had orgasms without penetration before, and felt like her breasts had filled with milk. What could than mean? I knew I couldn't bear the blasphemy of her Germanic rationalism if I brought it up now and she said, as she had with the tribal dancers in Delhi, that it was all a matter of technique. Why did I have to make it magic? And how could I mention it without sounding somehow petulant, as if I wanted it back again? Goddess, give it to me! It would destroy any possibility of the magic returning. I contemplated practising the ritual without telling her: secretly touching her heart area, crown, three eyes, throat, earlobes, breasts, upper arms, navel, thighs, knees, feet and genitals. It could be done, as intimate caresses. Then quietly I would mutter: "*Hling . . . kling . . . kandarpa . . . svaha.*"

"*What* are you talking about?" she'd say, her accent coarsely German.

"Oh, nothing. Do you mind if I lie on my left side a bit to get the air flowing through my right nostril?"

This was not going to work. The whole idea of slipping her a tantric tickle was ludicrous. You don't do that to a goddess, not if you want her to respect you in the morning. For all I knew, she did not want the intensity to return. At the time, I pulled away because I felt it would fuse us too deeply. Now, perhaps only a week away from having to leave the country, it would be foolishness to even bring the subject up. Really, what could I say about it that she didn't already know: that at the crucial moment it was me who pulled the plug, and the electricity had never come back. Surely, even if she could not or would not put it into words, this was the reason she had been angry after we had parted.

There was no point in further research. The power of Shakti had been aroused in our union, and now she had subsided. To arouse her once again—this would not be the result of following a textbook. There could be no predicting, no training rituals. Only waiting, as Ramakrishna had done. I felt once more the presence of a phantom limb, a void where ecstasy once had been.

A KALI
CHRISTMAS
Calcutta

I WOKE UP early on the morning of December 23 to the sounds of splashing in the pool and taxi horns out our window. Sabina was still curled towards me in sleep. I stroked her hair, its blonde strands streaming through my fingers. For the first time since we had resumed travelling, I felt relaxed and calm, knowing we could linger in bed rather than race out to catch a bus, or attempt to hunt down a curator with a museum key. She stretched out a hand. Our fingers intertwined as we kissed each other's lips, undeterred as only lovers can be by the lingering taste of curry and garlic from the previous night's dinner. Her free hand reached down and teased me erect. She kissed my belly, ran her tongue along the length of my shaft. I lay back as if floating on an ocean, warm and shivering. Straddling my hips, her eyes holding mine, she began pulling herself up and down on top of me with a slow and steady stroke until I felt I was no longer floating but melting into her. She leaned forward and clutched my neck, gasping, squeezing me tight between her legs. I felt myself flowing into her, a quiet trickle. It seemed a most untantric tenderness. Eventually I put my arms around her and we rolled to one side.

How does shakti, if that's what it is, transmute itself so? I wondered. Perhaps the mysterious fire was gone for good—but something had taken its place. I felt I could see her so clearly. Certainly, she wasn't a goddess to me any more. I'd seen her dirty, mad, frustrated near to tears over her research, duped by dishonest taxi drivers, and had even noticed, superficial male that I was, the little bit extra she had put on around her waist since we began hitting the city's restaurants. I smiled when I remembered my first impressions of her: an improbable blend of Marilyn Monroe, Indiana Jones and the goddess Parvati. How utterly I had thrown myself at her feet, just praying that she would, in her infinite mercy, accept my adoration and maybe sit on me naked. It was all very self-absorbed, all too much like my religion. Now, here in poverty-stricken Calcutta, she was simply the one person I had to care for. Loving her was much more difficult than adulation, which was so simple in its single-mindedness. It still seemed to me that the sexually free life she had chosen left her hurting, afraid no one would ever touch her deep inside. This thought made me want to touch her almost more than my desire to touch just for the softness of her skin. But to touch and not hold on, that hurts.

"What is it?" she asked.

"I just want to stay like this with you, arms and legs all tangled," I said, kissing her lips, her cheeks, her eyes. "Sleep, dress, eat and walk around the city like the Greek four-legged hermaphrodites."

Or like Shiva and Parvati? No, she wouldn't approve of a metaphor that mixed her pleasure with her business. A thousand years of sex? Hmmm. But only after Parvati's long austerities had turned her dark skin to gold—sort of like a celestial peroxide blonde. And still he didn't give her what she wanted, damn yogi. Parvati couldn't make him lose his self-control. No, only Kali, the blood of demons dripping from her lips, could incite Shiva to dance with her and let loose the chaos that destroyed the world, and thus cleared the way for its rebirth. And so Kali, not Parvati, was the Mother. I was drifting. Suddenly I became aware of her eyes on me, jolting me back. Had she responded to my classical allusion without me hearing it?

"You know, Tim," she said, her voice strangely soft, "sometimes you talk a lot, but I think there is much more you leave unsaid."

"Lucky for you."

"Oh, I wonder." She pushed her lips into a smile. "I'm hungry. Let's go to the place with the curried samosa."

I nodded and somehow we untangled into our separate halves. At breakfast we munched our way through deep-fried little pouches of curried potato while discussing our plans for the coming celebration. We agreed to make it as close to an Austrian Christmas as possible, with a private "family" dinner in our room on Christmas Eve, and then opening our presents. Talking about family Christmases left us both feeling homesick. It was harder than usual to part, but she had to go to a Sanskrit class she was auditing and I had to buy her Christmas present.

I went to the main bazaar to search for a pair of jewelled toe rings, the kind I had seen Sabina admire on Indian women. I knew if I found the right pair, she would wear them every day. The quantity of Christmas kitsch for sale disturbed me. Shop after shop sported rows of plastic mini-Christmas trees and Santas and, the item of the season, little metallic battery-operated toy puppies that wagged their tails and made tinny squeaks. Even ritual object shops had these for sale, all of them turned on and squeaking hideously. After an hour or so of searching through what seemed like the robot miniature dog pound from hell, I wanted to leap up on the counters and crush the tiny toys with my sandalled feet. Finally I found my toe rings and fled for the quiet of a teahouse.

I met Sabina for dinner, then we scoured the bazaar and the imported goods shops along Jawaharlal Nehru Road, buying food for our Christmas Eve feast. We found imported cheese, fresh bread, and even discovered a store near the Oberoi Grand Hotel that sold German white wine. Supplemented with fruit and a mysterious bag Sabina told me not to open, we then walked three kilometres back to the Mahabodhi Society, just to avoid the inevitable fight with a cabbie.

Arriving home, we found a note under our door: an invitation from the head of the Goethe Institute for Sabina to join him for dinner Christmas Eve.

"Of course, you will come with me," she said.

"I dunno," I replied. Shopping bags still packed, our Christmas plans were being abandoned in the face of a better offer. I sulked, and she did not seem to notice. I took a shower and fantasized about going to one of Mother Teresa's shelters rather than the Goethe dinner. When I had towelled off and returned to the room, I saw she had lit candles and opened up the mystery bag.

It contained paper, paints, glue and a child's blunt-tipped scissors. She was decorating our room with a cardboard crèche, the figures cut out and painted on by hand with a new watercolour set. She cut out a tiny gold star and stuck it on top, completely absorbed in her work. Her hair fell forward, glowing in the candlelight. Once the star was in place she looked up at me and smiled, just like a child.

"So beautiful," I said, touching her hair.

"Yes. I used to make these at school. It's been so many years."

We might never understand even the simplest communication, I laughed to myself. Maybe it doesn't matter. I kissed her, and looked away.

"It hurt, you know," I blurted out, "that our plans were all forgotten the minute you got the letter. I know it's petty. I'm just jealous, and wanted you all to myself over Christmas."

She turned and faced me, voice soft. "Tim, I'd never leave you for Christmas. If you are not happy, we can just go for an hour, or I could go alone and come back."

"No, don't do that. I don't have enough faith that you won't run off with some professor with good information for your research." I smiled wanly.

"He's married to an Indian, I think. Besides, I'm sure it's a gathering of people. We won't stay late. Just for dinner, I promise."

She took my head in her hands and kissed me.

The tantric electricity was gone; but still I felt as powerless as ever in her hands.

The idea of a visit to one of Mother Teresa's missions stayed lodged in my head, so next day while Sabina went to the museum, I took a bus north to the holy woman's home for the old and infirm. It was located in one of the most desolate slums of the city. A bridge spanning the railroad tracks demarked the entrance to the slum. On the other side, the street skittered off in four directions. The roadside was littered with trash. Wide puddles reeked of human feces. I held my breath and walked. Shanty huts of corrugated tin, bits of waste wood and rag lined the outside of the bridge where the ground sloped down to the rails. In the heat of the day, few people were out. The dirty, fly-covered children sitting in the dust didn't even bother to ask for baksheesh. I walked down to the tracks, hoping to stroll along them for a while rather than heading into the thick of the slum to search for the home. But the tracks were full of shit and garbage. A dog carcass lay to one side of the rails. A few metres farther I found its severed head, the raw meat at the neck covered with flies, the eye sockets already sucked dry. A child's trick, I supposed, setting a dead dog up to be decapitated.

I scrambled up the graded bank on the other side of the bridge, towards an old wooden building. It was a tannery. Dozens of hog hides were laid out on the gravel. Hundreds more hung on racks. A trench of dark green liquid with gelatinous fatty masses suspended just below the surface ran around the place like a pestilential moat. The air was so thick and fetid I could no longer breathe. I pulled up the bottom of my shirt to cover my mouth and nose. Around the side of the building I saw great mounds of yellow hog fat piled on the street. Farther down, someone had shovelled out the gutter to get it flowing again, but where the shovelling ended, the thick slime merely oozed slowly into the trench. Choking and sweating heavily, I strode through the cramped alleyways, searching for the home. Three times I circled back to the tannery without success. I hated to appear like a lost tourist. I'd be easy prey. Head up, step sure, I told myself. Look as if you know where you are going.

When at last a rickshaw puller appeared, I asked him for directions. He motioned for me to get in. This put me in a moral quandary. Bicycle rickshaws were fine. But that first morning when I entered Calcutta and saw the fat, white-clad woman being pulled by a running human being, I vowed I would never sit in her seat. I told the man I'd pay what he asked, and walk beside him to the gate. He looked at me with a most peculiar expression, and we had to pantomime the deal before I could convince him I really meant it.

The home was behind a high yellow brick wall. Inside, I could see palm trees waving. I rang a bell. Sister Rosetta came to the gate. A glowing young Indian woman, she wore the blue-fringed habit of the Sisters of Charity. He face seemed kind and quietly self-possessed as she invited me inside. Passing through the gates, I entered a wide, clean-swept yard with three or four large buildings at the rear. It seemed much cooler, the open space and lack of clutter disorienting after the slum outside. The several hundred residents in the courtyard all wore bright checkered clothing, red and white for the women, blue and white for the men. Old men babbled in groups and hobbled across one side of the compound, while in the women's section, a younger woman teased a senior, who rose and flailed at her in futile senile anger while those watching laughed. Nuns in blue-edged habits radiated cleanliness and cheerfulness as they passed among them.

Sister Rosetta provided me with Dikha, a young servant boy, to act as my guide. He spoke excellent English. It had been some time since I'd seen a cheerful child in clean shirt and shorts. As he showed me the men's dorm he explained that the nuns search Calcutta for the aged and infirm who can no longer take care of themselves and are left out on the streets to beg or starve. The nuns gather them up and bring them to the home, like trash collectors, I thought. No paperwork, no licences, they simply scoop the discarded and the broken off the curbside and bring them here.

The main men's ward seemed larger than a basketball court inside, made of wood and plaster, purely utilitarian, but adorned with the same aura of cleanliness. A slight antiseptic odour hung in the air, and beneath it I caught a brief smell of feces, not entirely banished from the home. The ward held hundreds of beds, stretching wall to wall in immaculate, orderly rows. Some were occupied at midday. One nun was singing to a wild man who was jabbering and flailing his arms in the air while the other was giving him a sponge bath. At another bed, a sister merely held the skeletal hand of a dying man. I watched them, the man's eyes on her bent head, both wordless, unmoving, too intimate for me to bear. What would it be like, I wondered, to be an aged and mentally infirm Hindu snatched out of Mother Kali's embrace and taken to this sanitary place where white-robed women washed the shit off you, bathed your sores and gazed tenderly into your face? I remembered a poem to Kali I had read at the Asiatic Society Library:

Mother, Mother!
The child cries,
And as she beats him,
he clings to her all the more tightly.

I cry, Mother, Mother!
But I am no lost child
I cling to you, Goddess,
through my misfortunes and woes,
with all the more strength.

Was it Kali's three eyes the old man saw when he looked into the sister's face? If stepping into this haven was disorienting for me, what must it be like for them? Perhaps some of them thought they had already died, and been reborn in a heavenly realm. I remembered the warning of the dour monks from Bodhgaya: There's no escape from karma. Then what would happen to the Hindus after they died and departed this Christian heaven-on-earth? Would Kali grasp their karma like a leash, and lead them back to dance with her once more along the squalid Calcutta streets?

As Dikha and I traversed the compound once more on my way back to the gate, a retarded adolescent girl called out to me, her hand outstretched. I hurried by with my guide, embarrassed. Probably she was just in off the curbside, I thought, and she still associated a white face with good begging prospects. She followed, and her pursuit frightened me, as if all my hatred of beggars and loathing of my hoarded riches were suddenly about to be exposed, here, in this holy woman's compound of lost and found souls. The girl came closer, hand still outstretched. She caught me with it, clasped my palm in hers. As I turned to face her and wrest myself free of her craving for baksheesh, she pumped my arm up and down in a proper handshake.

"How do you do?" she said, smiling at me.

She giggled and ran away, leaving me wretched, horrified at my response to simple friendliness. Had the good sisters washed away much more than shit, after all? And had I, so intent on protecting self and wealth from all the clutching grubby hands, affected my karma so much that I was now only capable of relating to those who lived on the dark side of the yellow brick wall?

That evening Sabina and I met as instructed at the Max Mueller Bhavan to rendezvous with the Goethe Institute director, Herr Nagel, whom Sabina had met during the course of her research. He was somewhat surprised to see she had a date. Of course, since the collapse of Calcutta's telephone system some years earlier, advance notice for changes of plans was not a part of social etiquette, even among Europeans. Nagel drove us to his home, which was tastefully decorated, strictly Western except for framed samples of Bengali art on the walls. His wife, a Bengali, had prepared two roast chickens, spinach curry and Canadian wild rice for our Christmas feast.

The wild rice was in honour of the only other dinner guest, a visiting Canadian photographer named Bruce. I took an instant disliking to my fellow countryman, who seemed, after the initial surprise, to take a quiet revulsion to me. Bruce had shown up in a polo shirt, dress slacks and Hush Puppies. His arms and chest looked meaty by comparison to mine, and there seemed to be a layer of fat that surrounded his entire body. I realized with a start I must have lost about twenty-five pounds over the past eight months. In Canada, Bruce would be considered average, whereas I would be considered thin—though in comparison with the rickshaw drivers and street-hawkers, I still looked beefy.

Over dinner, Bruce talked about his latest photography project, which had brought him to India. He had been commissioned to do a picture book of Toronto and Calcutta, a coupling that turned out to be less strange than one might think. Both cities were founded by the British about three hundred years ago. And, as Bruce cleverly pointed out, both cities took their names from the original Indian settlements. The food was excellent, the meal awkward. It seemed to me an obvious fix-up for Sabina and Bruce. When he finished his assignment, he intended to travel by train across the countryside to New Delhi, but he was concerned, he whined, about making the trip alone. Nagel had obviously put one and one together, and not counted on getting three.

I gnawed my chicken bones, and wondered if Bruce had included the squalid slums in his pretty picture book of Kali's city. I detested his light banter about Calcutta, the superficiality of his observations. He said he had taken a ride in a foot-rickshaw, just for the fun of it. And when Sabina broached the subject of cabs, he remarked how cheap they were compared to Canada. He was surprised she thought she had ever been cheated. I chewed and chewed on the bones, broke one open and sucked on the marrow.

"Oh, Tim, don't spend your time on old bones," said Nagel, hearing the cracking. He offered me the plate of steaming hot flesh. "There's plenty! Take another piece, or it will just go to waste."

I spent most of dessert thinking of polite ways for us to excuse ourselves after dinner. But when Nagel suggested schnapps, Sabina agreed with delight, and missed my pointed "but you promised" look. I declined the drink and took coffee, explaining that hard liquor would let loose the legions of bacteria that had infested my gut since living in Ladakh. I said I stayed healthy enough as long as I didn't eat rich food or drink much alcohol. Bruce looked suitably discomfitted by these veiled references to nasty bowel problems, which gave me peculiar satisfaction. When Nagel poured the second round it was already nine o'clock. Conversation passed me by as I watched the wall clock, getting angry. I took it out on Bruce.

"You see, Bruce"—I returned to my earlier theme—"in Canada,

the outer body looks strong, big muscles, lots of bulk, but the inner body is weak. We drink chlorinated water and eat refrigerated foods and everything's wrapped in plastic, so our immune system doesn't know how to handle one-tenth the bacteria an Indian's can. Really, they are much stronger than us. Travelling a long time in India, you learn how to get sick little by little. That's the way to build up your guts."

This perverse form of muscle flexing felt just one step away from kicking sand in Bruce's face. I checked myself, remembering my other listeners were an Indian and two Westerners who spoke native languages fluently, although at the moment I was possessed with such arrogance that I didn't think any of them had lived as close to the land as I had. I caught Sabina's glare and glared back at her.

"Well, thank you for a lovely dinner," she said brightly.

We made superficial conversation on the way to the door, and then we were out in the night air.

"You were being horrible," she said.

"I was the uninvited guest who turned a cosy foursome into an awkward five. The only natural point of contact I had was with my brother Canadian who treated me like a pariah," I growled.

"Well, you didn't act much different. I thought you were trying to frighten him about India."

"You promised we'd leave early."

She was silent. I sulked. She hailed a cab. The driver said that his meter was broken. Sabina banged on his window with her fist and yelled abuse at him. I flagged another down. When he lowered his window, Sabina lit into him in a mix of Hindi, German and English, demanding to know if his meter worked, and did he know how to get to the university? The driver nodded stiffly, in what appeared to be fear-induced paralysis.

"Relax," I said to her once we were inside, which has got to be the stupidest thing a man can ever say to an angry woman.

"They *are* all liars, out to cheat us," she hissed.

I moved to take her hand.

"Don't touch me."

Suddenly my own ill humour vanished and I felt like laughing. Her anger seemed so funny, now that we were alone and it was Christmas Eve. There were fireworks going off in the night, and faint strains of brass band music. Somewhere, someone was having a parade. I rolled down my window. Yes, it was "Disco Dancer," a reassuring constant in a chaotic world. The streets were jammed, traffic slow. Sabina instructed our driver at every intersection, anticipating and preventing deliberate wrong turns. At the hotel, the meter read nineteen rupees. The driver asked for forty. Double for Christmas, he explained. It was a near-fatal miscalculation on his part, for at that instant Sabina transformed herself into the wrathful incarnation of Kali in her Cheated Tourist Aspect, and began spewing fire at the Bengali. His eyes bulged with indignation and then rage and he began yelling back.

This is it, I thought, the end of the world, the Kaliyuga spiral of destruction is about to reach its zenith. Like one giant nuclear bomb, all matter will be dissolved back into primordial flux. All over a taxi ride.

I managed to push her out of the cab and onto the street. She turned and yelled through the window at the driver, who was now gesticulating wildly with sharp stabbing motions. He was, he no doubt realized, in a very weak bargaining position. We were out of his cab and at our destination. This fact, combined with the impending end of the world, made me supremely calm. A few young passersby stopped and asked what was wrong. I explained, then asked if they knew the correct taxi fare for the trip. About ten rupees, they said. I handed the appropriate bill to the driver, who would not touch it. I dropped it through the window onto his lap, then grabbed Sabina firmly by the arm and turned her towards the society's gates. She did not struggle, but wrenched her head around to continue abusing the driver.

"And I am going to take a gun and shoot the next one of you taxi bastards that cheats us!" screeched the incoherent deity, pointing her trigger finger at the cabbie, while he flung every Hindu curse at his command onto our escaping forms.

Once upstairs, Sabina flung herself on the bed, face buried in the pillow. A minute later I heard a knock at the door. Alarmed that the driver had dared follow us inside the building, I opened with caution. It was not the driver, however, but one of the young men who had told us the correct fare down on the street.

"You must leave the Mahabodhi Society at once!" he spat at us. "I am a worker here, and we cannot have our guests threatening to shoot cabbies in the street!" He turned and marched down the hallway.

Sabina started throwing clothes into her duffle bag.

"What are you doing?" I asked.

"I am leaving, period. It's too much. Don't touch me! The bastards. Cheating, cheating, cheating, touching my breasts, doubling every price, killing their own politicians and murdering innocent people! I want to kill them all." She shook her fist out the window. "I hate the greed, the materialism, the poverty, the inhumanity of everyone, the fingers, always touching, grasping. How am I expected to do my work here? I have to treat everybody like shit just to get the simplest of things done. I can't do it any longer."

"Hush, sleep now." I put my hands on her shoulders. "I'll go talk to the abbot in the morning. That boy can't throw us out; he was just upset."

"So you are on his side?"

"Oh, no! Stupid bastard!" I shook my fist out the window. "I'm on your side. In fact, if you want to have a shower, I'll keep shaking my fist for you."

She smiled a weary smile and went to take her bath. The Mahabodhi Society was our one refuge in the city, the one place where we knew we would be treated fairly, a cool, clean place, like a mountain retreat high above the filth and squalor. Finding a replacement hotel within our budget would be impossible, and we both knew it. I went to Rev. Bandula and asked to see the abbot in the morning, but the monk brought me to him at once. He was a rotund, copper-skinned Singhalese who wore horn-rimmed spectacles that seemed to clutch the sides of his hairless brown head like a set of pincers. He listened with a placid, thoughtful expression as I explained our confrontation with the worker and his order of eviction.

"Thank you for telling me this," he replied. "Actually, the boy you have described is not a worker here, but one of several relatives of a worker, all of whom are living in our servants' quarters. This boy has many bad habits. He drinks, and it is most concerning to me that now he is bothering our guests and saying he is our worker."

The abbot spoke to a servant, who brought the troublemaker forth a few minutes later. Squirming like a worm on a hook, the wretched youth denied saying he told us to leave, and was summarily released. The abbot turned back to me.

"He did you a good turn," judged the abbot, "and this balances out the harm. You are our guest, please accept my apologies. It will not happen again."

Ah, a little Buddhist justice. Who could ask for a better Christmas gift?

When I returned to the room and told Sabina the news, she smiled, and said she knew it would not be a problem, that a peon could not evict us from the society. In my absence, she had lit candles around the little crèche, and invited me to sit on the bed beside her while we opened our presents. She gave me my own watercolour set and an incense holder, and one of the little squeaking puppy toys. I had told her how much I had wanted to stomp on them in the bazaar, and she said she wanted to gratify my every Christmas wish. She adored the coral toe rings that I gave her, and the poinsettia leaf I had pressed in my journals from Nepal, and carried south as a reminder of the northern Christmases we both missed. Outside, firecrackers thudded like gunshots in the silent night. We sang a carol together in our respective languages and went to bed.

Silent night. Holy night. All is calm. All is black, in Kali's great sleeping city.

CHAPTER THIRTEEN

DIRTY JOKES

Orissa

T HE DAY after Christmas we travelled south to Orissa, another state rich in buried Buddhist treasure. Sabina attacked its remote, tiny museums, visiting five in four days without turning up a single new statue. Rice fields, rooms of old stone carvings and arguments with rickshaw drivers all blurred together indistinctly in my mind, and my shoulders grew sore from carrying her duffle bag through a quick succession of cheap hotels and bus depots. At the museum of Khiching we missed our bus out and were stranded for four hours, forced, thank Krishna, to relax for a while. At the curator's suggestion we rented bicycles and rode off to explore the nearby ruins of yet another buried kingdom.

From his ancient capital near Khiching, King Kalinga had once ruled Orissa and the lands to the south until the year 260 B.C., when he fought and lost a bloody battle against the empire to the north. Records of the carnage have survived over two millennia, for it produced a most unlikely side effect: the spreading and nurturing of the Buddhist faith through most of India. The previous year, the northern ruler had nominally converted to the new religion. Nonetheless he went to war and, like a good monarch, obliterated his enemy. But as he surveyed the battlefield filled with the dead and dying, King Ashoka changed.

Cycling across the countryside, we passed outcroppings of stone that had been quarried, carved and buried long ago. I imagined the battlefield as Ashoka must have seen it: crushed chariots, dead horses, rats, vultures, crows pecking eyes, jackals and wild dogs snarling, pulling open the wounds to get at the meat. The victors joined the scavengers, stripping armour, weapons and jewels from the dead. The Dead. What was the difference to a warrior king like Ashoka between the enemy and the dead? The difference between a pig and a ham: an enemy is a corpse that has not yet received the touch of your sword. To such a warrior, death is the ideal state of the enemy; rendering him inanimate, a just cause for pleasure.

We parked our bicycles by the shade of a peeple tree and sat beneath it. Sabina closed her eyes. Shutting mine, I imagined Ashoka once again. I envisioned him riding through the field, savouring the pleasure of victory. He dismounts to piss, standing on mangled bodies. As he finishes, a hand reaches up and grasps him by the ankle. He wheels, draws his sword, but cannot slash, for the hand comes straight up from the ground, its wrist pressed against the line of his foot. To cut at it would be to wound himself. There is something peculiar about this hand; it is slender, dark like a root, but the nails long and feminine. A tingling shoots up from the hand through his leg, coils round his spine and shoots up through his head, as if he has been struck by lightning from below. He bends, pushes dead limbs aside to unbury this creature, but the hand slips beneath him as he clears his way to ground, and he sees the last of the fingers sliding straight down into the earth. He pales and blinks. He searches the ground once more for the vanished hand, but sees instead the nearby head of an enemy soldier, a youth, with black eyes open, as if the corpse is staring straight into him. It startles the king.

"Dead," he says aloud.

The eyes blink. "Alive," says the young soldier. He closes his eyes and dies.

Ashoka touches the face. It is warm, no hallucination. And suddenly, each human body on the battlefield has a life, a human heart and spirit. They come alive for the king in one great burst of energy. The light spreads across the battlefield, to the fields and villages beyond, as if in one second, from a single seed, the whole dark world has come to light. The next instant, the light implodes, the battle-field turns once more to ashes. But now it is living beings who are dead, and he, King Ashoka, knows he is to blame.

Subsequent to the battle, history—rather than my fantasy—records that Ashoka passed a new edict that henceforth it was his desire to govern, please and protect his subjects according to the Buddha's teachings. He announced it was his duty to improve the quality of his subjects' lives, so as to provide a framework for their following a moral and religious way of life, Buddhist or otherwise. He inaugurated public works, such as wells and rest houses for travellers, supported medical aid for humans and animals, and gave donations for the fostering of such measures in regions beyond his empire. Dharma officials were appointed to encourage virtue, look after old people and orphans, and to ensure standards of social justice. While he retained some judicial beatings, he abolished torture and the death penalty. Released prisoners were given short-term financial help and encouraged to do good deeds to improve the karma of their future lives.

The reformed king gave up invasions. He replaced royal hunting trips with pilgrimages to sites associated with the life of the Buddha, erecting religious monuments and great stone columns proclaiming his just edicts. In time the royal household became vegetarian. The sacrifice of animals was banned in the capital city, and, livestock excepted, all animals and birds in the kingdom became protected species. In short, Ashoka became the most beneficent, socially conscious king in Indian history. Buddhism flourished under this imperial nurturing. It grew in strength and remained a strong force across India for the next fifteen hundred years, until the Muslim invasions dispatched all unrepentant Buddhists with the sword.

Eventually we arose from our private reveries. The ground was damp, and I felt a chill as we pedalled back to the bus stop. To our annoyance, the bus had departed early, and we had missed it; the next one wasn't due until six p.m. Rather than travel at dark, we decided to walk to the paved road and hitchhike. We finally caught a lift with an upper-class Indian family who took us to the crossroads of a main highway, where we could catch the late-night bus to our destination. We were dehydrated, famished and exhausted. We ate greasy samosas at a dirty roadside restaurant, too hungry to question whether or not the food was safe. Days of tiring travel and similarly questionable meals had pushed me past my limit, and the afternoon chill had finally done me in.

My stomach churned as I ate, and I felt my bowels constrict in an urgent, painful way that was all too familiar: the "one-minute warning." Quickly I asked the server where the toilet was, and he pointed to a field outside the back door. I tore some blank pages from my journal and made haste into the dark. The field was mucky, full of tall weeds and grasses. I walked twenty yards or so away from the building, and then squatted most miserably to relieve myself. The exalted feelings of the afternoon over the glory of Ashoka were wrung out of me. For the moment, there was only me in the universe, me and the poison running out my gut.

I heard a rustle in the grass and tightened with fear. This was not the stance I wished to assume when fighting bandits for my life. I saw a black shape coming towards me, keeping low at the edge of the grass. A mongrel dog, skinny, with large hairless patches so that I could see the contour of its ribs in the moonlight. It ran towards me. I ripped up a handful of weeds and threw it at the creature, yelled at it. It wavered a second, then dived into the tall grass. I lost sight of it, and my belly twisted downward again, as if trying to push my intestines out. I clutched my knees. Suddenly I heard a lapping sound. The dog had circled round, so starved it was unable to wait until I left. It was eating my shit right as it was coming out. The animal dodged out of the way as I beat the air behind me, almost losing my balance and falling into my own mess. I squeezed back tears. I was too sick to stop. The spasms were wringing me dry. I clutched my knees again and panted. The dog kept darting back at me, whimpering, trying to get at the closest thing to food it could find. The thought of it touching me with its tongue made me want to kill the thing, put it out of its misery. Put me out of mine. Kill the rot, inside and out, the rot in my belly and the rot, the horrid rot, of this world.

It was a strangely familiar feeling, I later recalled, the same revulsion I experienced when pressed upon by beggars, their clammy touch upon my sandalled feet. Ashoka's world may have come to life, but mine, as I so deeply knew, had not. The Buddha attained enlightenment after thousands of lifetimes of practising self-sacrifice, literally offering his limbs and bodies to be eaten by wild animals so that they would not go hungry. And I, budding Buddhist, couldn't even bear to share my shit. I felt that all my time in India had produced no change at all. It had all been squandered. I cleaned myself as best I could with the torn pages. As I slowly straightened, the dog fell upon my remains. I staggered back into the shack, my jaws clenched to keep down the few mouthfuls left in my belly. For the first time in a long time, I just wanted to go home.

The bus pulled into Jaipur at two in the morning, and we had to hammer on the door of a hotel for fifteen minutes before a coolie let us in. We had grown used to humid, stale air and greenish mildewed sheets, but the room we were given stank as if an open sewer ran through the floorboards. We rinsed and threw ourselves onto the dank bed, not touching, not speaking, but the stench was too strong to sleep. I shook the coolie awake in the lobby and told him our problem. He rubbed his eyes, selected a different key, and dragged himself down the hall. The room was humid but did not reek.

"I can't believe he would put us in a room like a cesspool," I said.

Next morning I looked at my face in the cracked remains of the bathroom mirror. Sick, pale, skinny. This was not my style of travelling, a forced march through the ruins of India. Even had the conditions been sanitary enough to make it appealing, we were mostly too worn out for sex. And where was the tenderness? Where was the tantric ecstasy? What was the point of trying to love in this muck? I ached because I loved her, and, at the same time, I was relieved that the decision was out of my hands. Three more days and I would have to return to Calcutta so my visa could be rejected. I would be ejected from the country and on my way to Thailand, and perhaps another monastery there. Frankly, I was ready to go. We had planned a detour to Puri, a seaside resort town where we were going to rest, celebrate the New Year, and once more say goodbye. But there were two more museums she wanted to see first. We were behind schedule, and possibly going to end up with only a single night together by the sea.

"What will you do if you get your extension?" she asked as we rode through the dust on yet another bus.

I shrugged. "You'll be somewhere in the wilds of Orissa, or maybe backtracking through Bihar. I doubt I could find you."

"But I have an idea. You could wait for me in Calcutta. I'll call the Mahabodhi Society to check. Then we could travel through Bihar together again."

"I think that if by some remote chance I can stay, that it is time I tried something I really wanted to do in India, but never had the chance to try: living without money, you know, like a sadhu, a wandering, penniless holy man, maybe in South India. Complete detachment from all possessions. I've been so lax with my spirit lately; I feel I've learned nothing. This is just something I have to do, maybe for a month or so. After that, perhaps when you are doing the museums down there, we could travel together again."

She looked at me as if I had slapped her hard across the face. Her voice came hot and rang hollow, as if she was at the far end of a cave.

"So what am I supposed to do with you in a month's time? Put you in a hospital until you recover? Nurse you back to health?"

"I'm not afraid of living dangerously. I'm just so attached to things—my backpack, my money, books, all my security. I want to let it all go, like your father did during the war."

"My father was a prisoner of Stalin, waiting to die," she said fiercely. "He didn't *ask* them to strip him of everything he possessed."

"It's just time," I said, setting my jaw.

"You stupid man," she spat out at me.

I thought she was about to slap my face, and braced for it. But when she spoke again, her voice had softened and she seemed close to tears.

"I know this is not much fun for you, Tim, this way. You carry my big bag and fight with the rickshaw drivers and we go bop, bop, bop, from town to town. Maybe you should just go on to Puri, and I will meet you there on New Year's Day, if you want to wait for me."

"No," I said flatly. "I'm just tired and I feel like shit. I want to settle for a few days. I'll keep going with you, but we will stop in Puri for New Year's before I go? Good. I don't want to leave you, and I don't want to leave India. I don't know what I'll do if I get more time, but I don't want to carry on like this."

She looked me square in the face; no smile, no anger, just a flat look of understanding. She nodded. There was something I liked about it. It seemed the most honest exchange we had ever had.

We spent the evening in the Ratnagiri guest house, in a room furnished with two chairs and a single narrow bed. The sheets were crisp and clean, the mosquito nets untorn, the bathroom free of mildew. Iron bars adorned the glassless window. In North America, it might have passed for a prison cell. But for us, it seemed the most decadent luxury.

"We can take a shower together," she said to me, tentatively, "and then make love a bit, if you like."

"Did I hurt you so much that you have to ask?" I replied softly. "I hate to feel you so distant." I sat on the bed for a while, silent. "You never did tell me why you were angry after we parted in Patna," I said bluntly.

"Hush," she said, and put her finger to my lips. "It doesn't matter any more."

We washed each other's backs with soap, then crept beneath the netting. She placed my hand between her legs and clung to me as I caressed her, drawing her waters to the surface, then ducked my head to drink. She pulled me up, placing her legs against my chest so that her ankles rested on my shoulders, and I sank into her, rocked hard against her on the bed. She opened her mouth wide and uttered short gasps. I took long, slow strokes that felt like bowing the strings of a violin—until I stroked too far and my bow plopped out on the bed. She opened her closed lids and looked at me, raising an eyebrow.

"You're not as long as you think you are," she said, then reached around and reinserted me. "Oh, but strong!"

I laughed, "Thanks a lot for stroking my male ego. Don't worry though, it's not about to go limp."

Later, curled together beneath the mosquito net, she said, "I worry about you going to Thailand, Tim. All the whores in Bangkok."

"Don't fret. For me, sex and economics don't mix."

"You sound so virtuous."

"Being on a cheap budget does wonders for one's virtue. I'll probably head to another monastery soon as I get there."

"Mmmm, such a virtuous monk. If I were a Thai whore, I would take you for free."

"Hell, if you were a Thai whore, I'd pay double for you."

"But what will I do if I come to Thailand looking for you, and you're a monk!"

"Well, find me and make me break my vows. Or don't you do monks any more?"

She turned suddenly quiet, averted her eyes. An ugly name flashed unspoken between us.

"You saw him after Patna, didn't you?" I asked bitterly.

"No."

I sat up in bed, pulled up the netting to go. She put a hand out to stop me.

"He invited me to his villa in Bombay."

"Shit, Jerry—of all people." I dropped the net and just sat there. She put one hand on my back. "Just give me a minute," I said.

This was like a boot in the stomach, or even lower. I was surprised how much it hurt. Such a great opportunity to just slough it all off with a good Buddhist laugh. What had gone wrong? Or did it matter what was past? She was with me for the present. Her freedom with men was part of what made me desire her, what made it so easy at first, because I thought I couldn't possibly hurt her. I thought she could take care of herself. And so she had.

"It's just dumb male pride, Sabina," I said at last. "I want to think that I'm someone special to you. And yet, since I can't stay to make that happen, why should I get upset?"

"But do you want to stay, really?" she said softly, tugging gently on my arm. Her pubic bone pressed gently against the side of my hip. I could feel it, still wet. I felt myself stiffen, against my will. I said nothing.

"Even if you don't want to, perhaps I will have to spoil you like this much more often. Give you so much pleasure you can't live without it."

"Make me addicted to you?" I turned and saw her gazing into my eyes with the look that held me.

"Umm."

"If I'm going to be an addict, I want you to be my vice." I turned to her. She smiled and squeezed me between her legs.

A single officer was on duty at the subdivisional office compound where we reported for directions to the ruins of Ratnagiri. The rest were recuperating from election duty and vote counting, and anxiously anticipating the results. The compound had a collection of several statues, including a magnificent Earth-Touching Gesture, with Mara depicted in two poses beneath Buddha's lotus pedestal. It excited Sabina because there was no record of it in New Delhi, and would count as a genuine find for her research: a nugget of gold after five days prospecting in the wilderness. The officer kindly arranged for a driver to take us to the ruin, fifteen kilometres away, to see what additional treasures we could unearth.

The entire population of Ratnagiri village turned out to welcome us, about sixty people in all, mostly schoolchildren and old women, including an ageing transvestite in a red-trimmed sari. Most of the men were off at work, in the fields or pedalling rickshaws in the nearby towns. The village teacher informed us that the tiny museum was locked, of course, and the curator had gone away for some weeks with the key. He added that many great foreign researchers had come to see the excavated monastery site. The whole happy crowd led the way up the hillside to the treasure.

Heaping mounds of ruined stupas ringed the two main temples. Large Buddha heads six feet across lay on the earth nearby. The ground floor of the main buildings appeared to have been excavated and reconstructed; new plaster held the walls together. Each surface was carved with relief statues of Buddhist deities and *devas*. The carvings were wild and ornate, from a later, decadent age in which Buddhism and Hinduism had begun to interbreed and mutate, as the pure essence of the former was gradually subsumed back into Hinduism's many-armed embrace. Sabina pointed to one of the dancing figures. The snake around his neck and trident in one hand were the symbols of Shiva—yet in his other hand, the Great Destroyer carried the vajra sceptre: a tantric Buddhist symbol.

But the entire complex reeked. To the residents of the hamlet, the ancient treasure also served as a colossal latrine. Human feces dotted every room of the foundations; a lump rested on the eye of one decapitated Buddha head. Inside one alcove, we found a life-sized Buddha, his head still intact, face visible, serene smile gracing his lips, and a decaying turd in the middle of his lap. I admired his composure in the midst of decomposure. In his crumbling, befouled serenity, he continued to preach his message: Everything is transient, so don't get too attached to great temples or plans of glory.

The villagers pressed close to us, watching our faces intently. We rounded the next corner and discovered a stone relief of two women and a man, sexually entwined. On the wall next to them, like a lonely voyeur, was a carving of a seated meditator, his two hands gripped in a bawdy self-touching gesture. There was a dopey look on his face, and it was hard to tell if the carvings were expressions of tantric mysticism or a practical joke, perhaps constructed by the ancient monastic school's engineering undergraduates. Our audience, especially the children, laughed outrageously the moment we caught sight of the panels.

In another courtyard we found two more panels, one on top, one on the bottom, with a punch line so plain we didn't need to read the curlicues of the ancient script to get it. The top panel showed various animals in the act of copulation: monkeys, elephants, water buffaloes and other mythical beasts I could not recognize. The lower panel showed humans in the exact same postures as the animals, only the rear figures were women. In each couple, the man's ludicrously extended penis was bent back between his legs like a monkey tail, arching over the head of his partner, then curling back so that the tip of each penis was wedged firmly in each woman's smiling mouth. I thought of the student-monks of that long-destroyed culture walking past these panels every day while studying their esoteric texts and practices. Their world had been savagely obliterated, but the raucous laughter of the village children was testimony to the eternally enduring nature of what remained—the tantric dirty joke.

We spent two nights at Puri, swimming, sleeping, shopping and dwelling in an increasingly sexual haze, washing away the crust of shit and dirt and frustration that covered us both. We ate fresh shrimp and lobster for dinner New Year's Day, and then began, once more, the painful act of parting. We repacked our bags, separating our things, and agreed to leave messages for each other at the Mahabodhi Society (telephone calls from outside of Calcutta being much easier than calls within the city). If I got the extension, I would travel south, and a few weeks later she would meet up with me. We relished these plans, knowing full well that the higher up the official channels my request went, the less likely it would be granted.

The last bus I could take to Calcutta left town in the middle of the night. After dinner, we walked the beach. Returning to our room, I lit the last of our candles and stuck it to the wooden side table, then wafted a stick of sandalwood incense over the soft flame. Sabina's skin glowed in the orange light. I gazed at her naked body, hoping to sear each curve into my memory. Should I worship her as goddess, try to arouse the tantric flame once more? No, for the present moment, which was all I had left, I was just going to love her as flesh and blood.

"Tim," she said softly, touching my face with her hands, "you remember the distance you felt from me in Ratnagiri, and before that? Well, it's gone. It's all gone. I'm so close now, and you're leaving."

"I don't want to leave. Call me in Calcutta. Or I'll leave a message, don't forget."

"But we don't have to separate. There is a way."

"You think?" I smiled and traced her lip.

"I can break my contract, pay back the money later, and travel to Thailand with you."

"You would do that for me? No, no. You finish your work, then we'll see. After all, who else is going to find all the Earth-Touching Gestures in India? Our time together has been beautiful. If it continues, wonderful . . ."

She stared at me in the candlelight, and I smelled the stench of my own hypocrisy.

"You know," she said, her voice low and sad, fingers stroking the hair of my naked chest, "men interested in Buddhism, they say these things, and it is so frustrating."

"You mean because they don't want to act to make it happen?"

"Yes."

"I'm not a Buddhist."

With a deft move she clutched my left arm and flipped me, rolling over so that now she was on top of me. Her voice was quiet but intense. He eyes flashed in the candlelight.

"If you were thirty-five and finished with all this craziness you have yet to go through, I would never let you go."

"You would drop your thesis?"

"Yes."

"But why?"

"I'm a woman."

"Yes, that you are."

She smiled at me.

"What if at thirty-five I'm a frustrated, unpublished and impoverished writer?"

"Doesn't matter."

"So who says it has to end? If I have to go, find me in Thailand."

"But if it breaks now, it may never be the same again. I've had it happen. You meet again and everything's changed."

"I remember meeting you in Bodhgaya, after looking for you for three days. I was crazy to touch you. Of course everything changes. But I can't imagine changing so much that I wouldn't feel just the same at the thought of seeing you again."

"Oh, stop talking, Tim," she said, her voice sounding suddenly weary. "Just come close a bit."

At 1:15 we awoke to my alarm. Time yet to clutch each other once more. Afterwards, I lit the candle and dressed.

"My breasts will miss you, my love," she whispered. "And when I'm alone, and feel like making love, I will touch them and think of you, and it will excite me very much."

I bent and kissed her breasts, and felt her hands slip under my shirt and rub my belly. I pulled away, shouldered my bag, and walked out into the dark, alone, in time to catch my bus.

CHAPTER FOURTEEN

AROUSING THE GODDESS

Mamallapuram

January 3, Calcutta

Dear Wendy,

Sorry if this is hard to read. I've been on an overnight train ride and haven't slept. I need to talk to you. I've just left Sabina in Orissa to see if my application for a visa extension in Calcutta will be accepted. I know it won't. I'll probably have to leave right away. In the meantime, I'm sitting in front of the Foreigners' Registration Office, writing on my knee, waiting for the doors to open.

Sabina told me last night that if I were thirty-five, she'd never let me go, even if it meant abandoning her research. She's right though, at twenty-six, there's still a lot of craziness I've got to go through. Could it have worked? If she was serious about giving up her research, should I have asked her to come to Thailand with me? When I think about it, I can't get the image of her driving her Austrian boyfriends' Porsches out of my head, and I think, no way. She's used to a lifestyle, or rather, a man-style, that I'll never provide. Okay, perhaps it takes more devotion to ride the tin buses of India together and fight with rickshaw drivers and fend off the beggars than to lend your car keys. But for a lifetime, this would not be much fun.

Today I just miss her like hell. I remember this woman in

Varanasi, Wendy, an Indian beggar who got beaten with a club right beside me because people thought she was stealing something from my bag. She seemed numb to the pain as they thrashed her. Standing right next to her, I felt numb too, as if I couldn't move. I didn't do anything to help her. I just watched. It feels as if that's how I've lived out my emotional life, numb to love, numb to pain. I sometimes wonder if the fiery physical sensations I experienced the first weeks of having sex with Sabina wasn't just feelings coming to life in my physical body. Feeling receptors being turned on for the first time ever.

In some crazy way, the hurt I feel today is bringing me out of that numbness. A poor woman hit me up for baksheesh just outside the train station this morning. She wasn't crippled, no kids, not really elderly enough to fit into my categories of who I give to. She approached with a rasping voice and stuck her hand in my face, squawking. I gave her a rupee, which is a lot for a beggar to receive, and frankly, though it seems cheap, a lot for me to give. I know this kind of giving changes nothing, solves no problems. She didn't thank me or touch my feet or mumble any prayer, just went off searching for another soft touch. It was not a great moment of human contact, but for the first time, it just felt good to give. Usually, when I refuse, or argue over fares with the skinny old rickshaw pedal pushers, I feel angry, abused and impoverished. But with this ungrateful old woman, it felt like a blessing. I don't know. I think I'm just heartsick today. Half of me longs for my good old Buddhist detachment. The other half just wants to hold her.

Either way, the task ahead is clear: beat down the door of the FRO. If the extra time comes through, I'll head south for a quick look at Madras, and maybe check into an ashram for a little while just to settle again, and wait for Sabina to join me for one more round.

I miss you, Wendy. I'm glad I've got your ear, even if only on paper.

Love, your brother,
Tim

I was first in line when the FRO opened. Mr. Besares smiled crookedly at me. He took my empty passport and shuffled papers for half an hour. Eventually he wandered back to the wicket and told me my case had been transferred to the HPO, the Home Passport Office in the Writers' Building across from BBD Bagh Square. I was to report to Mr. Mukherjee.

I marched to the complex, a great grid-like brick structure several floors high, taking up an entire city block. Inside was a human anthill filled with wall-high stacks of yellowed papers, dirty halls, garbage, peons delivering tea and armloads of more paper. Every corner was crammed with battered desks and ageing bureaucrats labouring over their documents, reading newspapers, or chatting and sipping tea. It was a catacomb of writers and scribes, a civilization unto itself. Walls of paper files blocked some corridors. Here and there, entrances to stairways had been walled off, and from some stairwells, certain floors were inaccessible. As a result, despite the regular grid shape of the building, navigating it was a task for a lab rat. No one knew where to find the office I was supposed to report to, nor could even tell me where to go to find out where to go. At least with all the tea coming up and down the halls, I knew I would not succumb to thirst, as many bored scribes invited me to stop for a cup. Eventually someone said he knew a Mukherjee who worked in the Urban Squalor Office, or something like that. He speculated that the USO Mukherjee might have heard of the HPO Mukherjee. I found the man, and indeed he did know his fellow caste member. He indicated the direction in which he thought the Home Passport Office might be.

Following his directions, I soon found myself in another dead end. I backtracked, walked down a flight to get around the obstruction, got lost, and, in an attempt to relocate the USO Mukherjee I had just left, got mistakenly directed to his namesake in the HPO, just several desks down the hall. My Mukherjee was a bespectacled Brahmin in his fifties, with thinning, silvery hair combed straight back over his semi-bald head. There was an ashen pallor upon his skin, due, I assumed, to spending years and years in a windowless office. He wore a dhoti, homespun Indian shirt and a vest, and spoke slow yet eloquent English. I explained my case, which he had not yet read.

"Frankly, Mr. Tim, there is little I can do for you, being that you entered with a tourist visa. You will have to go home and get a letter from your university, then apply for an education visa."

"Could I just make the request for a visa, even though it would certainly be denied?"

"Yes," he said slowly, seeming puzzled. "Of course, I will read your file and determine what to do. Please return in three days to my office."

He escorted me down the stairs and through the catacombs to the outside world.

At the Mahabodhi Society, Rev. Bandula gave me the room overlooking the swimming pool. Our room. I slept until late afternoon, then roamed the streets Sabina and I had wandered, ate at our favourite restaurants. The streets were packed with people celebrating the election victory of Rajiv Gandhi. I spent much time in my room, avoiding the crowds, just lying on my bed, gazing up at the ceiling. In the evening I joined the monks for a prayer service, a rite I had never attended with Sabina. The shrine room contained a bright and shining silver stupa, ornate and inlaid with gems. The Rev. Bandula told me in his soft voice that just before his death, at age eighty, the Buddha had instructed that his body be cremated and his ashes divided into eight portions. Over each, a special stupa was to be built, and at the sight of these, the followers of the teachings would be blessed. The silver stupa at the altar contained relics from one of the original boxes, he explained, making the society's building a sacred site.

"Do you know the story of the Buddha's passing?" he inquired.

"Please tell me." I had read several accounts, but Rev. Bandula's offer seemed so unusual, I didn't wish to deflect him. Although polite and friendly, he was a monk of few words. He had never before initiated a discussion with me on any subject, let alone something so weighty as the death of the Buddha.

"He was an old man," the monk began, his voice soothing just to hear. "He fell sick and knew that death would soon visit him.

Propped up on one side, he told his disciples to gather around. They asked him for final instructions, and he said he had withheld nothing from them. Now, it was up to them to practise whatever truth they found in his teachings. He reminded them that all things decay and pass away, to train with diligence, and rely only on themselves. Then he passed through the four stages of meditation, entered Nirvana, and left his body behind. The younger monks wept and rolled about on the ground. But the elder monks scolded them and reminded them again of the teacher's last instructions."

I thanked him for his account, and the intention behind it that I read in his compassionate eyes. All things decay and pass away.

Next day I decided to finish what I could of my "research" before I had to leave the country. I went to Belur Math, the headquarters of the Ramakrishna Mission, hoping to discover something more about Hindu tantric practices. Although Ramakrishna's ecstatic devotion to Kali did not particularly attract me, it was the best lead I had. The mission, following the founder's pan-spiritual approach, was built with a Buddhist gate, a Hindu facade, Muslim windows and balconies, and laid out like a cathedral, in the shape of a cross. Inside, a white-clad clerk gave me some pamphlets and indicated that I was free to look around on my own. I wandered the cool, vacant halls. Despite the culture-clashing architecture, the inside of the main building seemed weirdly modest.

I looked through a doorway and saw an Indian woman in a plain white sari sitting alone on a cushion, eyes half-closed in meditation. Although her hair was heavily streaked with silver, her body was slender as a dancer's, and she held the lotus posture with such attractive grace that I stared at her openly. Her painted lips curved slightly upward in a delicately chiselled smile. As I gazed, spellbound for that moment, the woman looked up straight at me, her eyes black and shining.

"I . . . I'm sorry," I stammered, flushing red. "I'm just looking around."

"Come, have a seat," she said, indicating a sitting cushion by her side. Her accent was slight, inflected more towards the North American than the Indian lilt.

Hesitantly, I entered the room. My shyness felt silly: it was the Indian taboo about being alone with a woman, and though she was old enough to be my mother, her beauty had cast such a spell over me that I felt awkward, as if some watchman would come and surprise us in the indecent act of conversation.

"My name is Aditi," she said, extending her hand for me to shake. Her wrist was small, the fingers long and cool, yet the grip firm. She shook with a single strong downward stroke, then smiled at my disorientation.

"Perhaps you have been in India such a long time, Western manners have become strange to you? I assume by your accent you are Canadian? Yes? Perhaps you have some purpose here at Belur Math?"

"Thank you. Actually, yes. I've got just one day left in Calcutta, perhaps in India. Before I left, I wanted to find out more about the tantric practices of Ramakrishna."

"Tantric? Then look to the moon, not to the finger pointing at the moon."

"Excuse me?"

"To penetrate his secrets, look not to Ramakrishna, but to she who filled his life, to Kali Mahadevi, goddess of Tantra."

"What does 'Mahadevi' mean?"

"*Maha*: great; *devi*: goddess. Devi is the Sanskrit root of your English word *divine,* and you still use it today for the closest thing to goddesses your culture can bear to recognize—divas."

I laughed. "That's not my current image of Kali."

"No, it is not," Aditi said sternly. "To you, if you are typical, and I think you must be, she is a fearsome goddess of blood sacrifice."

"But also a devourer of demons," I added, eager to seem more than typical, "the personification of feminine power that can destroy male aggression, the wrathful aspect of Shiva's wife. And I know behind this, she is shakti, life-force energy, the half of Shiva's nature he split off to make birth possible."

I suppose I expected some sort of gold star for my good answer, and when her eyes glinted dark and hard, I felt afraid.

"Oh, I see you have been well indoctrinated," she said with heavy scorn. "No, Kali is no derivative goddess. Before the male priests ever dreamed of Shiva, Kali *was*. The oldest relics of the Indus Valley civilization are stone and terracotta statues of her as fertile mother, belly swollen, breasts full. For thousands of years she was worshipped across the land. She was the Earth, the Mother who brought forth life, who fed it with her body and then consumed it back into herself in order to begin the cycle once again: Goddess the Creatrix, Goddess the Preserver, Goddess the Destroyer. Could men create life out of their bodies? Could they nourish it? No, their worthless teats bore witness to their derivative, secondary nature.

"When the Aryans invaded the Indus civilization more than three millennia ago, their Brahmin caste of priests set out to conquer goddess worship. They assigned Kali's triune Godhead to the male deities, Vishnu, Brahma, Shiva, and tried to banish her. They made her unclean, a creature of cremation grounds, an outcast, a demon of wild places worshipped by the uncivilized jungle tribes who remembered her. Did you ever wonder why Kali is black? That is the colour of the pre-Aryan race, thought by Indians to be so ugly.

"But the Brahmin couldn't keep Kali out. They couldn't explain the universe without her, as the creation propaganda of the Vedic scriptures so well reveal. Just like the priests, the male gods of their invention did not possess the power to create regenerative life. They needed shakti, a principle undeniably feminine. So the gods pleaded with Shiva to split his universal nature and produce Shakti as his derivative half, so that the goddess could come into existence, and from her, woman, the obvious source of life. Such a convoluted, tortuous, cosmology they devised to reduce the Mother of All to Shiva's consort! Even so, the priests still feared her powers. They named the present age Kaliyuga—an age of degeneracy and destruction—because they knew the goddess they had failed to banish was not just an icon, but the force of Shakti itself. And when the goddess arises once again, it will literally be the destruction of the male cosmology, and the birth of a new age.

"Until that time, the Black Goddess still embodies for us the entire truth of the Great Mother: As Shakti, she is sex, the most unfathomable power in the universe. Kali gives birth, Kali suckles the living, and Kali eats the dead, welcoming her children back once more into her womb. Never forget, women are the stronger, more lethal sex: we have the power to create, and this must be balanced with the power to destroy."

Hackles raised along my neck as Aditi spoke. Was Kali the primordial Earth Goddess, the shakti energy of the Tantrists, *and* the destructive force of Kaliyuga? I could hardly hold it all together. Aditi continued.

"But back to where we began. Divas, so blindly worshipped in your society, also embody the presence of Kali. Think of your divas, conjure their appearance: in what explicit way do they resemble the goddess?"

I thought hard. The force of Aditi's words was making me sweat. What did Kali look like? Four arms, necklace of severed heads, girdle of severed arms, tongue stuck out of a red and bloodied mouth—

"Lipstick?"

"Yes," she said vehemently. She seemed pleased. At last I got a gold star. "Now, the blood on Kali's lips represents each aspect of her divinity: as Destroyer, she takes life and consumes it. As Preserver, the blood represents the vital force that nourishes. As Creatrix, it symbolizes the triune blood that flows from her lower mouth at first sex, menses and childbirth. You are not shy, no? We are talking metaphysics? Good. So even in your spiritless culture, your divas and all those who imitate them adorn themselves in the likeness of the Great Goddess."

"But why do we only call singers divas? Why not actresses or beauty queens?" I asked.

"Of course there is an aspect of the goddess in them too. Although this cannot be clearly demonstrated etymologically, I believe there is a special aspect singers alone reveal. Do you know the meaning of Kali's wreath of severed heads? No? There are, in faithful renderings, exactly fifty of them, the same number as letters of the Sanskrit alphabet. Kali, you see, is also Mother of the Word. Logos, singer of the song of the original creation.

"Ah, perhaps this strikes you closer to home, the claim of Kali's divinity over the territory of the Christian God?" She laughed without a trace of ill will. "But you came here searching for what you can learn from her. Now that you know better who she is, perhaps you are ready to receive, for she has already offered you her boon. You have noticed, no doubt, that her statues have four arms. The upper right is raised in blessing; the lower right extended towards you, offering her bounty. The upper left holds a bloody sword, and the lower left, a freshly severed, bleeding human head."

"So how do you get the blessing and avoid the machete?" I asked.

"No," she replied fiercely. "The boon is won only when you accept both sides of her, including pain, sorrow, decay, death and destruction. These are not to be overcome and conquered. Run from her horrors, and you run from her blessings. To deny death, to act as if your ego is the centre of things, that must be protected from pain and preserved as long as possible, this is the real death. But embrace Kali as she is, kiss her bloody tongue and feel all four arms embrace you at once, then you have life, you have freedom. This, my young friend, this is Kali's boon."

Aditi went on to tell me how Kali was known throughout the ancient world: *Kele* to the Irish, *Cale* to the Saxons, *Caillech* to the inhabitants of Caledonia, now known as Scotland. The Aztecs called her *Coaticue*, and in parts of Europe she wore the disguise of the Black Madonna. I couldn't hold much more in my mind. I was reeling when Aditi said she had to go, and our interview came to a sudden close. I pressed my palms together in the gesture of respect and bowed low. I asked if I could visit her again. She said no, she was leaving next morning for her ashram in Orissa.

I passed safely through the confusion of the Writers' Building the following morning and presented myself to Mukherjee for his verdict. He informed me that my visa request would definitely be turned down. He explained that his office had the authority only to say no or pass decisions on to the head office in Delhi. But if I insisted, he would accept my application nonetheless, although the effort would be futile. I nodded and he wobbled his head from side to side. He instructed me to contact security control ten days hence.

"Ten days?" I struggled to keep my voice calm. "Do you think a decision will be reached by then?"

"Fifteen days then."

"Ah, do you think it could be as long as three weeks? That would give me time to take a trip to the south."

"Three weeks."

I thanked him, smiled, left, turned around and asked, "Four?"

"Come back as soon as you can," he told me with a smile that seemed benign, though not necessarily benevolent.

Rev. Bandula agreed to pass along a message to Sabina, if she should telephone, that I was headed south and would call in frequently to get any message from her. Then I took the long, two-night train ride south to Madras.

From Madras I visited the temple ruins of Mamallapuram on the Bay of Bengal, and wandered through the great eroded carvings of yet another vanished kingdom. I sat on the beach near to a great Shiva temple barely a few metres from the tide line. Grain by grain, the stone was turning back into sand, worn away by wave and wind. What, I wondered, had urged the builders to place a temple here, defying the elements, denying death? I closed my eyes to meditate. I could feel the sun penetrating my exposed skin, turning it raw and red. A steady wind whipped away the moisture of my sweat and caused my lips to crack, while I let my mind go free.

After a time, a picture of Buddha under the Bodhi Tree came to me, and, in a state akin to lucid dreaming, I decided to let the familiar scene unfold. I saw Mara, peeking around the corner of the Mahabodhi stupa. In this incarnation, he wore a white blazer and black turtleneck, his red hair cut short. In fact, the Devil was the spitting image of Jerry. He sent his demons to torment the meditator. Some were multi-headed, half-human and half-beast, but as each wailed out its fearsome call, and elicited no response, it shrivelled and fell silent. Other chimeras then took shape, bent on breaking Buddha's concentration: showroom automobiles, colour TVs, a radio, telephone, home computer, stocks and bonds, piles of cash. They swirled around him like a storm and then fell to the earth like ash, like snowflakes, melting as they touched ground. The next wave of Mara's forces took the shape of humans, chattering their pleas and promises in Buddha's ear: teachers, policemen, tax collectors, priests, politicians, bureaucrats (one looking exactly like Mr. Besares), soldiers, beggars, saints, parents, each squeaking out its last, false note, then turning into dust.

Then Mara sent out his three prize lures, his lascivious daughters. They draped their feather boas around Buddha, ran their fingers down his cheek. Noticing his eyes were only half-closed, the Devil's daughters started to strip, removing their veils one by one while Mara conducted a sleazy Bourbon Street band in the background. Now naked, they threw their hands around his neck, rubbed their breasts against his arms. One thrust her chest out to put a nipple in his mouth, and at that moment, without breaking from concentration, the Buddha, with his inner eye, undressed them further. His gaze stripped them of their youth, causing their skin to wrinkle and sag, their flesh to shrivel, teeth grow long, mouths cave in, hair fade to brittle grey. With his mind he peeled away their skin, layers of subcutaneous fat, slack sinews, innards. He pared them to the bone, and saw that there was nothing desirable in the three heaps that remained, like so much refuse from a tannery.

Mara was furious. With a gesture, he turned the band to toads, his face red, eyes blazing fire. Then, in an instant, he was calm again. He pulled the cuffs of his jacket, examined his sleeves to make sure they were of neatly equal length, then approached the Bodhi Tree.

"Ah, excuse me, O revered meditator. I can tell you are in the midst of something you think is important, but I just wanted to give you a little advice. See, I know you just want folks to be happy, but you're meditating up the wrong tree if you want to blame their misery on me. I know my turf, and I tell you, delusion's the finest thing ever happened to the human race. I'm a man of principle, and my principle, as you well know, is that pleasure is good, and pain is bad. What's wrong with that? Look what it has produced. Folks doing good deeds. Folks giving alms to the poor. Folks being kind to their children. Why? might you ask. Because if they don't—" Mara stepped dramatically aside, allowing a whoosh of flame to appear from his feet. "Because if they don't they know they're going to fry in hell for many lifetimes. But if they're good, they know they'll get their reward: a cushy rebirth. See, desiring pleasure and fearing pain is the beauty of the system. Get folks thinking about that, and they'll keep their noses clean. And in the meantime, they don't have to think about what to do. Just run towards pleasure, and flee the pain. Life is simple. Call it delusion if you must, but all the religions that are ever going to bring order to the world depend on it.

"You want to break it all up? Then you are going to rain down misery upon the planet. Imagine, people not fearing pain, not desiring pleasure. How could you even run a business, let alone a moral order? Who would buy stuff if they didn't think it would make them happy? And look at you, what kind of an example do you expect to be for humankind? You quit your job. You deserted your wife. You're a deadbeat dad, and you're a welfare bum dependent on handouts. You're a loser. It's not you who should be sitting under that tree, but me. I've thought it all out, I've got a system that works, and I've got the market share to prove it.

"But, say you really want to accomplish something: you join up with me. Preach goodness. Talk about the just reward, and warn people away from sin! They can always use a little pep talk, and, you know, I think you've got the right stuff for it. You could make a real name for yourself. What do you say? Go back and be prince again. Pass benevolent laws. Don't just sit here on your ass.

"Still won't talk, huh? Going to do it your way? Well, then you're just one more set of bones to be rattled, rolled and tossed in the dustheap. Who's going to stand up for you when you try and preach your message? The deluded aren't going to get it, so who? I've got the crowds on my side. Hey, everybody, who's for Mara?"

The demon army reappeared in a huge stadium, roaring, cheering and waving red, white and black pennants with "Go Mara!" written across them. With a wave of his hand, they fell silent.

"You got no friends here, Buddha boy," Mara concluded with a sneer. "No witnesses that there's any merit in your path."

The Buddha looked up. He frowned for a second. Mara smiled a sickly sweet smile. Then Buddha gave a short laugh, as if, suddenly, the answer was so simple. He lifted a hand from his lap and pushed his fingertips into the black earth.

A woman's voice pierced the air, held a single note, loud and clear. The ground shook like an earthquake and opened. Climbing up a subterranean golden staircase she arose, microphone in hand. Her skin was black and seemed to glisten. From her head a hundred black braids fell like shining leather whips down the length of her back. Her cheekbones were strong, forehead broad, her eyes large, black and flashing. All she wore was bright red lipstick and a necklace that looked like pearls, but were in fact a string of tiny skulls. Her breasts were large and round, coming out to pointed tips even blacker than her skin, her belly firm, hips solid yet undulating with every motion. She glided as she walked, and looking down, one could see her ankles merged into the earth; below the surface, instead of feet, she had roots. Her voice was rich and resonant, and the note she held now swelled into a song:

"Ooooo, how I love that Buddha man!
He's the one can touch me,
Like no other man can.
Ooooo, the way he touch me.
Ain't no right or wrong.
Ooooo, the way he touch me.
He knows pain and pleasure are one.
So won't you dive in, baby,
You're gonna know
That Mother Earth, Oooooh,
She's gonna love you so."

Then she flowed towards Mara. She was taller than he, and he shrank back, his red face turning ashen. She pointed one long, strong, red-tipped finger at him.

"Now what *you* seem to have forgotten," she said, her voice sliding up and down, but her tone severe, eyes fiery, "is that you were not, in fact, here first. Whenever you use the word 'turf,' you just remember who you're talking about. Principle? Ha! You scare them with ghosts and reward them with baubles, like those three little bitches of yours. Not a crumb of earth in them. Or riches? Not worth the leaves on my trees. Freedom's the only currency in which my shakti flows, and all your powers can't generate a single spark. You leave me cold."

As she spoke, Mara began to change. His white jacket becoming transparent wings. His black body grew additional legs and eyes, all the while shrinking so fast that in seconds he had assumed the size and shape of a fly. He buzzed, circling wildly, and then flew off, round the corner of the monument.

"That's right," the Earth Diva laughed as he fled, "you go lord it over the flies."

Then she turned and smiled at the Buddha, and she noticed that although he remained immobile, his robes had shifted subtly in his lap.

"Hey, is that Ashoka's pillar in your pocket, or are you just happy to see me?" she said sweetly.

She looked at him fondly, sighed, and slowly shook her head. She approached the Bodhi Tree and kissed him briefly on the mouth, leaving a smear of red on his lips.

"Later, babe. I know you got work to do," she said, her voice husky and tender. "I'll catch you when you're through." She winked at him, and walked down the golden staircase.

And at that instant, the Buddha was enlightened.

CHAPTER FIFTEEN

ELEPHANT POOP HAPPENS

Mysore

January 18, Mysore, South India

Dear Wendy,

There is a saying in India: Patience is the sandal which the wise man wears because he cannot pave the road with leather. This past week has been one full of blisters. I'm writing you from a bench at the Mysore Zoo, just across from a pair of rare white tiger cubs recently born here. There's lots of palm trees everywhere, and the breeze is refreshingly cool. I'm resting for a bit in this oasis, and putting my sore feet up for a rest.

I spent a little time in a puritanical and celibate ashram near here, and when I left, called the Mahabodhi Society in Calcutta, where Sabina and I stayed. I've called four times now, without word from her. On my last call, the monk said I had a letter from the Home Passport Office. He opened it and read it for me. It said I had seven days to report to the Calcutta office and then leave the country. The letter was already two days old, so I went to the FRO here in Mysore. I explained my problem to the passport officer, and asked if he could grant me permission to leave India for Thailand via Madras. He assured me it would be a simple procedure. At his request I wrote a two-page report of all my particulars, and agreed to come back the following day.

I returned to my room and unburdened myself of passport and moneybelt, being careful to cover them up with some papers before I left, as an instinctive traveller's precaution. When I got back to my room that evening, there was a different lock on my door. It was the little padlock I use to keep my bag closed during train travel, not the heavy-duty lock the hotel provides. Using my Swiss Army knife, I managed to take the little lock apart and get inside. My room had been burglarized. My backpack with all my possessions was gone.

Now, here's where karma comes in: for some months I have fantasized about travelling possessionless through India like an ascetic wanderer, truly free of all worldly cares like books and clothes and money. Just following my bliss. (I know this sounds crazy, but trust me, tens of thousands of Indians do it.) Obviously, this burglary was a gift from the gods. All afternoon, I had been just the penniless, wandering ascetic I had always aspired to be, and hadn't even noticed. All I had to do now was turn, walk down the hall, and away, into the embracing arms of Mother India. Instead, I felt like an icicle severed from the rooftop, speeding towards the concrete below, ready to shatter. Suddenly I remembered my moneybelt. I looked at the table. There were papers on it still. I couldn't breathe. Hands trembling, I reached out and pulled the papers away. My moneybelt, traveller's cheques and passport were all intact. I exhaled. I was myself again—a rich tourist from Canada. I was so happy.

I called the police, and the local inspector came down, made me fill out another report. Two days later, the hotel manager told me the occupant of the room next to mine had disappeared, and he thought we should check out his room together. He opened the lock, and inside we found the contents of my backpack, minus my instamatic camera, which I never used, and my Gore-Tex rain jacket, which I will miss. But it was a cheap price to pay for getting my journals back. We called the inspector to come wrap up the case. He came down, collected everything back into my bag, and then took it with him to headquarters. He said it was evidence in the case. To make the story short, I had to hire a lawyer, go to court before a judge and post a bond for 150 rupees, promising to return the bag and all its contents should the case ever come to trial. All in all, I spent three days fighting to get the damn burden back on my shoulders.

Meanwhile, every day I'm going back to the FRO. When I show up, the official thumbs through my report as if he has never seen it before and asks me to write a new one. I was going crazy. When he finally gave me a signed document, it said, in summary: "The foreigner has requested exit permit to leave India via Madras; therefore we grant him permission to return to Calcutta to obtain exit permit to leave India via Madras." The damn point of my request was so that I wouldn't have to return to Calcutta! He was granting me absolutely nothing. Something snapped in me, Wendy. I stormed into the chief officer's quarters and began haranguing him on the stupidity of his subordinates. Unimpressed, the chief told me not to insult his men. "You have your choice," he said. "I will sign this paper as is, or you can go with nothing."

And so, here I am, a humiliated, exhausted man, resting my feet on a park bench, and wishing I was wearing thicker leather.

Now, something interesting is happening . . .

Back to you now. While I was writing this letter, a zookeeper was taking an old elephant out for a walk along the zoo paths. It had mottled skin and a bad limp in one leg, but it was big. Just past my bench, it stopped and spread apart its back legs and pushed out three great bales of steaming elephant poop onto the walkway, and then lumbered on. Well, no amount of shit can surprise me in India any more, but what followed next did. There was a family on the other side of the path that rushed to the scene as the elephant began to poop. The husband wore a dark suit, the wife a bright sari, and the young boy and girl were clean and well dressed. They seemed a model middle-class family. As soon as the elephant moved on, they kicked off their sandals and jumped in, tromping up and down over the hot, spongy mound, laughing and squelching with their feet as if it was the greatest game. I couldn't stand it. A man in a white shirt with pens in his pocket walked by. I accosted him in English, which he understood, and asked if he could explain the scene. He was embarrassed.

"You see, it is not very scientific. Just superstition," he stammered. "But, there is a custom that if you step in the dung of an elephant, you will become strong. It is *not* scientific," he said again, as if by way of apology.

"Hmmm, the energy of an elephant remains in his dung, and people can draw some of its strength upward through their feet by stepping in it. It is logical," I replied, sounding like Spock. "But I think I'll give it a miss."

"Thank you," said the embarrassed Indian, and hurried on his way.

I tried to call the Mahabodhi Society again three times today, but couldn't get a line through. You see, I wrote Sabina when I got the FRO's notice. At that time, I thought I was going to get permission to leave from Madras, and so I wrote her a letter, explaining it all, and saying goodbye. What if she gets the letter and leaves before I get to Calcutta? Or what if she's there, and I have to leave at once because my seven-day deadline has passed? These are not pleasant thoughts to take with me on a three-day train ride. Now that the family members have their sandals back on, maybe I should slip mine off and give the poop a try. God knows, I can use all the strength I can get.

Love you Wendy, your brother,
Tim

At Madras I changed trains and rode the rest of the way to Calcutta in the company of three educated Madrasis who shared with me their bananas and polite conversation. The second morning, after we had finished a breakfast of biscuits and coffee from my companions' Thermos, a clan of six emaciated villagers boarded our car and tried to settle in our compartment. The Madrasi woman was visibly repulsed by the intruders. Her husband tried firmly to shoo them out of his territory, preferably into another car, smiling apologetically at me all the while.

"These rural folk, they are terribly dirty and ignorant," he said. "Look! They can hardly understand a civil word one tries to say to them!"

"Why not let them sit with us?" I replied. "There's room for at least two more on these seats." I slid over towards the third Madrasi so we were pressed against the window, and motioned to the villagers who stood clustered timidly in the aisle.

"My dear fellow!" the Madrasi protested, uncomfortably aware that it was too late to argue and too gracious to insist further when he had already lost. "Well, come and sit over here then," he conceded at last, motioning me to come and fill up the empty place on their side of the compartment, and leaving his male companion to hold on to the window seat on the other side while the villagers made camp around the vacated open space. The Madrasi woman looked at me as if I had most villainously betrayed her hospitality.

The newcomers slid two great burlap bundles under the seat benches and heaved the rest onto the luggage racks which hung overtop and along the aisle. Gaunt, shrivelled people, they looked more like nomads than farmers, and the bundles probably contained all their worldly possessions. The two younger men crawled up into the luggage rack and squatted next to their belongings. The other four squeezed into the space for two on the opposite side of the compartment, leaving ample room between themselves and the third Madrasi, who sat by the window and set his eyes on the passing dry fields.

Conversation died, giving me the opportunity to study the old peasant couple up close. The patriarch of the group was grey-grizzled, with frightened, dark-circled eyes. The rim of his eye sockets stuck out from beneath his brow with no flesh padding to soften the lines of his skull. He sat with his feet planted flat on the seat, legs folded up like an upright lawn chair, so that the great knobs of his kneecaps came up to his chin. His limbs were just worn skin loosely drawn over bones. The contours of his femur could be distinctly traced to where they disappeared in the grey folds of his waist wrap.

His wife wore a grey sari of the coarsest cloth I had ever seen on an Indian woman. There was no pattern to the material and she wore no blouse underneath. Every now and then a long nipple would slip out from under the front swath of her garment. It drooped against her flat chest like a limp purple worm. She had the face and eyes of an old camel: dull, unintelligent, worn out. Her bare feet were camel's feet. The soles, covered with thick calluses, were so cracked and blackened that one could not tell where flesh ended and earth began. Around the middle toe of each foot a dull metal ring was wrapped, matching the simple pewter bands she wore on each wrist. Her teeth were long and rotted black at the gums. She never spoke, never raised her eyes.

The six accepted their place as lower beings, coughing quietly throughout the journey. Although we shared the same compartment, which they had taken eagerly enough, it was clear we inhabited two concurrent but separate universes. And that from their viewpoint, the Madrasis and I were as indistinguishable as coconuts. I wondered what they could possibly hope to find in the noise and rushing streets of Calcutta. Were they some of the many thousands who travel to the city because the countryside has starved them out? It seemed likely. They would search for a piece of earth under a bridge or alongside a railway track or gutter to set up a burlap tent. The younger ones would try to pull rickshaws for the few rupees a day they would be allowed to keep. And the old woman—it was hard even to imagine her raising her arms to beg.

"And this is how ignorance is reincarnated, in as pure a form as you will ever see it," said Philippe, perched on the luggage rack next to the younger members of the clan.

I could see his skinny legs inside his robes as he sat kicking the air with his feet. He was, in fact, not all that much heavier looking than the old man. He still wore the tattered sandals he had on during our prayer flag planting trek, which made his feet look large and duck-like on the end of his spindly legs.

"Your mind has grown soft, Tim," he continued. "Lured by the lurid promises of Kali worshippers, your imagination, your fantasies, your ever-hopeful dick, are binding you to the endless wheel all the more firmly. And you call it freedom? Take a look. This is how the human spirit inures itself to eternal rebirth, suffering and death. Look closely. You will see no phantom spark, no divine candle in the darkness. Just a karmic twitch, the urge to eat, shit, fuck, until the final spasm of death."

"And why do you condemn it, as if their earthen lives are any different than yours—except, of course, that you, monk, have stopped your fucking?" It was Aditi, sitting where the third Madrasi sat. She smiled on the wretched villagers, and ran her graceful hand along the camel woman's dusty cheek. "Yes, their misery is very real: it is *tamas*, the path of ignorance. Yet Mother Kali enfolds them in her arms as equally and completely as these"—her delicate hand swept towards the Madrasis and to me. "To her, and her alone, the universe is one."

"And this is why I prefer the mountains and the instructions of my guru," retorted Philippe, "a way off that stinking wheel."

"Your aversion reveals itself, monk," she spat out the last word with distaste, "and will forever keep you bound to that which you would escape. What repose can there possibly be for one who flees from Kali's embrace?" Aditi raised her dark arms towards Philippe and simultaneously towards me. For the first time, I realized she had two pairs of them. The open gesture made me respond, instinctively, leaning towards her as if towards my lover. For an instant, the face of the disgruntled Madrasi broke through her mask. He looked annoyed at me, and I leaned back, allowing the fantasy to resume.

Philippe pulled his dangling legs up into meditation posture, but it looked like a defensive move. Aditi had crossed both sets of arms and was awaiting his response.

"It's not these human worms who repel me, nor Kali's arms," he said, "only the illusion that in them lies bliss. You say there is no escape from death and destruction, so celebrate, slaughter goats to the

Black Goddess, wear flowers in your hair. You say, 'Surrender up to life, and this way touch the divine.' I say, then you are an accomplice of Mara's: just another daughter putting garlands on a corpse."

Aditi's eyes flashed. I noticed now that when she spoke, her tongue and lips were bright red. Her lipstick began to smudge along the edges of her mouth.

"You may escape my most intimate embrace for now, monk, by my caprice. But there will be a time when it tightens and you will cleave to me and call me Mother."

"Phhh, *mon Dieu*," said Philippe with a dismissive wave of his hand. "Break this body as many times as you please. But every mantra, every ritual, sharpens my mind as a hard flint which one day will pierce your veil."

Aditi laughed scornfully, red lipstick now running down the sides of her black cheeks. "And you, O Buddhist, what exists besides your form, and the sense impressions it engenders? Within what abstract realm does your immortal karmic twitch seek its peace?" Her upper-left hand held a machete now, and she pointed it at him as she spoke.

Philippe jumped down from the upper berth and sat on the knee of the camel woman, right next to Aditi. He smiled an arrogant smile and looked her in the eye.

"In this realm, right now, right here, I seek my peace."

"Then you shall have it," cried Aditi.

"No!" I shouted, thrusting my arms forward. Hot liquid burst upon my hands. Philippe's corpse, convulsing in spasms, fell to the floor at our feet. His head hung in Aditi's lower-left hand. Because he had no hair, she was holding on to him by his left ear, which stretched and left his face dangling at an angle.

He smiled at me out of one side of his mouth and said, "Women, phhh . . . ," then rolled his eyes up into his head, and was still.

Aditi dropped the head with a hard ceramic thunk onto the compartment floor.

The Madrasi next to me was dabbing at my wet arm with a cotton cloth. His friend on the opposite window seat picked up my fallen cup. I had spilled coffee from the little table beneath the carriage window, as if due to a violent twitch in my sleep. My Madrasi companions eyed me a little nervously now. The camel people did not seem to notice, but continued their dull staring at the floor all the way to Calcutta.

I found the abbot and Rev. Bandula in the carpeted lounge of the Mahabodhi Society. They were both surprised to see me, and quite relieved that I had a letter from the Mysore FRO since my seven-day period had expired three days ago. Rev. Bandula, noticing my anxiousness, answered the question I was afraid to ask.

"She's here."

"When?"

"Three days ago."

I mumbled quick words of thanks, and tried not to race out of their presence. I ran down three flights of stairs to the entrance, out into the lane, and down to College Street where a small roadside stand sold garlands as temple offerings. By the time I had flown back up the stairs to our room, yellow flowers in hand, I was panting and sweating heavily. The light was on, the door closed, but no answer. I pushed it open. The shower was running down the hall. I would have liked to shower too before seeing her, but she would be here any minute. I had not dared hope for this, all through my time in the south, and not dared to dream we would be given a third chance. I left the door ajar, to avoid complete surprise, and sat on the bed to wait. Her footsteps slowed as she noticed the open door. Her face peered in, and her mouth fell open in surprise. I garlanded her and kissed her lips. She did not respond, just stared at me, a tight smile frozen on her face.

"You're crazy!" she said. "They will put you in jail. Your letter said you had gone to Thailand. Now I will have to visit you in some rotting cell in Calcutta. Ugh."

"No, no." I waved my note from the Mysore FRO like a truce flag. "I tried to get out through Madras, but they wouldn't let me leave. My letter, you see, they insisted I return to the office here."

I was still sweating, and thought I sounded incoherent and insecure, as if she was the detaining official, rather than my lover to whom I had, however momentarily, returned. I had the overwhelming sense of being a great inconvenience, as if the garland was a lasso meant to drag her off her path once more.

"Are you on your way to a meeting?"

"Yes. Well, it's a few hours yet. Have a shower and we'll go have lunch. You look awful."

"Two nights on a train," I grinned.

"So you win a prize for dirtiness."

At lunch, I filled in all the details of my visa battle, and she in turn told me her tale of closed museums, obstreperous curators and missing men with the keys. She would have to retrace her path once more, and it was highly unlikely she would be able to complete her research within the three months remaining in her sponsorship. She looked worn down, the circles under her eyes had darkened. Her skin had lost the golden tan that had deepened in Puri, and now looked grey. Her conversation seemed mechanically animated, as if she feared quiet moments when one of us might say something that mattered, or reach out a hand.

"But look," she said, brightening a little, "I'm thinner. You were making me fat with your eating all the time."

By the end of lunch she had me half-convinced that the FRO was simply going to throw me in irons, and as she went off to her appointment, I steeled myself once more for the Writers' Building at BBD Bagh Square. I said I would call her from jail that evening. I found my way swiftly through the familiar part of the maze to Mukherjee's desk. I sat and waited for an hour until the official arrived. When I presented him with my Mysore papers, he nodded and asked if I was ready to leave. I said I only needed to buy a plane ticket for Bangkok, which could be accomplished as quickly as necessary.

"No hurry," he said munificently. "You may have ten days to organize your affairs."

I restrained myself from kissing his semi-bald head. It took him twenty minutes to complete the paperwork and stamp my passport, giving me a valid document for the first time in over a month.

I rushed outside and headed across BBD Bagh Square for my meeting with Sabina. Not watching where I was going, I bumped into a child. He reeled back from me without a word and kept on walking. He was tethered by a leash around his waist. A sickly, icy feeling ran through to my bones. It was the boy with no arms. In a second, the blind hag passed. I could see her milky eyes, the wrinkled and collapsed mouth, one cheek horribly distended. She spat a gob of red blood in my direction. I leapt away, too late to avoid its spatter on my feet. I choked back my scream. Betel nut, I realized with relief. She was sucking pan.

I met Sabina on Park Street at a hidden treasure that Nagel from the Goethe Institute told her about: an ice-cream cone stand.

"You've got a problem now," I said in mock seriousness when she arrived. "What will you do with me in the country for ten more days? God knows, I'll follow you all the way back to Bhagalpur."

"What are you talking about?" She actually seemed to blanch.

"I'm legal for ten more days. I can go with you."

The server handed her her butter pecan, and me my chocolate cone. Sabina took a long slow lick, twirling the cone so that her tongue swept the entire surface of the ice cream. She was stalling. Before she said it, I felt like a fool.

"Well, maybe the three of us can travel together then."

"Three of us?"

"You remember Bruce, the Canadian photographer we met at Nagel's? Well, he has finished his assignment in Calcutta and he said he wanted to see a bit of village life before returning home." Her voice trailed off.

I raised one eyebrow. Inwardly, I felt my heart contract as if a hand with long fingernails was squeezing it.

"It's not like that," she said.

"I thought something might be up when you seemed so anxious to get me out of the country, or into jail."

"I thought you *were* out of the country."

"I tried to get through."

"But it's nothing like that, anyway. He's not my type."

"Not one of your types."

"Somehow these things just happen, though. It will be very good for my work. You see, he will be able help me with photographs, and travelling in Bihar alone, for a woman—"

"Stop, Sabina. Forgive me. Look, it's my premise that any emotionally mature and physically healthy man would fall over at first sight of you."

"He's changed his tickets so he can make the trip with me, but I don't think he would mind the three of us travelling together."

"As long as he doesn't mind having his own room."

She looked as me reproachfully, licking her cone.

"I'll try not to get aggressive," I said.

"I haven't been so good with my pills since you've been gone. When we make love, we will have to be careful . . ."

This was the closest to a tender remark she had made since my return, and I had to press back a sudden trembling.

"I didn't know if I'd ever see you again," I said, looking down at the trash and decaying curbside. "I didn't expect just to drop my pack on your bed and my head on your pillow."

She smiled for a fraction of a second. She seemed distant, aloof, self-possessed.

"Now I have to run to meet Bruce for coffee, and then I am to have dinner with Nagel. I will tell Bruce that maybe we can go as a threesome"—I winced at the word—"and we'll see what he says."

We agreed to meet up after dark, back at the Mahabodhi Society.

I wandered the shops, and caught a glimpse of myself in a large mirror. I looked skinny and sunburned. My clothes, none of which had been washed since they had been fondled by a thief, were grey and greasy. As a returning lover, I was not a pretty sight. But it hurt to be so swiftly replaced, especially by Bruce. It was just what she had done after we parted in Patna, running straight to Jerry. Maybe she just can't exist without a man after her, I thought. But that didn't make sense; her reputation demanded she be on her own at the university. There was another possibility I didn't like to contemplate: that our parting had hurt her and finding another man was a necessary compensation.

Maybe her protestations of love were more than a colour on her artist's palette. What if she too had felt the unspeakable ecstasy of shakti, understood what we had touched together, and yet watched me pull back? I had said it plainly then: the force would bond us too intimately for what either of us wanted or needed. Why did I speak for her, when what I was really saying was that I didn't want to be deeply bonded to her? No wonder she was angry, diffident about travelling together when we met the second time.

In Puri she had offered to abandon her research to stay with me. I didn't really take her seriously. My answer had been a brush-off decorated with pretty words, and it had made her sad: a second blunt rejection. Last she heard of me, I was flitting around the south—not tracking her down—and on my way to Thailand. Perhaps I had taken a big chunk out of her armour, and she just wanted it to heal up as quickly as possible. Bruce might just be a bandage, and here I had come back to rip the wound wide open once again before skipping the subcontinent for good. Nice guy. So why was she being so aloof?

Of course, it was also possible I was just another lover in a very long line, and the time had come for me to let her go. No, whatever truth dwelled behind her artificial smile, the gods and bureaucrats had conspired to bring us together a third time. Twice I had pulled back from her. Maybe in ten days, the outcome would be different. I wanted this third chance. If need be I would break Bruce's teeth, spiritually speaking, just to get it. I felt suddenly giddy, and began, almost recklessly, to shop.

I bought papaya, incense, candles and fresh bread, sandalwood soap and a packet of razor blades. Street urchins began to cluster around this frenzy of spending, begging for alms. I motioned to them to follow me and led the way to the produce market, where I purchased two pounds of fresh carrots and distributed them to the children one by one. Some nibbled with glee, while the hard-core professionals snubbed the offering, and in one case I had to drop it down the front of a dirty shirt before the boy would clutch it in his hands.

Dusk was approaching. I smelled burning buffalo dung and curry as the evening cooking haze filled the air, and for the first time I felt love for this great heaving, wretched city. The poor, the maimed, taxi drivers, rickshaw pullers, shopkeepers, Kali priests, missionaries, bureaucrats: I could feel how their prayers and scams and suffering made up the music of the city; and if Calcutta often plays a dirge, what a sweeping, grand, complex one it was, not to be tampered with lightly, nor cured by those who would simply eradicate its pain. For the first time I could feel the suffering without the need to turn away from it, burdened with guilt for the rupees pressed in my pockets. Rather, I could take my place within it, add my voice, every note of it, with all its lust, despair and hope.

I bought a poppy-red kurta of finespun linen, almost translucent and flowing, then wandered home through the back streets to prepare myself, once more, for my lover's return. First I dug the grit out from under my toe and fingernails, showered with the sandalwood soap, shaved, washed my filthy clothes, and then dressed in a white-and-purple sarong Sabina had given me as a New Year's present in Puri. I slipped the red kurta over my head. It felt light and billowy. The same feeling swept over me from that first night in the Maharajah Hotel in Varanasi: something delicate, beautiful, almost feminine in its sweetness. She would come home. I would embrace her, seduce her, open her heart once more. I lit the incense and sat on the bed to await my beloved.

She arrived. Her hair was pulled back, wet with perspiration, her skin grimy from the traffic.

"Where did you get that awful kurta?" she said.

"You don't like my kurta?"

"On a woman maybe. But on a man! No. The colour is too bright. Why did you buy such a thing?"

"I like red. Perhaps a darker colour. It looked darker in the shop. But, well, I like it. Is it so bad?"

"It makes your lips look pink."

"So what's wrong with being beautiful?" I said defensively.

"I'm hungry. Let's go for a walk in the Muslim quarter and get some hot milk," she said.

I nodded and jumped up off the bed, laughing.

"Aren't you going to change?"

"Are you kidding? *I* am a Disco Dancer!"

She rolled her eyes and muttered something in German under her breath all the way down six flights of stairs and out into the dark streets.

"Hey!—You're looking splendid!" called one young man from a table at a streetside café. All through the Muslim quarter I got cat-calls and admiring compliments as I picked my way through the dirty alleys. I had to hold up the edge of my sarong to keep it from trailing in the puddles. Sabina, however, was barely speaking to me. She pulled me in to what seemed to me the filthiest milk-stall she could find, with wet floors and grimy benches. A crowd clustered around the bubbling pot at the front, too intent on buying milk to notice the freak-show foreigners.

She told me Bruce had reacted poorly to the news of my return. He said he had expected something like this would happen, after he had gone and changed his air ticket. She seemed sympathetic towards his whining.

"Poor Bruce," I concurred. "It's just awful to think how he would manage all alone in, say, that stinking hotel in Jaipur."

"But he has promised to help with photography for my research," she said pointedly. "And that is important to me."

"So he'd still come with us?"

"He didn't say definitely yes. He said he was going to think about it, and buy some more film tomorrow."

"So a lover being along might make the difference in his coming or not?"

"It's not like that!" she hissed angrily and stood up.

I followed glumly and let my sarong trail in the muck on the walk home.

"If the guy is any kind of a gentleman, he'll know it's time to bow out," I grumbled to myself. "It's what I would do if the sandal were on the other foot."

Back at the Mahabodhi Society, Sabina announced she had some international phone calls to make, and left me alone in the room again. She was gone for an hour and a half, returning just before midnight.

"I'm so tired," she said. She quickly changed into a long cotton nightshirt I had never seen before and lay down on her stomach. "Would you mind?" she asked. "A little back rub?"

I lit a candle on the bedside table and straddled her hips.

"But I may fall asleep," she murmured.

"You do that."

"In the morning, there's a young monk, he brings me tea."

"Oh—that's a new service."

"Yes. He was being very friendly to me. He smiles out the side of his mouth. I told him that's a sign of sexual frustration and he said he's often wondered what sex with a woman was like."

"Oh great, so you're teaching monks?"

She laughed, sleepy. "Of course not. I'm in India to study Mara's daughters, not become one of them."

"So what did you tell him?"

"That sex is like a drug. Very addictive. You have it once, and you want to have it again and again. I told him it's not a good thing for a monk."

"Amen."

I watched the candle flicker as I kneaded the familiar knots along her spine. After a while, I heard the steady rhythm of her breathing. Perhaps she was just pretending. It didn't matter. I stopped, blew out the light, then lay still beside her, eyes open, looking up.

"What are you doing?" she said drowsily.

"Nothing."

She turned on her side. I didn't move. She pressed her cheek against mine, and I reached out to pull her onto me. Then, feeling her resistance, I let go and lay back once more. She slid her head down over my belly and took me in her mouth, her fingers deliberately milking me so that I quickly came. The orgasm was painful, and I bit my fist to avoid making a sound. It left me confused. Was she doing me a favour, doing the best she could without birth control, or just fending off further intimacy in the surest possible way?

CHAPTER SIXTEEN

THE CIRCLE BREAKS

Gangtok

WHEN I AWOKE, Sabina was gone. She returned a few minutes later, hair wet from the shower. She said she had a lot to do, and needed an early start. I went with her to the American Express Office where she received her mail, and while she stood in line, I visited the nearby West Bengal Tourism Office. I had the inspiration that there might be Buddhist sites around Darjeeling relevant to her work. I returned to AmEx and dragged her to the tourism office.

"So you come with me to Darjeeling for eight days, then if it's still what you want to do, you can travel with Bruce to Bihar," I said, showing her the pamphlets. "Wouldn't that solve everything?"

She shook her golden head and showed me a letter. "I got this today from the Indian government. Some problem with my visa extension. It seems complicated, and I will have to go back to my professor in Varanasi to get him to help me with it before travelling into Bihar."

"It couldn't wait a week?"

She gave me a pained expression, as if to say, "Are you, too, blocking me once more?" She sighed a weary sigh. "I just hope Bruce is still willing to go now."

She rushed off to a meeting.

Bruce, I muttered to myself. I wouldn't hang on like he is, whining about changes in plans as if he's dependent on her already, as if he can't travel without her. If he were Jerry, we could fight. But she wants him along for whatever reason. It's got to be up to him to do the honourable thing. If I was him, I'd know it was him she wants, not me. I—Suddenly the world turned inside out. Everything was clear. She never said she wanted me. She's been saying all along she wants him. God fucking Kali Shiva Buddha Christ damn it all. I'm the inconvenience. I'm the one she hoped would have to leave the country. I'm the one, I guess, who just can't take a hint.

It hurt to be so blind, and then to see the light so swiftly.

We met for lunch. She slid in across the white vinyl table from me.

"Sabina," I said, "I've thought about it, and I've decided not to go with you and Bruce to Varanasi. I'll fly to Darjeeling on my own instead."

"But Tim, you know if you come to Varanasi, you will have to stay alone in the Tourist Guest House again. I know you don't want that."

"Sabina, I'm going to Darjeeling. I want you so badly that going my own way is like a wound, but between work and visa problems, I know it would be better for you to be without me. So it's time to let go."

"And in Bihar, we will have to go back to the places you have already been, so I just think you would not—"

"Sabina!"

The commanding tone in my voice stopped her. I spoke slowly and firmly: "I am not going with you. I already bought my airplane ticket to Darjeeling. I leave tomorrow."

"Well, maybe it will work together, the three of us."

"It's done. Let's not talk about it. You've probably got a meeting to get to."

I watched her sink a little in her chair. Relief, I thought, as the muscles around her neck relaxed. She looked at me and smiled.

"Okay, we talk about it later."

I spent the afternoon at the one museum in Calcutta that Sabina had not visited. According to her records, there was no Earth-Touching Gesture there, but to be sure, I had agreed to check it out, as the last act of a dutiful research assistant. I squeezed into a packed tram, inhaling exhaust and human odours, savouring the smells like the last sniff of an expensive wine. I was going to miss this city. The museum was situated by a quiet lake, and after a thorough search for Mara, I settled down beneath a bo tree by the water's edge. The shore was sodden with decomposing orange and yellow wreaths from countless morning rituals, and in their midst was an old sadhu taking a bath. The twisted grey curls of his hair floated like octopus tendrils among the waterlogged yellow and red blossoms. He dunked and spat out water and emerged naked, shameless, with not a glance towards me. He assumed the lotus posture, dripping wet, and let the afternoon sun dry him. I laughed when I recalled my unknowing stint as sadhu for a day. Now, I had neither the freedom of the sadhu nor the ecstasy of a lover: just my backpack and a visa for nine days with nothing to do. It was so damn hard to let go.

I arrived home well ahead of Sabina. There was a message from Bruce under the door, saying he had bought tickets for the morning train. She burst in an hour later, waving her arms theatrically.

"Oh, the traffic! I'm so sorry I'm late! It's the Saraswati Festival, blocking everything."

She looked around the room. "Has Bruce come by?"

"No. Were you expecting him?"

"Well, we were supposed to meet for coffee, and then the traffic—he was going to book tickets for the train tomorrow."

"Hmm. You came late and he was gone?"

She nodded. I laughed.

"And you thought he might show up here instead? Is that why the dramatic entrance? Did you expect us to be fighting? Or find one of us dead on the floor?"

She glared at me.

"I found a message under the door," I said and handed it to her. She read it quickly without comment.

"Come, let's see the parade," she said.

Painted goddess statues and brass bands paraded up College Street. We sat at a restaurant booth and watched the crowds revelling in the sacred strains of "Disco Dancer."

"And who is Saraswati?" I asked.

"Wife of Brahma, goddess of learning."

"No kidding?" I mused. "You know, it's always amazed me, Sabina, that you know so much about Indian religion, and yet you believe in none of it."

Her eyes danced. "And it has always amazed me that you know so little about Indian religion and believe in all of it."

The drums still beat and the lights reflected in through our upper window when we returned to our room to say one more goodbye. She gave me a porcelain bead on a leather thong to wear around my neck: a Buddhist good-luck charm for travellers, she explained. I read a poem I had written for her by the lake that afternoon:

We have eaten our love like a ripe fruit
And these last mouthfuls, I savour with sweet longing,
Knowing that now it is finished.
In the moment we first tasted the tender flesh,
We foresaw we would discard the core
And let our love's seed fall barren in the dust.

Other ripe fruit hold no pleasure for my eye or tongue,
For I have shared the sweetest taste with you.
Yet one future joy awaits: the joy of planting.
And if another fruit is found, the seed I'll nurture
To sprout, shoot, stretch to sapling strength,
Rise to flower and harvest all my life.

I hurt now only because such a tree,
Had it unfolded between you and me,
Would have blossomed with radiance
And borne much joy.

234

Where now our love's seed falls barren,
Even as I lie, panting, on your breast.

"This is another reason why I am leaving you," she said, flushed. She sat down on the bed and clenched her fists.

"It's just a poem," I said lamely. "What don't you like about it?"

"How can you say what will happen next?" She turned her face away from me.

"Maybe I'm not understanding you. Look, so often I want to make a special claim on you. My ego doesn't want to be just one man among many, and I have to beat it back down."

"But you are special."

"I love to hear it, but how can I believe it?"

"Oh, why do I bother!" she yelled.

She grabbed me by the shoulders and pushed me back on the bed. She pulled off her kurta and kicked off her pantaloons. When she touched me, my skin felt like it was leaping out towards her. I penetrated her at once, pushing in as deep as I could. Our lips fused, tongues pressed hard against one another. For a while, we could barely move, just lay locked together, muscles straining as tightly as they could to mesh us together. It was as if I was trying to pull myself inside her, pull her inside of me. Nothing else mattered. I rolled us over to press deeper into her. Her ankles locked around my calves, and I felt the muscles inside of her clench fast around my shaft. She pulled her lips away from mine and groaned. Her mouth opened wide, eyes half-closed, head turning slowly side to side. Our bodies were vibrating now, not the normal pulse of sex but a shared tremor. I closed my eyes. My sense of my body as a thing which housed my brain disappeared; instead I knew only pathways of sensation, whirling currents that rushed through my flesh. Where did I stop and she begin? The centre throbbed, expanded. The core of energy felt like an arrow, the bow drawn back within me to send it home.

"Be careful"—the memory of her warning of the day before echoed in my mind—"I have not been so good with my pills."

Her arms clenched tightly around my back. The bed was shaking. Spasms shook her hips, driving us up and down on the mattress. The bow released, the arrow sung towards her, and in the violence of the instant, I drew back. My penis hit cool air and was slammed between our bellies, bleeding out its semen. The pain was excruciating, a severing, a current cut. We kept clutching, shivering, limbs still locked hard in place, and for a long time, we did not move.

We awoke next morning to a timid knock at the door.

"It's Bruce," she said, bolting upright. "He's come early! Bruce?"

No answer.

"Maybe it's the monk who brings you tea?"

"No. He didn't come yesterday. I think he must have heard you were here."

I crawled out of bed and pulled on my sarong. I opened the door, ready with anger. But it was an Indian youth, probably in his late teens, slender, with unusually bad acne, or perhaps the scars of some childhood disease. He was well dressed in grey slacks and a white, collared shirt, but his voice sounded strained and high-pitched, and his eyes seemed slightly glazed as if drunk or on drugs.

"Is the lady in there?" he asked, trying to peer past the crack in the door.

"*Mein Gott!*" hissed Sabina.

"You know him? Just a minute." I closed the door on the young man and turned to hear her explanation.

"Before you came back, he was following me around. I asked the monks, and they said he is harmless, but he follows women sometimes. They said he has a troubled mind."

I slipped on pants, shirt and sandals, reopened the door, and shut it behind me. Gently I took him by the elbow and began guiding him towards the stairs. My grip had some sort of calming effect on him. He floated by my side like a balloon on a string, looking back over his shoulder, but without the will to resist. I felt sad for him. Of course he had fallen in love with her beauty, and his "troubled mind" had made him bold enough to act on his infatuation. I saw so much of myself in him, and gladly undertook the job of cutting him loose.

"Where, where is she?" he said, still craning his neck around.

"I am her husband, and she does not wish to see you," I replied calmly.

He stopped and shook free of my arm. The look in his eyes grew wild and hostile. "Sir, are you insulting me?"

"No," I said, turning and looking straight into his eyes. "Can't you tell?"

He looked at me, turned his head a little sideways, a bit confused. He smiled.

"You, you love me?"

"Yes, that's right. Now come."

I walked him all the way to College Street, and set him adrift. When I returned to our floor, I heard Bruce's voice. He must have come up the other staircase as I was going down. I hesitated just outside the door.

"Were you able to get some extra film for me yesterday?" she was asking him.

"Nope. They only had ten colour rolls of Kodak left, and I'll need them all myself."

I stiffened. Maybe now was the time to escort him down the stairs too. Or out the window, unspooling his film roll by roll and throwing it after him like streamers. When I entered the room, he turned. His face was red from carrying his backpack through the heat. Sabina had washed and dressed.

"You remember Bruce?" she said.

I nodded. He put out his hand and I shook it. I could tell she had already told him I was not coming.

"Well, let's get ready," he said. "Train leaves in two hours."

"That's really more time than we need," she said.

"Well, I like to get there early," he replied, hefting his backpack.

She reached down to her duffle bag, bulging with books, and heaved on the straps.

"Ugh, I don't know how I'm going to manage this bag on the street." She had not lifted it off the ground.

"Me neither," said Bruce. "I'll give you guys a minute alone." He walked down the hall to the stairs.

With Buddhist calm, I noted the urge to make Bruce eat his own film.

"I'll wave from here," I said, looking out the window at the street below.

"You're not coming down? I thought . . ." She tugged at her bag again, only sliding it across the floor. "Please, help me."

"Of course, always." I blinked back tears, and slung the bag over my shoulders. The familiar burden felt good to bear, one last time, down six flights of stairs.

"I'm crazy," she said softly as we walked.

"What?"

"Not to take you with me. Not to change it all . . . It's just so difficult to change, in India."

I wobbled my head and spoke like a coolie. "Memsahib, I pick the bag up, I put the bag down, as you wish."

"Don't. Perhaps I will travel to other parts of Asia, to Thailand, later in the year."

"I should be easy to track down. Check the Canadian Embassy. I'll leave word."

"Ha, you'll probably be in a monastery in the jungle, your head shaved, chanting Pali and renouncing the world."

"So, promise me again you'll make me break my vows."

"I promise." Her eyes flashed blue for a second.

We walked down the stairs into the morning haze and met up with Bruce at the entrance. People were washing out their clothes in the swimming pool, and we could hear the wet slap slap as they beat their garments clean on the concrete. Sabina began hailing taxis. I knew in morning rush hour she wouldn't find a single working meter. A driver quoted her a price. She swore, slammed the first taxi's door, then the second, then the third.

"Oh Jeez, I'll pay the darn fare if it costs a thousand rupees!" said Bruce. "Let's just *go.*"

She shot him a withering look, which he missed entirely. He

fumbled for his wallet in the street and waved a hundred-rupee note above his head. The next cab swerved sharply in and almost ran him over. She pushed him inside the rear door and told him to put away his money, fast, then climbed in next to him. The driver helped me put her bag in the trunk. I watch him slam it shut.

She rolled down the window.

"Take good care of you!"

I bent to peck her on the cheek, but she put a hand behind my neck, pulled me forward, and kissed me full on the lips. She held me there, leaning through the window in the back of a cab, in the middle of College Street, for what seemed a very long time. When we let go, Bruce was fuming.

"All right, let's go, let's go!"

I waved as the yellow cab veered into traffic. My lungs ached. My lungs? Since when had life become so visceral? I just stood there. The cooking haze seemed to be lifting, and everything snapped into sharp detail. I wandered the streets a while. It was a perfect morning. The beggars had crawled out from under their sacks of bedding and blankets, and had already begun crying for alms. Hawkers and coconut sellers set out their goods on the sidewalk and accosted potential customers. Rickshaw runners padded by on callused feet. Traffic blared. Buyers and sellers haggled, and a tourist walked by, crying and smiling at the same time.

February 10, Gangtok, Sikkim
Dear Wendy,

I'm sitting here in a bar in the tiny state Sikkim, once an independent kingdom nestled right up against Tibet. I'm drinking hot fermented millet called tong-ba, trying to stay warm. It's snowing out, and all I have had to wear for shoes since Nepal were my sandals and one pair of socks. I'm shivering in my Indian cottons and have only one felt Tibetan jerkin to keep me warm. Fortunately, I'm going back to nearby Darjeeling and then south again in two more days. I decided not to go to Thailand for a few months, and instead to travel overland into

Bangladesh. I guess you could say I can't bear to leave the sub-continent yet. Until a few weeks ago, I never would have even considered entering the poorest part of the region. But I have come to really appreciate what I found in the midst of Calcutta's poverty. I don't know how to say it, but remember what I wrote you, long ago, about hoping Buddhist detachment would get me through India intact? Well, it didn't. And neither did my fanciful ideas about sexual restraint. I'm not intact, I'm broken open.

I have to leave the country. Leaving Sabina four days ago was even harder. But something has happened that I can't explain that makes Bangladesh seem a desirable place, that makes stepping into the crush of poverty not so fearsome any more. I spent my last day alone in Calcutta, my heart unbearably full. I don't expect it will last. Nothing does. But it's a good note on which to leave India. As I go, I have a final image to share with you.

There's a beggar boy in Calcutta with dull eyes and no arms, bound by a leash to a blind hag who uses him to collect alms in a busy city square. She sits in the middle, and he wanders round the perimeter of his leash with a tin can tied around his neck, rushing back to her when he gets a coin, so that she can pocket it. Now imagine one day a foreign man stands at the rim of this perimeter. As the boy approaches, the man pulls out from his pockets not a coin, but a pocketknife. With one smooth stroke he severs the leash entirely, then disappears back into the crowd. The boy stands still. The old hag, feeling the tether drop slack, calls out sharply. He has a second to respond. What will he do, Wendy? What?

With love, your brother,
Tim

GLOSSARY

bodhi	literally, "illuminated," enlightened
deva	a god or good spirit
dharma	truth, or the teachings of the Buddha
Diwali	Festival of Lights; Hindu celebration of the return of the gods Rama and Sita from exile to resume their thrones
ghats	stone stairways leading down to the waterside
hirja	Hindu caste of transvestites and eunuchs
japa	the repetition of a mantra
Kali	the Black Goddess
Kaliyuga	the Age of Kali; i.e., the current Age of Destruction in which we live
karma	the sum of a person's past actions which determines his or her actions in the future
kurta	a long-sleeved cotton pullover shirt
lingam	phallus
maithuna	ritual sex
memsahib	wife of a sahib or a female master
Nirvana	extinction of individual passion, hatred and delusion, and hence freedom from the endless cycle of reincarnation
paise	one one-hundredth of a rupee
pan	a betel nut mixture used for chewing; a stimulant
Parvati	Hindu goddess and wife of Shiva
Rama	god-king of the epic *Ramayana*; an incarnation of Vishnu

sadhu	a Hindu ascetic holy man
sahib	master; term of respect especially used for Europeans during the colonial era
samadhi	state of deep meditative concentration
samsara	"the world"; Mara's kingdom of delusion
sari	traditional Indian woman's dress, consisting of a long piece of cotton or silk wound around the hips and then up over one shoulder
shakti	life-force energy
Shakti	the feminine personification of life-force energy
Shiva	third god of the Hindu Trinity, along with Brahma and Vishnu; the symbol of higher consciousness and the Destroyer; husband of Parvati/Kali
stupa	Buddhist memorial monument, usually pyramidal or dome-like in shape
sutras	Buddhist scriptures
tamas	the power of inertia; one of the three qualities of nature of which the world is composed
Tantra	Hindu or Buddhist doctrines/books/practices of rituals, disciplines and/or meditations that regard enlightenment as the realization of the essential oneness of oneself and the visible world with the invisible Unity or Godhead
vajra	diamond or thunderbolt; symbol of the supreme power of Indra, king of the gods; Buddhist Tantrists transvalued the vajra as a symbol of great compassion
yogini	female yogi
yuga	one of the four ages of time, each worse than the last; after the fourth age, Kaliyuga, the cycle of time ends, only to begin all over again